ADVANCE PRAISE

"Janet Cromer has captured so elegantly and emotionally the ups and downs and roller coaster ride of experiencing a brain injury in her book "Professor Cromer Learns to Read." I found myself eager to turn each page, cheering on the little accomplishments and grieving with her at the very complicated loss and grief that accompanies this devastating life change. Cromer takes us beyond the injury and into the recovery, which, while painstaking, never fails to help us understand the beauty and the grace in little things and to cherish what we do have."

Lee Woodruff, coauthor of *In an Instant: a Family's Journey of Love and Healing,* and author of *Perfectly Imperfect*

"Professor Cromer learns to read is an intellectual and emotional road map for anyone who has, is currently, or may in the future navigate the swampy waters of caregiving for a loved one with serious disability. It is the compelling story of love and struggle in the midst of illness, of the strength and frailty of the human spirit looking straight into the eyes of the beast, a starkly honest and forthcoming account of the ins and outs and ups and downs of their lives following the transformation of Janet's husband by brain injury after a cardiac arrest. Extremely well written, I could not put it down."

Mel Glenn, MD, Director, Outpatient and Community Brain Injury Rehabilitation, Spaulding Rehabilitation Hospital; Associate Professor, Department of Physical Medicine and Rehabilitation, Harvard Medical School

"During the seven years of Alan Cromer's entry into the worlds of brain injury, dementia, and Parkinson's, his wife, an experienced psychiatric nurse, is there to observe and report upon the initial crisis in an airplane, the long rehab in which her professor husband learns once again to read and write, and his death at the age of seventy. She also observes the changes in herself as she adjusts to life as a caregiver in a new kind of marriage. "The original Alan was not coming back," so how to survive? Janet Cromer answers this question for herself and offers her strategies to others in her situation in this extensive examination of one well spouse life."

Maggie Strong, Founder of the Well Spouse Association, author of *Mainstay: For the Well Spouse of the Chronically Ill*

"Janet Cromer has written a valuable, detailed account of the nitty gritty of caregiving for a spouse through four major progressive, destructive diseases from heart attack and accompanying brain injury to Parkinson's disease. An "insider" on two counts – as a professional, a psychiatric nurse and therapist, and as a spousal caregiver – she writes from both points of view, of how the ravages of her husband's illness took over his life; and of how as his caregiver she went through rolling grief (repeated mourning) and some very difficult emotional readjustments in their relationship and intimacy.

This is a book that works on two levels: for the professional caregiver and spousal caregiver. For the former it cannot but help to increase the empathy for, and admiration of the family caregiver, supporting their loved one. As for the latter, as a former spousal caregiver, her descriptions of her ambivalent emotions, joys and travails, ring absolutely true."

Richard Anderson, Board and Executive Committee Member; Immediate Past President, Well Spouse Association

PROFESSOR CROMER
LEARNS TO READ
A Couple's New Life after Brain Injury

JANET M. CROMER

authorHOUSE®

AuthorHouse™
1663 Liberty Drive
Bloomington, IN 47403
www.authorhouse.com
Phone: 1-800-839-8640

First published by AuthorHouse 1/9/2010

ISBN: 978-1-4490-6421-1 (e)
ISBN: 978-1-4490-6419-8 (sc)
ISBN: 978-1-4490-6420-4 (hc)

Library of Congress Control Number: 2009913944

Printed in the United States of America
Bloomington, Indiana

This book is printed on acid-free paper.

Alan, I love you forever,

Janet

CONTENTS

FOREWORD 1

What does it really mean to live with the effects of a brain injury long beyond discharge from rehabilitation? How does one begin to redefine themselves with incredible limits on needed services? How much is needed of family caregivers and advocates? What are the human costs? How does this injury test the limits and capacity for love and devotion?

With daring honesty, compassion, and intense love, Janet Cromer has given many readers a gift. This book will serve anyone interested in the difficult journey of recovery after an acquired brain injury, understanding the huge commitment required of a family member in this recovery, and navigating and overcoming our healthcare and human service delivery system. This book provides the details of what it takes to undertake the awesome roles of survivor and caregiver.

Janet shares her insights with no holds barred. This is a story of very personal and emotional experiences. She uses her professional expertise and objectivity when appropriate, and she naturally exposes her special brand of humor and compassion for others. This is not only Janet's journey; it is also her husband's journey. She merges their shared attributes and gives us a picture of her loving and gifted husband to tell a very real story. I witnessed and learned from their story by observing and working with both Alan and Janet.

Having had the pleasure of knowing Alan as he was challenged in his struggle with his own rehabilitation and ensuing medical crisis with so much courage, optimism, and honesty was an honor. I could only imagine who Alan was before the brain injury, but imagining was not hard. I do know Janet, and reading her book will leave you better informed and a little anxious as we all know life can change in an instant...and through this story.

By reading *Professor Cromer Learns to Read*, we increase our understanding of the level of love, caring, and respect that makes a marriage or any loving relationship complete as it is so clearly described through the living of each day and of every stage of Alan and Janet's lives.

Marilyn Price Spivack
Co-Founder of the Brain Injury Association of America

FOREWORD II

...You and your husband have just boarded a plane to go home after a fun-filled weekend away with people that you love and that love you. Within minutes, your husband suffers a massive heart attack, cardiac arrest, and subsequent anoxic brain damage. An hour later, you don't know if he's going to survive. Days later, he's still alive, but that man connected to all kinds of machines with tubes and wires doesn't look or act like your husband. Your life as you knew it is irreversibly over...

...You and your wife have just boarded a plane to go home after a fun-filled weekend away with people that you love and that love you. Within minutes, you suffer a massive heart attack, cardiac arrest, and subsequent anoxic brain damage. An hour later, no one knows if you're going to survive. Days later, you're still alive, but you're medically unstable, agitated, confused, in significant pain, and you can't communicate. Your life as you knew it is irreversibly over...

This book, written by Janet Cromer about her and her husband, Dr. Alan Cromer, following his heart attack and cardiac arrest, is simultaneously a beautifully written portrayal of a couple's love and commitment to each other and an honest depiction of their experience of the health care system in this country. The book chronicles this couple's life from that fateful moment on the plane until Dr. Cromer's death seven years later. It describes two lives filled with dignity, integrity, and strength, lives that were united by love, passion, and a sense of humor. It candidly shares their unrealized hopes and expectations, conflicts and unmet needs, and successful and not-so-successful strategies to deal with these. It illustrates ongoing re-invention, re-prioritization, and survival of relationships and of self. Consistent with their dedication to their professional roles as college professor (Alan) and psychiatric nurse, teacher, and registered art therapist (Janet), this book TEACHES the reader about anoxia, brain injury, Parkinson's disease, and dementia. It portrays the shared and individual needs of patients and their spouses, the art and the science of rehabilitation, and the health professionals who commit themselves to the care of others. It highlights the strengths of our healthcare system and exposes its weaknesses.

Life is characterized by a series of ups and downs- some anticipated, and some not. Throughout it all, people continually search for dignified ways to peace, fulfillment, and love. Whether or not you are a husband, wife, daughter, or son; health professional; policy maker; insurer; we all share the responsibility and the desire to provide and receive life-long support with which to live lives of dignity, as Janet and Alan's "Odyssey" teaches us in the book.

Knowing Janet and having known Dr. Cromer, it is my honor to write the foreword to this beautifully written personal and professional legacy of life after brain injury. May it give you hope and inspiration.

Therese M. O'Neil-Pirozzi, ScD, CCC-SLP
Associate Professor; SLP Graduate Program Director,
Northeastern University
Spaulding Rehabilitation Hospital, Boston MA

INTRODUCTION

One minute, I had my husband, Alan. The next minute, he was dead. Our lives changed forever on July 5, 1998, when Alan suffered a massive heart attack and cardiac arrest on an airplane. Alan was left with a severe anoxic brain injury from lack of oxygen to his brain during the prolonged resuscitation effort.

In an instant, Alan went from being a professor of physics at Northeastern University, a prolific author, and an engaged and loving person to being someone with a life-altering brain injury who had to learn how to do everything all over again. And all at the same time. Alan lost his abilities to read, write, walk, talk, think, and remember. Over the ensuing months and years, he regained all of those abilities to varying degrees, and we made a new life with meaning and gusto.

But this story is not just about Alan's experience. As Alan's wife and caregiver, I went through many parallel changes, losses, and adaptations. We learned the art of composing a whole new life and marriage as individuals and partners through determination, courage, grace, mistakes, and humor. This is our story.

When Alan became ill, I read several excellent memoirs about life after brain injury. But they all covered just the first year or two of the experience, and often ended at the peak of improvement in rehabilitation. My intention for this book is to share our experience over several years, through the challenges and triumphs of rehabilitation to our adventures getting to know each other all over again and redefining marriage—at least a few times. Like many survivors, Alan developed additional major medical problems. For Alan, those were dementia and Parkinson's disease (PD). Those conditions brought their own complications and limitations to be reckoned with.

Alan was truly a "Real Professor" both before and after his brain injury. He taught all those who loved him and those who treated him a new meaning of courage, resilience, determination, motivation, and passion. He most loved to share his experiences with patients and families at Spaulding Rehabilitation Hospital's community and professional education programs. When he described what it was like to learn to read and write again, the college student with a traumatic brain injury (TBI) and the mechanic just beginning stroke rehab listened intently. Then they carried Alan's message of hope and motivation to their next treatment session.

I decided early in this journey that I wanted to write a book to make sense of all that happened to us, and to share our experience honestly with others on the same rocky road. This book is not meant to be a case study or an instruction manual. Every brain injury is different, and every person is unique. I humbly offer some of what we learned, what sustained us, what pushed us forward, the mistakes we made, and how we made a new life with love and meaning.

The main lesson I've learned about writing a memoir is that you have to leave out 93 percent of the story and focus on a realistic number of themes. I chose the themes that interested or troubled Alan and me the most:

- What is it like to relearn everything you used to know?
- How can you possibly build a new identity when you have forgotten who you are and lost many parts of that person to brain injury?
- How can individuals and couples grow in love and adapt to challenging circumstances?
- What makes life worthwhile, stimulating, and fun in the face of progressive illness?

- What does it mean to live a good life and prepare for a good death?

Medical treatments and medications recommended for specific conditions change frequently and vary widely with each person's needs and the preferences of his treatment team. I chose not to go into details about the particular medications Alan received, since the information would be outdated now. I describe the underlying principles when that might be helpful.

Most of the research and writings about brain injury focus exclusively on traumatic brain injury. I searched in vain for material specific to the long-term effects of anoxic brain injury and the different needs of survivors of cardiac arrest. I hope this book will contribute to our understanding of anoxic brain injury.

In recent years, there has been an exciting revolution in understanding the neuroplasticity of the brain—the brain's capacity to change and alter its structure and functioning. Neuroscientists and clinicians now know that the brain can continue to heal and adapt for years after injury with specialized treatment, including cognitive rehabilitation. The Brain Injury Association of America defines "cognitive rehabilitation" as "a systematically applied set of medical and therapeutic services designed to improve cognitive functions and participation in activities that may be affected by difficulties in one or more cognitive domains." In other words, the ability to think, remember, solve problems, make decisions, communicate, and get along with other people, which we all need to be independent, social, and productive people.

Alan benefited from intensive and sustained cognitive rehabilitation and made gains in several areas for years after the brain injury. Our story illustrates how building on his strengths and interests made life rich and worthwhile.

I've been privileged to talk with a few hundred brain injury survivors and their closest family members. Every family caregiver tells the story of the "Moment Everything Changed," with the emotional charge of an event that happened yesterday, even if the accident was twenty years ago. That's how dramatic the turning point is, regardless of the cause of the brain injury or the age of the person affected.

All of the statistics about brain injury are really about huge numbers of human beings whose lives are dramatically changed, often forever.

Every year, 1.4 million Americans sustain brain injuries from falls, motor vehicle accidents, sports concussions, assaults, illnesses, and accidents. Over 125,000 of those people who suffer a brain injury become disabled. According to the Centers for Disease Control and Prevention, at least 3.17 million Americans currently live with disabilities resulting from brain injury. Most of those people are cared for at home by family members and want to be part of their community.

I've been a medical and psychiatric registered nurse since 1970. However, like most of us, I'd had very little exposure to the specific deficits and ravages brain injury can impart. Brain injury is called the "silent epidemic" because the consequences are often not visible to a casual observer. The young man walking down Broadway who was hit by a car last year may look just like you or me, but his personality along with his abilities to learn new information, recognize you and say hello, and find a job he can do now may all be seriously affected. These are the functions that make us who we are and allow us to participate fully and independently in the world.

Now there is a new type of brain injury disrupting the lives of mounting numbers of veterans of the wars in Iraq and Afghanistan. A 2008 Rand Institute report states that nearly 320,000 individuals suffered a probable traumatic brain injury while deployed. Those injuries range from concussions to severe blast injuries from improvised explosive devices (IEDs). Brain injury is now considered to be the "signature injury" of this war. Many of these veterans and their families will require intensive rehabilitation followed by long-term treatment and services for the chronic problems that can be the consequences of brain injury. Only then will they be able to lead satisfying and productive lives.

Much has changed even since Alan's brain injury occurred in 1998. Advances in emergency and battlefield medicine, rehabilitation, and technology have improved survival rates. That means that more people are living with brain injuries they would not have survived even a few years earlier. For many, the chance of resuming a life with dignity and meaning is enhanced by excellent rehabilitation, community reintegration programs, and specialized educational facilities.

But here is what everyone should understand, which never changes:

First, a large percentage of persons who sustain a brain injury require and deserve lifelong support and specialized cognitive rehabilitation to reach their best outcomes and lead satisfying lives.

Second, there is an increasingly urgent need for research and clinical programs to prepare and coach family caregivers to manage the complex needs of the person with a brain injury as well as the family's needs for years after the brain injury occurs.

Once a person leaves a formal rehabilitation program, family members are expected to continue teaching the strategies necessary for daily activities, relearning cognitive and social skills, and managing psychiatric and behavioral issues. The best rehabilitation programs try to train family members to carry on the work of specialized professionals, while supporting the family's intense emotional adjustment. However, even those programs are not equipped to provide the training necessary when the survivor's needs change as the years go on.

Putting these services in place is a public health issue that will require collaboration and conviction between those affected by brain injury, medical professionals, policy makers, public and private insurers, and concerned citizens.

Only when the combination of ongoing specialized rehabilitation and improved family resources are in place can we, as a society and medical community, provide the treatment and quality of life every person with a brain injury and their family caregivers deserve.

Janet M. Cromer
Jamaica Plain, MA
August 2009

Alan experiments in his home science lab in June, 1998.

1. JULY 5, 1998

One night in early October, I arrived home from the hospital, exhausted and depressed. Flipping on the answering machine, I was deluged by a cascade of messages from my husband, Alan. In rapid succession, he said:

"Hi Janet, just want to talk to you before you go to sleep. Lots of things to tell you about if I don't forget them. I love you!"

Click.

"Janet, you were here today, right? When will you be back?"

Click.

By the fourth message: "First time I've called. Just want to see if I know how to use the phone. Nothing special going on. Forgot what I wanted to say. Call me."

Click.

"Hello? I'm lost. Come get me. They won't let me leave."

Click.

The eighth message really grabbed me: "Thank you for everything you've done for me and half the things you've done I don't even know about." That was the first time in four months he'd thanked me.

Click.

"Where are you? Are you ever coming back to me?"

Click.

The last message was in a tremulous voice: "Hello? It's Alan. Is anyone there? Call me to say hello to me, okay? Calling to ask you a question about something. I forget."

Click.

In the thirty minutes it had taken me to drive home, Alan left twelve messages. As soon as he hung up, he forgot he had called. So he called again.

Alan called me from his bed on the Brain Injury Unit of Spaulding Rehabilitation Hospital in Boston. As I listened, questions ricocheted inside my head: "How did this happen? Who is this person, this man posing as my husband? Where is the life we knew so well and were so happy to be living?"

Everything changed on July 5, 1998.

Alan and I had traveled from Boston to Chicago for a family reunion to celebrate the fiftieth wedding anniversary of Alan's sister, Barbara, and her husband, Sanford Kahn. We arrived Friday, and on Saturday, family and friends from across the United States gathered for a gala party at an Italian restaurant. Alan used his new digital movie camera to film the guests and record their messages to the anniversary couple. He always bought the latest technology and then enjoyed mastering the manual. While I sat at the table talking to his cousins, I could hear Alan's hearty laugh from across the room.

A few weeks earlier, Alan said, "I want to update my look for the party. I need some new clothes." Now my handsome, dark-haired husband looked like a PBS documentary director in his stylish black silk tee shirt and pleated linen trousers. When Alan buzzed by our table, I said, "Hey Larry, take a picture of Alan and me." Alan wrapped his arm around my shoulder as we added our congratulations to Barbara and Sandy. We looked like a happy and thriving couple in the prime of life. Indeed, we were. At sixty-two, Alan was a professor of physics at Northeastern University, prolific author, and developer of many educational programs. I was forty-eight, a psychiatric nurse, teacher, and registered art therapist building a private practice. We had been married for eleven years. Although we did not have children, we cherished our close relationships with several nieces and nephews.

All of the guests offered high-spirited tributes and reminiscences. Later that night, the family gathered back in the Kahn's yard for more conversation while fireflies flickered like stars.

On Sunday, the extended family shared lunch at a Japanese restaurant before dispersing back across the country.

Alan and I were running late as we drove to O'Hare International Airport. We weren't concerned. If we missed the flight, we could just take the earliest flight out on Monday. Alan was scheduled to start his favorite teacher-training program, Project SEED. I was due to facilitate support groups in a cancer program. We were in the thrall of the joyous weekend that put us back in touch with what mattered most: spending time with the people we loved.

Just that morning, we'd made love in our hotel room before joining the family on a three-mile, multigenerational walk. Alan jogged part of the route and then walked while quizzing the children about math and astronomy. Ever the science teacher, he was always good for explosive demonstrations and tricks that turned out to be elegant experiments.

I should have known something was wrong the second time Alan got lost trying to find the rental car return as we approached the airport. After the first wrong turn, I said, "No, Alan, Hertz is to the right." Even with two wrong turns, we made it to the terminal as the last boarding call sounded. We sprinted down the long corridors of O'Hare to the farthest gate.

As we handed in our tickets, Alan said, "Oh, I feel so sick to my stomach."

I replied, "I'll get you some Dramamine as soon as we get settled."

We figured he was paying the price for running on a full stomach, and it would pass. The flight attendant shut the door the second we boarded. Alan sat down while I stowed our bags. The plane began taxiing slowly down the runway.

As soon as I sat down beside him, Alan said, "Oh, I feel so dizzy," and slumped forward with his head in his hands. His face had turned pale.

I grabbed his wrist to feel his pulse. "Do you have any pain in your chest?" I asked anxiously.

Before he could answer, Alan fell back with his head resting against the window. I felt his pulse stop. I knew my husband's heart had stopped beating.

The crisis reflexes honed over twenty-eight years as a nurse took over. I started screaming, "Cardiac arrest! Stop the plane, call the EMTs, get us off this plane!" over and over. For a moment, I was stunned by how natural Alan looked. It seemed as if he was just taking a nap and his seat mate should wake him up when the flight landed in Boston. But his color rapidly faded to grey, then blue.

A doctor seated a few aisles forward jumped up to assist us. He and I dragged Alan's limp body into the narrow aisle, and the flight attendant joined the doctor in performing CPR. I kept screaming that Alan needed real oxygen while she tried to stretch the ridiculously flimsy overhead mask to reach him. There was no defibrillator on the flight, no medications, sparse medical equipment. I felt desperate and furious because the equipment was so inadequate. I wanted to do mouth-to-mouth resuscitation while the doctor did cardiac compressions, but the flight attendant told me to stand back while she used an ambu bag to squeeze air into Alan's lungs.

I knew I should be tracking the elapsed time since Alan's heart had stopped. I kept glancing at my watch, but didn't want the answer to be true. I knew that soon an emergency room doctor would ask me, "How long was he down? How long until he was defibrillated, until he got a pulse back?" The answer was already starting to be, "Too long."

The emergency medical technicians (EMTs) arrived and attached Alan to a heart monitor that showed the wild pattern of ventricular fibrillation. The chambers of his heart were quivering erratically in an uncoordinated rhythm, so blood was not being forcibly squeezed out to provide oxygen to his vital organs. Each time the EMTs slapped the defibrillator paddles on Alan's chest and yelled, "Everybody off!" my heart jumped into my throat. Once, twice ... they zapped him. His body leaped off the ground and then thumped back down from the power of the electric current. But the rhythm stayed wild.

They seemed to do everything simultaneously. Now Alan had an endotracheal tube in his throat so the oxygen piped through the ambu bag could be delivered to his lungs more effectively. An EMT inserted an intravenous (IV) line into his vein to give medications. Kneeling at my husband's head in the cramped aisle, I was horrified to see that his face was turning as dark as his black tee shirt.

My head churned with confusion and disbelief. I mumbled my questions to the backs of the high upright seats forming a canyon along the aisle. Why didn't I know? What did I miss? Why didn't we know that Alan had serious heart problems? What didn't I know that had caused my precious husband to drop dead so suddenly?

Here and there, a passenger's face dared to crane back toward the unfolding drama, but everyone seemed frozen.

The EMTs and doctor kept up the CPR, defibrillation, and medications until we had to move to the ambulance. As they struggled to maneuver the stretcher toward the open door, I was at eye level with the faces of the shaken passengers. I grabbed our books and luggage and cried out, "Why didn't I know? What did I miss? Pray for my husband, please pray for us," all the way off the plane.

One minute, I had my husband. The next minute, he was dead.

From my seat in the front of the ambulance, I could hear everything and peek back through a window between compartments. At one point, Alan's heart responded to the treatments and began to beat at a steadier rate of 130 beats per minute. He moved around in pain and showed purposeful movement when he tried to pull out the endotracheal tube in his throat. I sat stone still, chanting to myself, "Alan is going to live, Alan is going to live," in time to the rapid drumbeat of my own heart. I felt a leap of hope when I heard him gurgle and struggle—it meant he was *alive.*

But then Alan's heart stopped again, the EMTs shocked him and kept pushing medications into his body, and the ride to Resurrection

Medical Center seemed to take forever. Resurrection was the closest hospital with a trauma unit and intensive care units.

When the ambulance pulled into the Emergency Department (ED) at Resurrection, we all ran in. Where was the Code Team? Why weren't they awaiting our arrival at the entrance? I was shuffled into a small, windowless waiting room while the staff fought to bring Alan back to life.

I sat staring ahead at the yellow wall. At first I kept up my chant: "Alan is going to live. Alan will get well. Alan will come home with me." My words were like a script scrolling down the length of the wall. My mind careened between a wife's absolute belief that my husband would live, and my belief as a nurse that it might be more merciful if he did not: "What if Alan dies? Should I have his body cremated here or brought back to Boston? But we only came for a reunion weekend. What if he lives but comes out a vegetable? His brain has been without oxygen for a horribly long time. He would never forgive me." Those words felt terribly disloyal, so I shifted back to my optimistic chant until they cycled through again.

Then I started making resolutions to change things that had been recent sources of disagreement or dissatisfaction in our marriage. I resolved that we would eat dinner together every night. As a psychotherapist, I led therapy groups or worked with clients in three different settings a few nights a week. No more late evening therapy sessions. No more, "I haven't seen you all week" from my neglected husband. Now my priorities were shifting from others to just Alan. I would take care of him in every way possible to restore him to good health.

I resolved to stop "bleeding out loud," as Alan referred to my prolonged descriptions of stressful situations or other problems. Alan hated it when I told stories about my clients (without identifying them, of course) who had major mental illness or end-stage cancer. Their circumstances terrified him, and he couldn't propose a ready solution to their problems.

While I was at it, I would give up nagging. When I went on about Alan's habit of not rinsing the sink after shaving, he would adopt a droning voice to say, "Thank you for making me a better person, dear."

I resolved to slow down my brisk walking pace to meet Alan's slower pace. Alan was a jogger, but when we walked together, he landed up several steps behind me. He had recently complained, "I feel like a dog trying to catch up to you."

We had both been unhappy with our pattern of not giving the other full attention when they wanted to talk. I'd said, "Please turn off *The McNeil-Lehrer News Hour* and listen to me," more than once. Now I resolved that we would give each other our full attention, be fully present when communicating. We would stop moving so fast.

For the last year, we had both been under a lot of stress. We had taken care of my mother in our home until she died of metastatic cancer ten months earlier. I was still in the throes of grieving her. I'd been spending my days off clearing out her home of fifty years in Somerville in preparation for selling it. Alan made frequent trips to New York and California, where he was consulting on educational standards and presenting at high-level conferences.

Just a month earlier, we'd made time for a few weekends at our vacation home in Narragansett, Rhode Island. There we relaxed, kayaked, and played as the loving couple we really were. Alan said, "This is what we need: time to just be together. We used to be good at this." I agreed.

The years of our marriage and hopes and dreams we shared going forward played out in snatches of imagination. I alternated between praying, chanting, resolving, and staring at the wall.

All alone.

Finally, a young resident physician in wrinkled scrubs approached from the trauma room. He sat down beside me.

"Alan has been down for forty-five minutes and is probably brain dead," he said. "You should be prepared."

I tensed up my shoulders and screamed at him, "No, it's not fair. He didn't get a chance on the airplane, there was no defibrillator, no meds. You keep doing everything possible. I want to give him a fair chance."

Because Alan had suffered a massive heart attack and cardiac arrest so suddenly, I felt that we couldn't stop treatment if he had any possibility of a meaningful life. We didn't even know the underlying cause of the heart attack. Alan was a vital, intelligent, active man. He looked much younger than his sixty-two years and was proud of his muscular physique. My moral compass, the guide I combined with medical information when making decisions, became making sure Alan received every treatment that would give him a chance at recovery and decent quality of life. But even then, I had a sense of uneasiness about all the factors we couldn't know or control. Even as minute-by-minute decisions needed to be made.

"You get back in there and keep resuscitating him!" I yelled.

The resident sighed, nodded, and turned back toward the trauma room.

I resumed my solitary vigil, wedged into the corner of the chair in the oddly silent hospital corridor. *My husband will probably die.* I shivered, even with my arms wrapped around myself. I hope I never feel that alone ever again.

Fifteen minutes later, a young female resident sat down beside me and said cautiously, "We did get a rhythm back. He is on a ventilator." *Alan was alive.*

I rushed into the trauma room to see for myself, to touch him, kiss him. From the corner of my eye, I could see the scene I had been part of countless times as a medical nurse: miles of EKG paper, discarded gloves, a forest of IV bottles. But my total focus was on my sweetheart's face, now waxy white, but no longer black. *Alan was alive.*

I said, "Alan, this is Janet, your wife. You're alive, you are going to be all right. I'll be right here with you. You're going to be all right."

A new chant had begun.

Someone had called Alan's family, and now Barbara and Sandy stood in the waiting room along with Alan's brother Richard, his wife Pam, and several nephews. Most of them were preparing to depart from Chicago when they received word that Alan was in critical condition in the Emergency Department. Less than three hours earlier, we had been trading bites of tempura from our bento boxes.

As I stood with the doctor looking into their solemn faces, I felt myself slip over a transom and through a door into our surreal new world. I took on the roles of wife with a capitol W, advocate, interpreter, and decision maker. Titles that would shape my identity for years to come.

I already grasped that everything in our lives had changed in an instant. But how could I know what that meant? I didn't know we were starting an epic journey to reclaim Alan's mind, body, and spirit from a devouring beast. I couldn't know the husband I loved had gone away forever without a chance to say good-bye. That he and I were now strangers who would have to get to know each other all over again. And decide to fall in love again. I didn't know anything about our future. I was clinging to the fact that my beloved Alan was alive.

2. LESSONS FROM THE ICU

The first night of Alan's new life in the ICU was horrific. All the indicators of potential recovery were absent. His blood pressure (BP) kept plummeting, even with vasopressor drips to elevate it; his heart kept reverting to dangerous rhythms; his pupils were dilated and didn't shrink down when a light was flashed in his eyes, which indicated brain damage. He developed pulmonary edema from fluid building up in his lungs, aspiration pneumonia from vomiting during resuscitation, and gastrointestinal bleeding.

All this within a few hours.

"Mrs. Cromer, your husband's condition is grave, very critical," each new medical specialist told me.

"Mrs. Cromer, what do you understand?" each nurse asked repeatedly.

Impatiently, I repeated the latest crisis synopsis and added tersely, "I get it, I get it. My husband could die again at any moment."

No one had called me "Mrs. Cromer" in the eleven years we had been married. But now it fit. I wanted everyone to know I was attached to Alan Cromer and guarding him closely.

The nurses were very kind about letting me stay right beside Alan all night. Letting them know I was a nurse set up an unspoken agreement that I had more freedom to visit and stay during procedures than other families did. In exchange, I was not supposed to get in the way or become hysterical without warning. It was a fair deal. Alan's family gathered in the ICU waiting room, an uncharacteristically quiet group of grim people who usually talked, debated, and laughed all at the same time. And Alan, always the most gregarious but now unresponsive, was the most silent of all.

Stark overhead lighting intensified Alan's waxy pallor and the engulfing machines that pumped, wheezed, dripped, drained, and clicked continuously. High-tech equipment monitored his heart rate and rhythm, blood pressure, urine output, and oxygen level as well as giving sophisticated information about his entire cardiovascular system. He was in a coma, partly because of being so sick and partly from sedative medications he'd been given so his body could rest as much as possible. I carefully snaked my fingers through the bedrails and wires to grasp his cold fingers. I whispered, "I love you, Alan. You are going to live." I just had to touch him, kiss his forehead, watch his chest rise and fall. Let him know I was there.

Around midnight, a Catholic priest shuffled in and haltingly asked, "Would Mr. Cromer like to receive Last Rites?"

I didn't reveal that Alan considered himself a scientist-atheist and scorned organized religion. It was one of the areas on which we'd agreed to disagree. I just said, "Alan isn't Catholic, but I'd appreciate it if you said a blessing for him."

Bringing my mouth closer to his ear, I shouted, "Alan, there are no atheists in the ICU; I want this priest to pray for you, Alan."

The blessing did not have an immediate effect. His condition continued to worsen.

I'd been stoic and in control from the time of Alan's cardiac arrest at 5:00 PM Sunday. Somehow, I made numerous decisions and translated the medical jargon for the family. I made a list of people in Boston for Pam to telephone; I even called my sister and Alan's closest friends myself. But at 2:00 AM, as the staff rushed in to respond to another episode of Alan "losing" his blood pressure, I finally crashed into sobs of realization at all that had happened. I was terrified that Alan might die, even with the best medical care. I thought, *I don't know if I can cope with this. I have no reserves left after caring for Mom. It would have been better if I'd had a year in between to recover; what am I supposed to do?*

As if any of us get to schedule life's great catastrophes.

Regret gnawed at me for not reacting to something Alan said a few weeks earlier. One morning, he leaned against the door on his way to teach a physics class at Northeastern.

"Janet," he said, "I've never felt this tired, this exhausted. This is very strange."

I gave him a sympathetic look, but answered without fully taking in his concern. "Oh, honey, that's understandable. You've been flying to California, consulting nonstop, plus teaching classes. In two more weeks, we'll go down to Narragansett and collapse on our beach."

Now that scene haunted me. I should have known his exhaustion heralded heart problems.

Around 3:00 AM, I noticed with horror that Alan was hemorrhaging blood from all the wounds on his body. A young intern with red hair steered me to a chair in the waiting room. Kneeling on the floor beside me, he carefully explained that Alan had developed disseminated intravascular coagulation (DIC), a condition that combines excessive bleeding and the formation of hundreds of tiny clots. The treatment for DIC could have the adverse effect of causing bleeding within his brain and further damage. Untreated, the DIC could cause clots to block off major blood vessels, leading to a different kind of death. "What do you want us to do?" he asked. The optimism I was clutching slipped out of my grasp, and my heart plummeted.

I needed time to think and craved the familiar solace of lighting candles while offering intentions and hoping some greater power could intercede with fate. So, in the chapel with Barbara and Pam, I prayed to Kwan Yin, the Buddhist goddess of compassion, God, my mother, the Blessed Mother, St. Anthony: "Please give me guidance, guts, wisdom, and fortitude. Help me make these decisions the way Alan would make them for himself."

I finally turned in the bench and explained the medical considerations to Barbara and Pam. They were considerate, but Pam said, "You are Alan's wife and will have to make the ultimate decision."

Alan and I were no strangers to medical illness and loss. Alan's first wife, Margie, had died of Hodgkin's disease when she was thirty-five, ten years before we met. My father was killed in an industrial accident when I was twelve. I had been the nurse manager of a hematology/oncology unit and knew that life could be altered in the instant of diagnosis. We'd had many long conversations about our final wishes and agreed not to postpone the things we most wanted to do, such as travel. We had traveled around the world twice, a decision I was even more pleased by now.

But I couldn't remember a single conversation about sudden death, resuscitation, and probable brain damage.

I decided to sign the consent form authorizing treatment of DIC, but knew the attempt might be futile. My decision-making compass started to shift from "I want Alan to have a fair chance, I want to try everything" to a more tempered "I want to do whatever is in Alan's best interest." I was beginning to realize that we faced choices that could keep Alan "alive," but with no quality of life.

Because DIC is so difficult to treat, the doctors told us we should take this opportunity to let Alan know we loved him and, essentially, to say good-bye. Sitting on the edge of the bed, I cradled my husband's machine-driven body in my lap, while one by one, his family members whispered their anguished love and gratitude to him. A solemn procession of the people Alan loved most in the world said the things we never can tell each other often enough in life. Alan had played a major role in each nephew's childhood, and now they reminisced about learning to swim or being tutored for an important exam.

Toward morning, I noticed that the lap of my dress was soaked with Alan's blood. I thought, *I'll have to go home to Boston carrying my husband's ashes in a box on my lap. I'll look like Jackie Kennedy: bereft, stricken, and wearing the bloody evidence of what happened for all to see.*

To the staff's amazement, the DIC treatment improved Alan's clotting mechanisms enough for the bleeding to stop. While I counted the hours since his heart attack, the ICU staff moved into a system of counting days. Monday was day one.

That morning, Dr. H., a tall, athletically built neurologist, asked me to recount the exact details of Alan's arrest and resuscitation. He nodded and shook his head sadly when I described the scene on the airplane.

"You realize that Alan's brain might not be viable, don't you?" he asked.

I shrugged my shoulders and said, "I know what the words mean, but I can't imagine how that will look on Alan."

It was implausible to me that Alan, the physics professor and textbook author, might not have his intelligence, engaging personality, or sharp wit. What would be left?

I came up with a manifesto: "If anyone has extra brain cells, it's Alan. He has the brain of one-and-a-half people because he constantly teaches himself hard subjects. His hobby is teaching himself computer languages. He's always looking up something in *Encyclopedia Britannica*. If anyone can bring his brain back, it's Alan!"

Dr. H. didn't dispute me. In fact, he said that people with higher intelligence tend to have better outcomes after rehabilitation. One reason could be that they are accustomed to the rigorous discipline required for rehab.

Running on a combination of adrenalin and sleep deprivation, I boasted, "I can go the distance with Alan." But no one could anticipate what that journey would involve or where the finish line might be.

The cause of Alan's heart attack was still a mystery. We never knew he had serious heart disease until his heart stopped. To investigate, the doctors needed to perform a coronary angiogram, even though his condition was so unstable. The results would provide critical information for the next series of treatment decisions. During the angiogram, a thin catheter was threaded through Alan's groin and advanced through the major coronary blood vessels to locate blockages or clots. The angiogram results showed that four main vessels were blocked from 80 to 100 percent.

According to the cardiologist, Alan would need coronary artery bypass surgery if his condition ever stabilized enough to survive it. He also said that Alan's family history was a contributing factor. Alan's father had died of a heart attack when he was fifty-nine, so Alan had led an exemplary lifestyle to avoid his father's fate. The cardiologist said that because Alan's father had severe cardiovascular disease, Alan had a fifty percent chance of having a heart attack even if he watched his diet, avoided smoking, and exercised regularly. So far, Alan had made it to sixty-two.

As I listened to the pieces come together, I felt a white-hot rage spread through me. How had this been allowed to progress so far? Why hadn't his doctors caught it earlier? Alan had an annual physical exam, kept his cholesterol around the 200 mg/dl level, and jogged regularly. Then, all of his strange, intermittent symptoms blew around in my mind. For months, Alan had pain behind his left shoulder that bothered him a lot. He thought he had pulled a muscle working out on Nautilus equipment. He went to the doctor a few times and had a course of physical therapy, which he thought helped for a while, but then the pain returned. Much later we learned that the pain behind his shoulder was indeed caused by a blocked coronary artery. Having less typical symptoms is a risk factor all its own.

There were times when Alan had to stop walking because he felt so weak, but it passed and he felt decent. And what were those blood pressure pills he took a few years ago? The ones that lowered his BP so much that he fainted when he stood up? And now I recognized that Alan's confusion finding the rental car return had been due to inadequate oxygen flowing to his brain. The heart attack had already started. I shuddered to realize that if his heart had stopped while he was driving, we would both have been killed.

I carried that rage about whether this heart attack could have been avoided for days. Then I had to make a choice. Alan's progress kept moving one step forward and two steps back. Each day that he clung to life became more complicated. I would be in Chicago for an indeterminate time. I needed every bit of my concentration and energy to put toward his recovery. I could choose to be consumed by my rage or set it aside and stay in the present moment in the ICU. But I couldn't do both.

Somewhat begrudgingly, I chose to set anger aside at least until we were home and I could track down medical records to put the pieces together.

On Tuesday, Alan's second day in the ICU, he had his first big breakthrough. His brother Richard, who was partially blind, maneuvered his way through the machines to stand at Alan's bedside. I stood on the other side.

As Richard cooed softly, "Alan, it's Richard. I'm here to protect you, little bro," Alan opened his eyes and turned his head in the direction of Richard's voice.

That was the first sign that Alan was capable of responding.

When I said, "Alan, this is Janet. Your wife is here too," he turned in my direction and tried to focus his eyes on my face.

We were ecstatic! Even with a ventilator breathing for him and an intra-aortic balloon taking over his heart's pumping action, Alan was in there. He could try to connect with us. Our hope shot sky high. But the staff emphasized that neurological responses are inconsistent and affected by many variables. Still, with each clear sign of life, we rejoiced.

Alan was bombarded by complications from not getting enough oxygen to his organs, along with the aftereffects of resuscitation. Dr. B., the chief resident who became Alan's ally and our family's best educator, explained that being resuscitated for an hour is the equivalent of being hit by a train. Alan developed pancreatitis, shock liver, bowel obstruction, infections, pneumonias, and renal insufficiency. His kidneys were not able to detoxify and filter the flood of broken down tissue and angiogram dye. The doctors started renal dialysis to remove toxins from his blood while waiting to see if his kidneys would be able to recover.

The only thing Alan wanted to do was to get comfortable. He wanted to get into his favorite position to relax by crossing his right ankle over his left, and folding his arms behind his head. So, he struggled. Alarms screeched and nurses came running to scold him to lie still. I implored the staff, "But he always sleeps with his ankles crossed."

Dr. B. understood that some of Alan's restlessness came from being restrained for hours in the same position. So, Dr. B. made sure to loosen the restraints and let Alan relax whenever he was in the room.

Some mornings, Dr. B. greeted me with, "Look Janet, Alan has a positive ankle-cross sign."

I was elated to recognize this little bit of my husband reclaiming himself. I asked the staff, "If the gestures are the same on the outside, does it mean the person is the same on the inside?"

No one knew the answer.

Alan's absolute worst problems were pain and agitated delirium. Each of his medical problems came with its own horrific pain. In his confused state, Alan frantically tried to pull out the endotracheal tube, IV lines, feeding tube, and catheters. When the nurses tried to restrain him, he kicked and hit at them. He was literally out of his mind from a combination of pain, metabolic imbalances, damage to his brain, the constant noise and lights of the ICU, and a buildup of medications. Who could blame him for wanting to escape from this torture chamber?

The delirium, which is common in seriously ill people, went on for days. The hospital did not have a specialized psychiatrist on staff who could evaluate Alan's extreme combination of conditions and recommend a sedative that would safely restore him to his right mind.

One day, I was reading to Alan when he tried to get out of bed despite the huge IV lines entering his groin. I grabbed his wrist and said, "No, Alan. Please lie down, you'll get hurt. I'll get you what you want."

Alan looked at me with a wild, unrecognizing stare. Suddenly, he seized my arms with superhuman strength, let out a growl, and twisted the flesh in a burning pinch that left me bruised for a week. Before the nurses rushed in, he pinched my breast in the same way. My own husband, or this man pretending to be, had just hurt me. Was this how he would be from now on: out of control and inconsolable? It took many failed attempts before the doctors found the right medication that would calm Alan down without making his blood pressure too low. Witnessing Alan in the throes of agitated delirium was the worst part for me.

Far from home, I camped out in the ICU waiting room for almost two weeks before a room became available in the hospital's guest house. I claimed a comfortable chair as my turf and set up my overnight bag. A bonded community soon formed among the waiting room families.

We took telephone messages for each other, followed their loved one's progress hour by hour, and agreed that the person whose patient had the most horrible day should sleep on the lone couch that night.

When I tried to fall asleep, my mind swam with images, information, numbers, and reminders. This was different from the undercurrent of anxiety from worrying if Alan would live or die. It was as if I could watch the process my brain undertook each night to sort through that day's mountain of data and organize it into a large file drawer. I visualized papers fluttering into files, tucked neatly out of sight. The work done, my brain let me grab a few hours of sleep.

I often felt powerless to help Alan with the extensive healing his body needed to do. All I could do was be there with him. I didn't underestimate that contribution, but I wanted to do more. I often composed relaxation/healing imagery scripts for my clients. So now I wrote a long, detailed script of all the changes that would happen to Alan's body and mind as he healed. It helped me to sit beside him and recite the litany of healing imagery that I fervently hoped would happen:

"Alan, you are wrapped in a blanket of blue light. The light of my constant love that keeps you safe and secure. Each breath you take is made up of your strong will to live, your body's capacity to restore and regenerate, and your resilience. You are recovering through excellent medical care, along with the prayers and healing energy sent to you from everyone who loves you ...

"As you breathe in, vital energy flows to your brain, cleansing the toxins, bringing fresh oxygen and nutrients to every cell to restore your tremendous mind.

"Inhale, and white light flows down to your heart, relaxing and dilating the coronary arteries, letting your circulation flow freely ..."

I detailed the healing changes happening from head to toe, within every organ and system. Several times every day.

One afternoon, a visitor told me I had a call on the waiting room phone. When I answered, an unfamiliar voice said, "This is Dorothy. I was the flight attendant who did CPR on your husband."

"Oh, thank you so much," I whispered.

"Everyone on the plane prayed for you and Alan, and as we landed at Logan Airport, the pilot announced that Alan had been brought back to life," she said. "I'm so glad to hear Alan lived. We attendants were so worried that if he died, you would annihilate yourself with guilt because you kept saying, 'Why didn't I know? What did I miss?'"

I cringed to hear my words repeated. "There's a good chance I would have felt guilty for a long time," I said. "But now we have another chance, and I'm trying to move ahead."

Five days after his cardiac arrest, Alan was awake and looking in my direction. I said, "Honey, this is Janet. You're in the hospital. You had a heart attack. You're safe and getting better every day." As I said the words "heart attack," Alan's blue eyes flew open, his blood pressure jumped ten points, his legs flew off the bed, his face screwed up around the endotracheal tube, and he began to cry. He twisted his head to stare at the cardiac monitor beeping above the bed. It pained me to cause him so much agony, but it was the first time he grasped an explanation. I stroked and kissed him until he calmed down. *But he understood.*

To my amazement, I had a sustaining routine within twenty-four hours. I began each morning in the splendid garden outside the cafeteria. I found solace in a "sparrow meditation," focusing on the bird's every move and chirp while I breathed deeply and tried to center myself for the day. I was jealous of the elderly couples strolling in the garden, and watched longingly as an elderly gentleman pushed his wife's wheelchair among the roses. Would Alan and I ever go outdoors again? Would he ever be free from all the life support machinery? Could we go back to being the couple who loved to explore nature on foot, kayaks, and bikes?

Then I went back up to the ICU and turned the page on Alan's calendar. I bent over the bed and whispered in his ear, "Good morning, darling; welcome to another day."

3. SHATTERED IDENTITY

One minute, I had my husband Alan. The next minute, he was gone. His disappearance became more apparent and disturbing to me daily.

After two weeks in the ICU, Alan was transferred to a cardiac telemetry unit. Now he was able to breathe on his own, but being more alert only led to confusion and fear. He still had periods of agitated delirium, which resulted in the staff sedating and restraining him. I watched in horror as he struck out, screaming for everyone to leave him alone. At night, I called my friends back in Boston on the pay phone that became my lifeline and pleaded, "What if the agitation never stops and Alan can't be comforted? How am I supposed to take home this man who can't understand or remember what I've told him for two minutes? He perseverates and asks the same question twenty times. It drives me crazy. How am I supposed to take care of him?" They didn't know either.

Alan required hemodialysis three times a week to treat kidney failure. He had frequent chest pain from his heart condition and was weak from pneumonia and being so ill. His broken ribs were healing gradually, but were very sore.

Alan's biggest frustration was constant hunger. He often begged, "Food, food, food, give me food." The muscles and nerves in his throat were traumatized by the brain injury and intubation. He was fed through a feeding tube stitched into his stomach and was only allowed small sips of liquids. It took several attempts before he could pass the swallow test, which is a special X-ray that examines all of the structures in the mouth, throat, and esophagus that must coordinate to swallow safely. His body was slashed with wounds from central venous lines and other equipment. He looked like a vanquished warrior who had not given up the fight.

Alan couldn't form many words, but he talked in a pressured gibberish—a stream of sounds and words he desperately needed to convey, but which had no common meaning. Whenever he spoke, he pushed his face right up into mine and pierced me with his beseeching blue eyes. I searched his dramatic expressions and tried to match my response to the emotion coming through his words.

"Are you scared, Alan? You are safe here. You are in the hospital. You've been very sick. I'll stay here with you," I said. Not very satisfying to either of us, but the beginning stages of communication. I touched him whenever possible—holding hands, kissing him, rubbing his feet, gently stroking his cheek. Touch was our more common language, as he gripped my hand tightly or reached through the bedrail to pat my thigh.

I appointed myself Alan's "Interpreter of the World" and spoke in short phrases when he jumped at a sound from the indecipherable environment. "That's the elevator door closing. It won't hurt you." Alan's memory was severely impaired, so any explanation had to be repeated often.

Each doctor involved in Alan's care repeated that he had a severe anoxic brain injury from lack of oxygen during the cardiac arrest. I was impatient with their repetitions, which didn't tell me anything useful. Of course he had a brain injury. We've all heard that brain cells start to die after three minutes without oxygen. I was the only person who had timed the entire resuscitation for over forty-five minutes. Well, okay, almost an hour. Part of what those doctors wanted me to understand was that brain *injury* is the polite word. What it really means is extensive, violent damage to tissue and neuronal connections caused by a cascade of chemicals and hormones.

The brain consumes about 20 percent of the body's total oxygen supply and uses oxygen to make energy to transmit electrochemical impulses between cells and to maintain the ability of neurons to receive and respond to these signals. Neurons are the cells that receive and pass on information within the nervous system by a cascade of alternating electrical and chemical events. Neurons have a small space between the cells, called a synapse. An electrical signal triggers the release of a chemical, called a neurotransmitter, which gets the chemical message across the synapse gap between two or more neurons and activates the target cell.

In an anoxic brain injury, where there is a reduced flow of oxygen-rich blood, neurons and other brain cells begin to starve and are prevented from performing vital biochemical processes. The person's neurotransmitter production and function can be very affected and contribute to severe impairments in cognitive skills, motor abilities, mood, and psychological functioning.

There are many types of neurotransmitters in the brain, and they contribute to how we think, feel, move, understand, and communicate. Alan's neurons and neurotransmitter system were very damaged. Some doctors consider the prognosis for recovery after an anoxic brain injury to be worse than that after a traumatic brain injury, but each person has a unique injury and potential for recovery.

I started to get glimmers of what this brain damage was about, which shook me to my core. One morning, I watched Raymond, an occupational therapist (OT/R), do a brief evaluation. Raymond held up objects from Alan's lunch tray: a glass, fork, spoon.

"What is this?" he asked.

Alan stared at him blankly. He couldn't say the names of the objects or show what to do with them. He couldn't name the color of my dress. He couldn't say the words for window or chair. He couldn't follow a two-step instruction to pick up a paper and hand it to the OT. A grim picture started to come together in my mind.

Out in the corridor, I asked Raymond, "Would it be anywhere near accurate if I imagined Alan's brain as a blackboard that has been wiped clean?"

He hesitated for a moment and then said, "Well … that might not be too far off."

We did not know yet that Alan had lost his critical abilities to read, write, talk, think, and remember. Even the simplest cognitive functions—which I came to understand are far from simple—would have to be relearned. I knew intellectually that the brain governs every function of the body, but I was just starting to grasp that the brain is also what makes us who we are as individuals and human beings.

Alan had very little idea of who he was. Occasionally, he could tell the doctors his name, but usually not. From the time he first awoke from the coma, he had a sense that I was his wife and wanted me close to him. When I walked away from his bedside, he howled in panic until I returned. But he couldn't call me by name consistently for several months.

When his family visited, Alan brightened up and responded to their voices with smiles and interest. His sister Barbara told Alan stories about his early family life in Chicago. Alan listened with curiosity, if not recognition. I tried to anchor him in the present by reminding him of our home in Jamaica Plain, where we had lived throughout our eleven-year marriage. I told him he was a professor of physics at Northeastern University. He listened politely, but all the information seemed to sit on the surface of his impenetrable memory.

We had no consoling answers to the pleas Alan moaned endlessly: "Go home. Go home. GO HOME."

Barbara brought in a copy of Alan's book *Uncommon Sense: The Heretical Nature of Science.* This was Alan's first foray into writing for the interested public after writing several textbooks. We propped *Uncommon Sense* on the windowsill beside his bed, along with dozens of get well cards from friends back home. I pointed out the book to the staff caring for Alan, saying, "Alan wrote this book. He is a well-known teacher and author." I wanted them to view him as more of a whole person, not just a brain-injured man whose behavior could be "difficult." When they had time, they did stop and congratulate Alan on his work. He smiled at their attention.

I began a campaign to see if Alan could recognize himself through his words read aloud. Every day, I showed him the book and said, "You wrote this book. Your name is Alan Cromer. See, this is your name," as I pointed to the green letters on the cover. Then I slowly read the same opening paragraphs from the introduction, gazing up often to check the expression on his face.

While being read to, Alan had the calmest composure he'd had since becoming ill. As he watched me with complete focus for several minutes, his anxiety abated, and tension seeped out of his body. This was in complete contrast to his frequent state of distraction, inability to concentrate, and difficulty sitting still. Alan couldn't comprehend his written arguments for why some cultures developed science while others did not, but on some level he was responding to his mother tongue: the language of science. Sometimes when I paused, he shook his head and said, "Good book, not mine," or even his ultimate compliment as a book reviewer for scientific journals: "Good writing!"

One Sunday morning, we enjoyed a peaceful interlude free of roommates, staff, and procedures. Alan, attached to a cardiac monitor and a collection of IV pumps, slouched comfortably on his elbow in an oversized recliner. His skinny legs stuck out from a wrinkled seersucker bathrobe. I sat across from him, enjoying the warmth of the July sun streaming in the window. My face softened and my shoulders dropped their perpetual load. When Alan was relaxed, I was relaxed. The scene felt so normal. Alan and I often sat together reading in companionable silence in our living room at home. When one of us came to an interesting passage, we read it aloud to the other and shared a brief discussion.

This was the first time I'd been at peace since Alan's cardiac arrest. Alan seemed responsive to the normalcy of this respite too. In one effort-filled motion, he swung his legs up and planted his feet in my lap with a huge grin. Ahhh, contact!

I smiled back and massaged his feet as I began reading *Uncommon Sense* for the twentieth time:

"It has been less than 400 years since Galileo's telescope and Newton's mathematics opened the heavens to human investigation, little more than 100 years since the realization that human beings are the result of an evolutionary process that has extended over unthinkable millions of years ..."

Suddenly, Alan shot up in the chair and exclaimed, "My words, my book. That's my book!"

I was overjoyed and hugged him, screaming, "Yes, yes, you wrote this book. You are a smart man!"

Alan smiled broadly and clutched the book to his chest. I telephoned everyone we knew to report that Alan recognized his own book. I felt a surge of hope that we could restore his sense of self and his identity. Maybe even make him the same person again.

We soon found out that after brain injury, remembering something once does not mean the information is in place and accessible thereafter. Alan's connection to himself would always be tenuous and require reinforcement in many forms. Repetition became the strongest tool in our arsenal. It took me a few months to understand that the original Alan, *My Alan*, was not coming back. It took much, much longer to accept that reality. Our mission would be to rebuild an identity that incorporated the essence of Alan that remained with the shards of this new person who was beginning to emerge.

Some days, I was almost as confused about my identity as Alan was. A stranger had taken over the battered body of my husband. My raconteur husband now said three coherent sentences, on a good day. I vaguely wondered who I was supposed to be as his wife, if *My Alan* no longer existed. I didn't even look like myself. Planning a two-day trip to Chicago, I'd tossed two dresses and a pair of sandals in my suitcase. When the ICU staff told me that Alan's condition was stable enough for me to leave the hospital for a brief errand, I asked his nephew Mike to drive me to a nearby Marshalls.

"Just stand by the door, I'll be fast," I said to Mike.

Zipping through the racks at the front of the store, I threw a few outfits and packages of underwear into my cart before sprinting back to the hospital. The elastic-waist trousers and matching beige tunic I now wore were far from my usual style.

I didn't think about my appearance until I caught a glimpse of myself in Alan's mirror. I'd dropped eight pounds in a few weeks, showered only when a Good Samaritan nephew brought me to his house, and wore underwear that was even the wrong size and style. My face looked haggard and pinched. The reflection in the mirror reminded me of the shell-shocked people interviewed on television after a fire has destroyed everything they own.

By the time I moved from the fishbowl of the ICU waiting room to a studio apartment in the hospital's guest house, I was on the verge of falling apart. As soon as I locked the door that first night, everything inside me let loose.

I flung my body from one twin bed to the other screaming, "Why, why, why? Alan, where did you go? Come back, come back, don't leave me. No, no, no, I can't do this."

Crying hysterically and slamming the beds with my entire body over and over, I kicked the closet door with all my strength and slapped the wood until the palms of my hands were blistered. Only the breathless onset of an asthma attack made me stop. I didn't care. I was desperate for physical release from being so controlled, so good, so attentive, so enraged at all that had happened.

During this period, I was agonizing over another critical decision in a chain of major decisions. We now knew that Alan's heart attack had been caused by blockages of 80 to 100 percent in four major coronary arteries. He was at high risk for a fatal heart attack or stroke at any time. He needed coronary artery bypass surgery, but I had to decide whether to have the surgery performed in Chicago or try to transport Alan back to Boston for surgery.

I questioned the doctors constantly about which Chicago hospital had the most experience with complex cases, what complications could occur after surgery, and what the worst scenarios might be during an air ambulance flight home.

When the cardiologist said, "Alan won't be able to fly for about four months after surgery, so you will have to stay in Chicago for rehabilitation," my mind was made up.

Four months! I had weathered four weeks of trauma far away from my main supports, and loneliness was making my heart hurt. Barbara and Sandy visited regularly, but I needed my friends around me if I was going to give Alan the best care. So, I worked with our doctors in Boston and Chicago to coordinate the complex transfer.

On July 30, a contingent of Resurrection Medical Center ICU nurses and doctors joined local family members in giving us a robust send-off. Alan and I waved gamely from the ambulance transporting us back to O'Hare International Airport. I quipped to the ICU nurse manager, "If this all works out, we'll come back next summer and do a billboard advertisement for you: 'I came back to life at Resurrection!'"

The med flight home was terrifying. Alan was strapped on to a narrow stretcher beside the window. The critical care nurse monitored him continuously from a tiny jump seat at his feet. Crammed into a tiny seat with my knees drawn up to my chin, I willed myself to breathe.

Alan's perseveration reached its highest, anxiety-driven level yet. For four hours, he recited a litany of unending questions but couldn't take in the answers. "Where are we? Where are we going? Why are we here? What's the matter with me? Who are you? When will we get there?" Over and over.

I wondered about those same questions, and not just literally. We tried distraction, singing, and reading aloud, which all helped for a while. Air ambulances can only fly at half the altitude of airplanes, so the flight took twice as long. Fortunately, the marvelous nurse was extremely competent, and I trusted him to handle any situation that arose. When the flight touched the ground at Logan Airport, I jumped down and kissed the ground.

An ambulance transported Alan to Brigham and Women's Hospital (BWH) for further evaluation and treatment. I will never forget the experience of sitting in the back of the ambulance, staring out the window on a glorious August day. All along the Esplanade, fluttering green trees framed the view of sailboats racing along the glittering Charles River. I was startled when a young woman on rollerblades darted across three lanes of traffic on Storrow Drive to greet her friends on the Esplanade path.

All of a sudden, it hit me: "Oh, it's still summer," I said to Alan, who was sleeping. "Oh, these people's lives just went on normally. They don't know that ours ended. Oh."

During my frantic phone calls home, I told friends that a giant hand had plucked us out of our normal life and flung us into the wilderness of catastrophic illness. Now I felt that same hand drop me back into the world I knew best, but nothing looked the same. We didn't fit. We were aliens.

A few nights later at BWH, unencumbered by tubes and lines for the first time, Alan climbed out of bed and stood in the middle of the room. Alan was bereft. Gaunt after losing thirty pounds in a month, pale grey skin stretched across his sunken cheekbones. His blue eyes overflowed with tears.

"All I need is someone to love me," he said. "Basically, all I need ... is someone to love me. Come here. Put your arms around here ..."

His most coherent words yet, his longest sentence, and the wisest words he had ever spoken. My heart broke and opened wide at the same time. I gathered my husband into my arms and climbed into bed with him. We wrapped our bodies together and held on for dear life.

"See, that's all I need," murmured Alan.

"Me too," I whispered back.

Following a full cardiac evaluation, we faced another dilemma. Dr. H., the cardiologist, laid out the choice we had to make.

Seated on the edge of Alan's bed to include us both in the conversation, Dr. H. said, "We don't have any clear-cut guarantees or exact precedents, but in our best judgment, if Alan had the bypass surgery now, his cognitive function and memory would probably stay at the present, severely damaged level." He paused.

Alan looked at him but didn't comprehend the words.

"He would probably not be able to make progress in brain injury rehabilitation. His ability to communicate would be frozen," he continued.

Dr. H. explained that there was also a calculated risk that the stress of rigorous surgery and the procedures involved could cause further brain damage.

Outside the room, Dr H. explained the problem to me more directly.

"Alan could live in a nursing home, watching TV, playing with his nephew's kids when they visit, and being dependent on others for his care. Would he be satisfied with that kind of life?" he asked.

I only needed to think for a second before replying, "Absolutely not. I know some people could be content that way, but Alan would hate it."

Dr. H. nodded and said, "If we delay surgery to pursue rehabilitation, there is no way of predicting whether Alan could regain the ability to read, write, communicate, or remember. And the process would be arduous for him. Without surgery, he could have another heart attack or stroke at any moment. This time, the event would be fatal. Think about it and let me know your decision," he said as he turned to answer his insistent beeper.

Alan had fought so hard to come back to life and progress this far. But he lacked any ability to understand his condition or the treatments being discussed. He couldn't participate in the decision. The need for me to make a decision based on two almost equally bad choices had started in the ICU and would continue for years. Each recommendation to treat a serious problem came with a warning that it could make another condition worse, or lead to dangerous side effects.

I mulled over everything I knew about Alan the man, husband, uncle, teacher, nature lover, and traveler. I thought about all the mosaic pieces that come together to form our portrait of a life well lived with integrity and involvement. I tried to picture the scenarios the doctors described. I talked over the choices with everyone who knew Alan best.

I concluded in my heart that if Alan could not learn to read, write, and have a conversation with those he loved, he would not consider his life worth living. Those were the abilities he treasured most: the life of the mind, above all else. It was just who he was.

Now I added a new factor to my moral compass. Now I considered which decision and which choice I could live with and survive the torment involved. It didn't take long to decide that I could eventually come to peace with leaving Alan at risk of a fatal heart attack or stroke if we delayed surgery, but I would never forgive myself if he survived surgery but lived locked in a world he couldn't escape and no one else could bridge. I decided to postpone surgery in service to pursuing rehabilitation.

When I explained my decision to the cardiologists, they recommended that Alan be transferred to Spaulding Rehabilitation

Hospital's specialized brain injury program for intensive physical and cognitive rehabilitation. With a mixture of apprehension and hopeful anticipation, I agreed.

4. Initiation into the Brain Injury World

On August 8, five weeks after Alan's heart attack and cardiac arrest, we were officially admitted into the world of brain injury. Alan was now one of the 1.4 million Americans who sustain some type of brain injury every year.

My first impression of Spaulding Rehabilitation Hospital's Brain Injury Unit could not have been worse. After Alan was admitted, the busy weekend staff couldn't give us attention for what seemed like an hour. Alan was confused and wildly agitated by the ambulance ride and new surroundings. The bed he was assigned to had not been cleaned, the carpeted floor reeked of urine, and his roommate's wife started right in telling me their problems. I tried to console and calm Alan while my own angry panic grew. I wanted to steal him away from this place right away, but knew it would be impossible to care for him at home.

After the bed was cleaned and Alan began to settle in, a resident physician came in to examine him. Alan failed every part of the neurological exam while yelling, "Take me home, get me out!" over and over.

The doctor turned to me and said offhandedly, "So you're a psychiatric nurse, huh? That will come in handy. Some people say brain injury is like chronic mental illness without the stigma." I got what he meant, but wanted to slap him. I thought of the people I'd worked with who have schizophrenia. Some of them shuffled down the city streets talking to themselves and never quite fitting into the world most of us take for granted. I couldn't bear to think of my husband that way.

As the evening wore on, a young woman ran screaming up the hall and hit a nurse who was preparing medications at the med cart. I watched the nurses escort the patient back to her room and tuck her into the security of a Vail bed: a net bed with zippered side doors used to keep agitated people from hurting themselves or others. To me, it looked like a cage, and I was horrified at the prospect that Alan might require a Vail bed if his agitation persisted. So much about brain injury treatment initially struck me as punishment. Incurring a brain injury was in itself the ultimate unjustified punishment.

In time, I understood the range of severe behavioral issues that accompany brain injury, both as the stages of recovery unfold and later as permanent conditions manifest their damage. But then, I was a novice. I scrutinized each professional who was responsible for taking care of my husband. My trust was hard-earned because there was so much at stake.

As I prepared to leave the hospital in tears that first night, the evening charge nurse put her arm around my shoulders. She said, "This place will seem chaotic to you at times, but miracles happen here."

I wanted desperately to believe her.

I had no idea how many types of brain injury there were until I got to know some of the patients gathered in the dining room every morning. Most had traumatic brain injuries caused by a blow or jolt to the head from an external force. This can happen from a fall, car crash, being hit by a car, or violent act. Even a sports concussion can cause a TBI. Alan was in the category of acquired brain injury (ABI), caused by something that happened within the brain. These brain injuries were caused by lack of oxygen, infections, tumors, or strokes. Each type of brain injury causes specific problems related to the area of the brain that was damaged. Most patients were in the early stages of recovery and had trouble with memory, communication, mobility, and controlling behavior.

TBIs can often be seen with imaging studies such as a CT scan or MRI. A blood clot, hemorrhage, or swelling can be seen and measured. I asked several times if Alan should have an imaging study, but the doctors declined and told me that (with the technology available in 1998) the damage from anoxia wouldn't be easily visible. I still thought there should be some kind of baseline study to use for comparison as time went on.

I carried a diagram of the brain and its functions to every meeting. Readers might want to have a diagram handy to refer to in this chapter.

Traumatic brain injuries usually affect particular, focal areas injured by the trauma. In contrast, the damage from an anoxic brain injury tends to be more generalized and widespread. Certain areas of the brain are particularly sensitive to lack of oxygen because they are located in "watershed areas." These areas are fed by the smallest blood vessels that branch off from main vessels. When the pressure in these watershed areas drops below the critical level to deliver oxygen-rich blood flow, damage happens quickly and is often not reversible. Some of these areas and the functions they serve include those deep inside the brain: the hippocampus (long-term memory and new learning), the amygdala (memory formation and mediation of fear, anxiety, and anger), the basal ganglia (body movements), and the thalamus (sensory and motor information).

The frontal lobe (language expression, cognition, motor planning, and short-term memory) is often affected. In addition, the other brain areas most impacted by anoxic damage include specific areas of the major centers such as the cerebellum (cognitive functions, speech, body's position in space), the occipital-parietal cortex (interpreting sensory data), and the substantia nigra of the brain stem (movement and mood regulation).

As a consequence of damage to these areas, people who have severe anoxic injuries often have major problems with memory and cognitive functioning, movement disorders, trouble controlling behavior, mood disturbances, and headaches. People who have TBIs also have many of the same problems.

Every patient on the brain injury unit was assigned a team of highly skilled specialists. Dr. B., the team leader, was a physiatrist, a specialist in rehabilitation medicine, as well as a neurologist. The team included a primary nurse, neuropsychologist, speech-language pathologist (SLP), physical therapist (PT), occupational therapist (OT/R), and doctors in training. Each professional did an extensive evaluation and discussed their findings in the weekly team meeting, where therapy goals were set.

Alan's first weeks at Spaulding were a combination of ongoing evaluation and intensive treatment. Medically, his nutritional needs had to be addressed so he could have the enormous energy required as the brain burns calories to do its work. He received medication to dilate his coronary arteries and control blood pressure, but he had pain in his chest or behind his shoulder with minimal activity and tired easily.

At the same time, some systems were healing surprisingly well. Alan's kidney function improved enough so that hemodialysis could be stopped after six weeks. His skin peeled off in sheets around IV sites and wounds, leaving baby pink skin underneath. I watched the bruises and incisions heal and thought, *Alan is shedding his ICU experience.* The lack of visible evidence of what had happened to him added to Alan's confusion. When he looked in the mirror at Spaulding, he said, "See, there's nothing wrong, nothing's broken. Get me out of here."

Back at Resurrection Medical Center, we considered taking a few photographs of Alan at his absolute worse. The idea repulsed me at the time, but now I wished we had proof of how critically ill he had been to explain why he needed rehabilitation.

Alan's most arduous and distressing times happened during the testing that made up the neuropsychological evaluation. Neuropsych testing provided information that gave important information about the likely location and extent of the injuries to Alan's brain. The results were used to formulate plans for cognitive rehabilitation and ways to manage behavior problems. There are many types of neuropsych tests. Some tests involve the patient answering questions verbally to check orientation, comprehension, and language production. Others involve listening to an instruction and then carrying out a task; for example, "Draw a clock with the hands pointing to 4:30." Other tests involve building patterns with wooden blocks, or pen-and-pencil testing of knowledge and logic. To check the ability to name objects, the doctor holds up a card with a picture of a bird or a tractor and the patient tries to identify the object.

One Saturday, Alan and I met with the team neuropsychologist, Dr. C., in his cramped office for another attempt at testing. Dr. C. began by asking Alan questions about himself: What is your name, what is your wife's name, where do you live, what was your mother's name? Alan started off with a confident air, but quickly dissolved into a state of mortified rage when he couldn't answer any of the questions.

"Let me out of here! This is stupid. You don't know what you're doing!" he screamed.

He tried to stand up and take a swing at Dr. C., then swung his wheelchair around and rammed it into the closed door in an attempt to flee the scene. I froze, held my breath, and waited to see how Dr. C. would handle the situation.

Dr. C. turned Alan's wheelchair until they sat face to face. In a firm voice he said, "Alan, if you leave this room you won't get any better, and you'll never know the answers. If you stay here, we can help you."

Pointing at me, he continued, "This is your wife, Janet. She loves you and wants to help you." My heart rate matched Alan's, but he returned to the table and did his best to answer the questions. I tried to imagine how lost I would feel if I couldn't call up my name or address. Like so much about brain injury, it was hard to fathom.

I was horrified as I listened to all that Alan no longer knew. Where did all his knowledge disappear to? How could he survive?

The neuropsych assessment, done over several days, showed that Alan had a range of impairments from damage to many parts of his brain. Language was a major problem. His ability to make, recognize, and say words was seriously limited, although he tried valiantly to generate the right word. Alan didn't know the names of common objects when asked what they were (anomia).

He made up words frequently (neologisms) and mispronounced the sounds of letters (phonemic errors). He struggled to find the words he needed (expressive aphasia) to express himself and couldn't communicate effectively beyond one simple sentence. This was an enormous source of frustration for Alan. And for those of us who desperately wanted to communicate with him.

Alan could not read a sentence. Nor could he write a sentence or copy a line of text. Occasionally, he could print a few letters.

The problem that complicated all the others was memory impairment. When Dr. C. did a standard mini-mental status exam, Alan scored poorly on all the cognitive abilities required for routine activities such as knowing one's name, location, and the date, and being able to remember a few words after a brief time. Anoxia had caused permanent damage to the most fragile areas that make and store memories (the hippocampus and amygdala), so now Alan had vascular dementia.

Every type of memory would be affected. Alan had amnesia for everything that had happened to him after the heart attack (anterograde amnesia). He had also lost many years of his life preceding the arrest (retrograde amnesia). He could neither access his long-term memories nor remember something that happened ten minutes ago. Alan's memory now began and ended with his early years. The extent of amnesia is one indication of severity of brain injury, and Alan was classified as having a severe brain injury. Additional tests showed that Alan could not form new memories. I couldn't understand how he could possibly relearn information and skills if he couldn't form memories or benefit from experiences.

The neuropsych testing introduced us to the term "executive functions," which essentially refers to the complex group of skills we use every day to plan, make decisions, problem solve, make sound judgments, monitor how we are doing, and get along with others. Many areas and functions of the brain are involved with executive functions, and Alan's combination of problems also meant that his executive functions were severely impaired. Intensive rehabilitation would be required, with no guarantee of improvement.

As the severity of Alan's brain injury revealed itself, I became numb from grieving the husband I had lost and the self Alan had lost. It was incomprehensible to me that Alan, the enthusiastic raconteur and visionary, the man capable of the deepest feelings and informed thoughts, could be gone.

I had to quickly master one of the hardest and most necessary tasks family members face. That is, to simultaneously grieve inside while showing up ready to participate resolutely in Alan's rehabilitation. Many family caregivers quietly see-saw between sorrow and duty every day.

Alan's speech-language pathologist, Jennifer, did an evaluation that also showed "profound cognitive-linguistic impairments," characterized by markedly impaired memory, orientation, and attention deficits. He now had a fluent aphasia, which meant that he had difficulty understanding spoken or written words, but he talked effortlessly. However, his speech was often meaningless and made up of malformed or substitute words.

He raced through the tests without recognizing his errors. He didn't recognize that the pen was for writing, so he held it upside down and tried to write with his fork. He couldn't recite the alphabet or read numbers or letters. He was unable to organize his thoughts, problem solve, or reason. Alan's problems with thinking and problem solving were ominous because they signaled that the frontal lobes and cerebral cortex of his brain were severely damaged.

In spite of all these impairments, Alan had enough self-awareness and an unusual ability to share flashes of brilliant description about his inner experiences. "I'm in a world where everything is different. I'm scared, I'm scared …"

Or, "I'm in a boat months and months away from my real life." His next sentences would be a mix of real and made-up words, but we could respond to the emotions he expressed so eloquently.

I soon realized that one way I could help Alan was to sit beside him and wait patiently for him to form tangled thoughts into words I could catch and give back to him. I believe that he made much more effort to communicate because I, or another family member, was right at his bedside so much of the time. A process I thought was automatic took inordinate effort and skill. When he used words incorrectly (paraphasic utterances), I could guess what he meant and repeat his statement using the correct words.

For example, when Alan said, "I'm cheating right now, my message," rubbing his arms, he meant, "I'm chilly right now, my muscles." He added, "I was staying in another temperature before."

Alan's all-time favorite book was Homer's *The Odyssey,* about the Greek hero Odysseus, who must fight legendary battles and endure years of hardships before the gods allow him to return home to his wife, Penelope. I began to refer to the battle to save Alan's life and embark on this voyage of extreme reclamation as "Alan's Odyssey." Over time, that became our shared way of framing this journey through the netherworld. I started to read chapters of *The Odyssey* to Alan like a bedtime story. Once again, he listened with pleasure. Odysseus's ordeals had nothing on Alan's.

Cognitive rehabilitation is the foundation for every form of treatment in brain injury because the goal is to restore or compensate for cognitive impairments by working on the functions needed in the real world. But that's just the beginning of the definition. Everything that goes on in the brain is connected, so an emotional state such as depression or the physical pain from broken bones influences and is influenced by our cognitive abilities.

Brain injury affects the whole person: cognitive, physical, social, and behavioral areas. So rehabilitation specialists employ an integrated model based on the patient's strengths and abilities to work across all of the four key areas. Ultimately, the goal is to empower the patient and family and provide compensatory strategies and tools so he can be as independent as possible. Even though the neuropsychologist and speech-language pathologist worked very directly on cognitive rehab, the principles were inherent in the treatments Alan's physical therapist and occupational therapist offered also.

Dr. B. explained that treatment often starts with whatever physical or cognitive function is working for the patient. When an area is stressed by repeated effort, the brain gets the message to increase that function. Repetition and gradually increasing the challenge can lead to improved abilities. For example, at first Alan could focus attention on a task for three minutes. The therapists structured his sessions to build up to five and then ten minutes, and eventually twenty minutes. All the therapists liked the motto, "Use it or lose it." Alan and I heard it and repeated it to each other so often it could have been on the Spaulding tee shirts

The Spaulding staff encouraged family members to participate in the sessions and continue specific exercises during the day for maximum effect. I was an avid student in this new world. I found that this type of intensive family training was essential to prepare me to guide and care for Alan at home.

The morning began with Heather, Alan's occupational therapist, teaching him the basic routine of "activities of daily living," known as ADLs. These are the routines we do every day such as using silverware to eat a meal, taking a shower, shaving, and putting clothes on the right places in the right order. Her evaluation showed that Alan had lost the ability to plan and perform motor tasks in a logical order (apraxia). Apraxia came through as he tried to dress. He couldn't sequence his clothes at all, and often tried to put his tee shirt on over his legs as pants. I had to stack his clothes in a pile on the bed with the items he put on first on the top.

He didn't remember how to do anything without being shown many times. None of the standard tools were familiar or intuitive. I flinched when he tried to brush his teeth with his disposable razor and drank soap from the dispenser when thirsty.

Sometimes, humor would carry the moment for us. Teaching Alan to shave was my job, and Alan found the process absurd.

"You're kidding me, right?" he said as he lathered up his face all the way to the scalp. "Guys don't really do this."

I replied, "Yes, they do, because men haven't evolved as far as women."

We both had a good laugh. Sometimes, we had to laugh at the absurdity of it all before trying again. Our motto became, "Practice makes perfect."

One of the most dramatic lessons was how profoundly exhausted Alan's body and mind both became from the enormous effort required to focus and learn in every therapy session. He often said, "My head is so tired. I need a nap right now." Alan felt and worked better when we planned long rest breaks throughout his daily schedule. This was a permanent condition that always needed to be considered.

Alan's physical therapy evaluation showed that his balance and coordination were poor, so he couldn't stand safely or walk more than a few feet. Beth, Alan's PT, began working on Alan's ability to focus and pay attention to her instructions for the exercises. The biggest impediment was the sights and sounds of the large gym, where he was surrounded by other patients trying to master different equipment. Alan couldn't benefit from PT until Beth reserved a private room for his treatments.

In the beginning, Alan couldn't even sit up on the edge of the bed without toppling over. He needed to rebuild strength in his core muscles as well as extremities before he could stand safely. In PT, he worked his way up from sitting to standing with support from two people. Then he and Beth worked on regaining balance by rocking on a tilt board, followed by cautious steps between the parallel bars. Physical therapy was Alan's favorite time because he had always been an avid exerciser, and now he wanted to walk again.

Over several weeks, the connections between Alan's nervous system and stronger muscles were repaired to the point where he took hesitant steps with a walker and then the handrail lining the hall. He told Beth, "I like driving (walking) with you."

From then on, there was no holding him back. Safety was a foreign concept to Alan. His insight and judgment lagged behind his urge to move, so he lurched off in every direction at all hours. Alan wasn't the only patient whose urge to flee the hospital was coupled with a fledgling ability to carry through, so he and several other patients wore special identification bracelets that triggered an alarm if they got too close to a door or the elevator.

Alan's primary nurses, Kristen and Kevin, were also involved daily. They helped me understand what was going on in Alan's brain that made him perceive things and behave as he did. They coached me how to talk with Alan and let him do whatever he could for himself. Their frequent presence and knowledge of Alan's idiosyncrasies and multiple medical issues made them astute observers of effects whenever there was a change in medications or interventions. They explained the rationale for any medications and treatments, and helped me find specific information.

Along with Alan's other therapists, the nurses got to know me as a person and gave me enormous support along with education.

Jennifer, Alan's speech-language pathologist, was responsible for addressing Alan's problems with swallowing, memory, and language early in therapy. She began by working on helping him to swallow safely. This was a major concern because Alan was at risk for another aspiration pneumonia. As Alan prepared to take a bite of food, Jennifer told me to cup his face in my hands and say, "Alan. Look at me. Pay attention. Chew. Swallow." Over and over.

If Alan felt like his wife was always in his face, it was an accurate perception.

Jennifer made recommendations about specific cognitive therapy approaches for the other therapists to try in their work with Alan. For example, she suggested that they rely less on complex verbal instructions and instead demonstrate what to do. So I also adopted a "show more, tell less" approach with Alan.

Jennifer also introduced Alan to the memory book every patient used to get to know themselves and the basic facts about their life. The red, loose-leaf binder had pages containing single lines of information such as "My name is Alan Cromer."

Next page: "I am in the hospital. I had a heart attack on July 5, 1998. I need therapy to improve my memory and strength."

The next page held a labeled photograph of Alan with his age and birthday. It read, "I am a physics professor." There was a photo of me on another page. Then a photo of our house in Jamaica Plain with the cherry trees in bloom and our address.

But this was a tough textbook for Alan. Day after day, we drilled on his full name, where we lived, and the name of his nephew Tom, with whom Alan shared a father-son relationship. I could overhear Alan's roommate Fred reciting the contents of his memory book too. Fred had a severe traumatic brain injury from a fall from a ladder, but he could recall his name. I sat on our side of the curtain, sulking about Fred's faster progress.

"How pathetic is this?" I mumbled. "I'm jealous of a guy who knows his wife's name 40 percent of the time."

The extent of his losses began to crystallize for Alan on his sixty-third birthday.

On August 15, my sister Sherry came to visit with her husband Jack, fourteen-year-old son Hank, and eight-year-old twins Sammie and Cassie. The children were shy around their formerly athletic and gregarious uncle, now frail and seated in a wheelchair. We gathered in the dining room with Alan at the head of the table, basking in their love and attention.

He smiled as he opened his presents and took some time to put his words together. Stumbling over his words, he said, "Thanks for being here, thanks for being here," as he stood up and staggered to give each person hugs and kisses.

Seated again, he turned his attention to the birthday cards. He opened Sherry's card, smiled at the cartoon on the front, and then looked puzzled as he tried to decipher the words inside. Suddenly, Alan screamed, "I can't read, I can't read!"

He threw the cards across the table and began to weep and hyperventilate. The little girls looked shocked.

The rest of us jumped in to say, "It will be okay, Alan … you'll be able to read again … you will get better." Our attempts at reassurance couldn't penetrate Alan's anguish.

Now he understood the bitter truth: Professor Cromer could not read.

Late that night, Alan asked the nursing assistant to call me at home.

"You're in our house," he sobbed. "But I'm in the house of misery.

5. Professor Cromer Learns the Alphabet

Every morning began the same way: We sat in the dining room overlooking the Charles River, going over Alan's schedule for the day. Alan picked up the milk carton on his tray and scrutinized the print as he tried to read. Then he screamed, "I can't read, I can't read," and hurled the carton across the room. No amount of preparation prevented him from this daily discovery. Because he couldn't remember what he had already experienced, he was doomed to repeat the discovery over and over. Each time, his outburst of sorrow, horror, and fear was as intense as the first time. If I reminded him that he was starting to learn to read, he said, "Let me just try ..." and failed again. But that willingness to try repeatedly and not give up turned into Alan's biggest asset.

Everything in rehabilitation is a series of links, like a long chain. Jennifer explained that before Alan could even begin to learn to read, she would need to find a way to connect with him and get him to focus his attention for several minutes. Working on attention and memory would have to come before working on reading. Before Alan could sit calmly to pay attention, the room had to be very quiet, he had to be physically comfortable, and the people with him had to speak softly and move slowly. Everything made him anxious, since he didn't understand anything that was going on. The therapists told me that Alan would pick up signals from me, so the more at ease I could be, the more he might try to be that way too. I happen to have a calm temperament, but believe me, there were plenty of times I had to fake being calm and confident.

We started with relearning tasks that used to be automatic and involved procedural steps, like getting dressed, or going to the refrigerator to pour himself a glass of juice. At first, Alan got distracted within seconds. Everything had the same importance and mystery to his battered brain. He had to do things many, many times before there was a hint of familiarity to the task. It took weeks of walking down the same corridor to the sunroom and back (a straight line) before he could recognize the door to his room with his name and room number prominently displayed. The severity of his memory impairment made everything much harder.

The only thing Alan thought was important was learning to read and write again. So, eventually Jennifer used that interest to form an alliance with Alan that led to sustained attention, concentration, and repetitious practice. Reading is one of the most complex neurological processes human beings are capable of learning. Jennifer told us that learning to read is a completely different process for an adult with an injured brain than it is for a child. For Alan, it all started with the alphabet. Jennifer began with the random letters Alan was already scribbling (usually his name), telling him the name of the letter and sounding it out. She wrote out the whole alphabet and said the names of the letters. Alan was fascinated by the sight of the alphabet. He started by tracing over the shapes of letters we had drawn, gripping his pencil and moving slowly and methodically.

Then he moved on to connecting the spaces in letters shaped by dashes. The hardest but most satisfying part was copying the letter below the one written by Jennifer. Each progression took concentrated effort and many hours of practice. Alan liked Jennifer and called her "my teacher."

On weekends, Alan's SLP was Margaret, whose presence exuded an easy calm. We met in a conference room, where Alan could spread his elbows on the table and bend his head low to the paper to carve short sentences onto the lined paper.

Copy this sentence: Alan is my name.
Alan is my nawm namm
Twis is my mnar Name

Copy this sentence: This is my wife Janet
This my wtyf Yanet
I can rtht a scy word.

Sometimes, he recognized his mistakes, but more often, he didn't. Alan was fervent about practicing, even when he couldn't understand what he was doing. He said, "All I want is my reading back. I have to get my reading back."

As I watched Alan's efforts and grasped the enormity of his losses, I knew how much was at stake. I was terrified that if Alan could not learn to read again, he would not consider his life worth living. He loved to sit in his recliner beside his bookcase reading science, history, politics, or religion for hours. Discussing the content was equally important since ideas, questions, and countering arguments to what he had just read filled his mind.

He wrote constantly: letters to the editor of newspapers, book reviews for scientific journals, articles for education journals, class lectures, and chapters for his latest book. In earlier years, he even tried his hand at science fiction and fables. I could not imagine what could possibly give his life meaning if he couldn't read or write.

In Alan's room, words surrounded us. To help with his inability to name objects, a select number of items were adorned with index cards bearing their names: cup, window, chair, telephone, book, clock. Oh yes, the clock. When we are children, we learn to do things in a developmental sequence. One step builds on the preceding one. The tasks get harder as we master the easier ones. But people with brain injuries have to learn to do everything all over again at the same time. Just think about that for a moment.

Alan was trying to learn the alphabet at the same time he was learning to walk and count money and tell time and hold a conversation and remember who he was. This astounded me, and I often summarized his condition for people who had not visited by saying, "Alan is learning to do everything all over again, and all at the same time. Just imagine all the automatic and deliberate things you've done today. Now imagine not knowing how to do them, and having to learn again all at once. It's unbelievably hard."

Friends couldn't conceive of what I meant until they spent a day at Spaulding. Then they said, "I don't think I could handle trying to grasp and do twenty things at the same time like Alan is doing." Observing a whole day of rehab therapy gave everyone a deeper respect for the enormity of what Alan faced, as well as respect for the intelligence and skills of the professionals who were guiding him.

Alan and I didn't have children, so I felt at a distinct disadvantage teaching him to tell time or tie his shoes. We fumbled along together, approving of digital watches and shoes with Velcro closures.

On the days when he felt discouraged and downhearted, Alan asked, "Isn't there anyone like me who did this? Isn't there anyone who used to be smart and now is stupid? Isn't there anyone like me?" Alan's friend Mike found just what Alan was searching for. Mike brought in an article written by the former president of MIT, Jerome Wiesner, about his experience following a stroke that left him paralyzed on the left side, unable to speak correctly or read, and with "black holes" in his stored knowledge. In the article, Dr. Wiesner, who was also treated at Spaulding Rehab, described his frustration in eventually recalling all the letters of the alphabet, but not in the right order. It took Dr. Wiesner two more weeks of concerted effort to get the letters in order. Having a peer he could relate to gave Alan the hope and determination he was desperately seeking, so he insisted that I read him the article daily.

Alan practiced his writing around the clock. When I arrived in the morning, he would be asleep amidst the labors of his nocturnal scribbling. He covered the sheets, tissue boxes, old menus, and any available surface with his letters and words.

A B C B F G FF E H …

Copying the calendar: Januwayy, Neubary Mauch, Aphr, ... Octom, Nobember ...

I can rt a woed if I try to be it.

I shoud try to trit more, because if will insteal the moud fo by trit ...

That meant "I should try to write more, because it will instill the moves for me to write."

During the day, we sang the alphabet song countless times. Yes, that universal song, "A-B-C-D ..." became the soundtrack to our days as we sang it over and over, matching each letter to a note. We practiced writing and sounding out words intensively.

Alan's debut performance came on the morning of September 6. As I entered his room, he sprang from the bed, stretched his arms wide, and gleefully sang "A-B-C-D-E-F-G ..." all the way through to the end, with no mistakes!

I have never been more proud of my husband! I really mean it. His other academic accomplishments paled in comparison to the effort of learning the alphabet. I hugged him as we bounced up and down, saying, "You did it, you did it! You got your letters!" It had been eight weeks since his brain injury, and Alan had his alphabet back.

Alan asked me to bring in the books he wrote. He assumed he could learn to read by studying physics again. I didn't want to break his heart, but he caught on soon.

One morning, he sat me down and said, "I think I have to start from the beginning. Like a kid. Go buy me some first grade books."

I said, "I think that's a very wise idea, honey." I had been waiting for Alan to suggest such books, knowing that if I brought it up, he would feel insulted. Later that day, I scanned the level one reader shelves at Barnes and Noble for books that would appeal to Alan, the books with illustrations that matched the words he might recognize. Alan accepted his new books with dignity and got to work.

Every afternoon after Alan's therapy schedule was over, we curled up on his bed and practiced reading. His favorite book was *My Dog's the Best*, by Stephanie Camelson. Adults learn to read by a combination of phonetic sounding out and recognizing words. Alan sounded like a first grader as he haltingly sounded out, "My ... dog's ... the best. He's ... shaggy," without any inflection or rhythm.

At first, we made a list of the "target words" that were problematic: smooth, tail, pompom, waggy: most of the words in the book were on the list to be drilled. Alan couldn't look at the pictures for clues to the words because that broke his concentration and added the problem of describing a scene. But he never gave up. Over the next few weeks, Alan aced *My Dog's the Best* and managed to read it aloud all the way through to Jennifer and me. Again, we celebrated his achievement. We were both very fond of this emblematic book, so I framed it and hung it in our bedroom at home. Alan was on his way to reading and writing again!

Celebrating progress was very important. I felt genuinely proud of Alan, but at the same time, I realized that I was asking his family to congratulate him for things young children practice. I tried to convey that the effort Alan's injured brain expended on counting or reading was the equivalent of passing a graduate school course, and I'd appreciate it if they responded to his news accordingly. Their sincere praise made Alan proud and kept up his motivation to practice.

Learning the alphabet and beginning to recognize words made up the early stages of regaining reading skills. The next steps involve comprehending the words and message, retaining the information, and being able to recall it at will. Alan's memory impairment interfered with each stage. To practice, I read him newspaper headlines and the first paragraph of the story, then asked what the story was about. He always loved current events, and this became a favorite exercise.

When Alan was particularly interested in a subject, we worked to copy or summarize the text in his logbook. Retention and recall remained problematic for years, so Alan's books were bedecked with post-it notes with a few words at the top to remind him of where to find a favorite story.

Once again, Alan felt most like himself when he had a book in his hands.

6. COAXING MEMORY, CONNECTING COGNITION

When we were preparing to transfer Alan from Resurrection Medical Center back to Boston, Dr. B. leaned over the bedrail, looked Alan in the eye, and said, "Professor Cromer, you've studied hard and taught all of your life. You have written many physics books. But in the next year, you will have to study harder than you have ever studied in your life."

Dazed and critically ill, Alan looked up at him and said, "Okay. I will."

Now we were deep into three months of brain injury rehab at Spaulding. How do you start to rebuild a person's sense of self, his identity? How do you explain a rich and full life that's been forgotten? Well, we had one custom-made tool. For a few years, Alan's sister Barbara had a videography business producing videotaped interviews with people as they reviewed key time periods and people in their lives. In 1990, Alan recorded his biography with Barbara. I could never have filled in the information about his childhood and formative educational experiences that he detailed on his tape.

We played the videotape during speech therapy sessions, in the evening, and when family members visited. Spellbound, we watched my movie-star-handsome husband talking with pleasure about his early fascination with a catalogue of prosthetic devices (artificial limbs) given to him by the family doctor: a harbinger of his interest in science. Hands waving, eyes bright, Alan spoke passionately about being a Ford Scholar: an advanced placement college program that enabled him to attend the University of Wisconsin after two years of high school. Listening, I was struck again by Alan's intellect. He finished college in three years, and earned his Ph.D. in physics at age twenty-five.

On the videotape, Alan's distress was raw as he talked about his parent's divorce when he was twelve years old. Sometimes, he cried when we watched that part of his story, or when he talked about his first wife Marge's death from cancer when she was thirty-five.

Alan never tired of listening to himself recount his life's journey. Repetition was a crucial part of everything we did, especially as he got a grip on who he was. I had a mental image of the process of taking in, imprinting, and holding on to information. It seemed as if Alan was kneeling by a pond, using his hands to scoop up water filled with darting silver minnows. As he raised his cupped hands to a pail, the minnows slid out from between his fingers on the rivulets of water before his hands could reach the pail. On Monday, he might remember one fact from the video, on Thursday, another. He and I made lists of questions to ask his family to get more details about his favorite parts.

Alan started to recount specific information to his treatment team: "I went to Camp Martin Johnson. I learned to swim and sail. I think I like boats."

After a brain injury, some knowledge and memories gradually emerge on their own. The rest has to be put in place or relearned all over again, if possible. It was amazing and sometimes disconcerting to watch Alan's memories re-emerge, especially those that had a strong emotional content. One morning, he awoke crying hysterically. "My mother, my mother … my mother died, she died," he wailed inconsolably. The emotion that accompanied the memory was always as immediate as if the event had just occurred. This happened many times. For a few days, he grieved Marge's death.

He called his brother and sister in tears. "Did you know my wife died?" he wept.

The responsibility for restoring another person's memory is daunting, strange, and even morally complex. Alan constantly asked me questions about his life, relationships, and career. He had so much to relearn, complicated by the burden of cognitive and memory impairment. Everything he heard was a challenge to comprehend, and he didn't remember it for long. I wondered what to leave out of my answers, even more than what to include. Does he really need to know about the hard times, the family quarrels, and the professional skirmishes he waged?

Alan's sense of chronological time was pretty well shot, which complicated everything. To help Alan grasp events over time, we drew a series of timelines. Each time period was diagrammed on a separate sheet of paper. Then family members could anchor the event they described to Alan by indicating it on the timeline of his twenties or forties, or his career.

One day when we looked at the timeline of Alan's marriage to me, he noticed there had been a ten-year gap between Marge's death and our marriage. This led to a bombardment of questions about his girlfriends in between.

"I must have had lots of girlfriends," he said. "What were their names, what happened?"

By this time, I had been living at his bedside in various hospitals for three months, and I had zero interest in tackling this topic.

"How should I know?" I snapped. "I wasn't there. They were all mean and ugly, so you married me. I'm the only one you need to know now!"

I even felt a twinge of jealousy toward his absent memories.

But it wasn't over. One morning, he woke up screaming, "I had another wife! I had another wife ..." The story I'd decided not to tell him. Indeed, Alan had a second, very brief marriage a few years after Marge died. It ended in a bitter divorce. Now she was back. This information thrilled and frightened Alan.

For days, he marched up and down the hall, asking every nurse, "Did I tell you I had another wife? How many wives am I going to remember?"

Of all the memories that flitted in and out of Alan's mind, Wife #2 latched on. When he raved about her for the twentieth time, I called my friends and pouted, "If she's so great, let her get in to Spaulding and sit with him for a day."

Alan's memories that did return did so in a patchwork pattern, generally starting with those from childhood and early adulthood, occasionally mixed with a teaching scene. He had no sense of the year these events happened or even how old he was at the time. I wasn't surprised that he didn't remember our dog Molly, since we'd only had her two years, but I was curious about his reaction to the photos of Molly I hung in his room. Alan looked at the pictures and said, "Cute dog," in a flat voice. He shrugged his shoulders when I said Molly was our dog.

One day, my friend Kathy joined us for dinner and said she'd taken Molly for a walk before coming to Spaulding. All of a sudden, a light went on in Alan's memory. He threw down his fork and exclaimed, "I know Molly, Molly's my dog. I love Molly! She's our baby, right?"

That weekend, Kathy brought Molly to Spaulding for a joyful reunion. Alan asked dubiously, "Do you remember me, Molly? Do you know me?" Molly's squirming snuggles and licks confirmed that she knew Alan well. Molly curled up in the forefront of Alan's memory, and a relationship was reborn. He even left messages for Molly on our home answering machine: "Molly, this is Daddy. Be a good dog. Take care of Mommy."

Jennifer introduced several great memory strategies. "Strategies" is the word you hear most in rehabilitation. All treatment is geared to learning and using strategies to relearn material or compensate for deficits. One of the best tools was a simple Polaroid instant camera. Alan loved to take pictures of me, friends who visited, and views from the outdoor deck. He asked people to take photos of us with our arms around each other. I wrote "Janet loves Alan!" and hung the photos where he could see them at night. Having the photographs immediately available helped form connections and memories. He was fascinated by watching the development process happen right before his eyes. I took photographs of the rooms of our home to plant those seeds and assure Alan he would be coming home eventually.

We filled small albums with his photos, all labeled in Alan's tentative new script: *Alan and Alan's Molly, My nephew Tom.*

Later, Jennifer asked Alan to write a sentence to describe what was taking place in the photo. Over many months, he built up to writing two-paragraph stories.

Alan was completely dependent on external memory devices from the time of the brain injury onward. The most consistent and helpful tool was the plain notebook he used as a logbook to record three things he did each day to help organize his thoughts, practice writing, and track the hard work he did. Alan took several minutes to compose each sentence, then several minutes to get the misspelled words on paper.

The labor was worthwhile when he could look back a few days and say, "Oh, I cooked an egg. I walked five laps. I wrote a story. I thought I was just sitting here in prison but I guess I'm accomplishing something."

Near the end of Alan's Spaulding stay, the neuropsychologist introduced him to a small personal computer system that could help him track appointments. The plan was that he could store more information in it as his abilities increased. Before the brain injury, Alan was a computer whiz who loved buying the latest software and upgrading his beloved Macs. Alan had one of the first Palm Pilots and raved about its efficiency.

Now he stared at the device quizzically, the way I used to stare at him when he explained the inner workings of a computer to me when all I asked was how to do a simple function. We did try to use it, but I think we underestimated the extent of Alan's hearing loss at the time. In the hospital, Alan had trouble hearing the alarm on the device, so it couldn't jog his memory to take his pills or go to an appointment. Months later, we found out that the early hearing loss Alan had before the brain injury had progressed to the point where it interfered with conversation, and he needed hearing instruments.

That taught me that sometimes there are simpler, non-cognitive explanations for why a strategy isn't working and we should check out the basics. After he started wearing hearing aids, Alan did use the Palm Pilot at home with better results.

Jennifer used a computer to work on reading and writing exercises with Alan, and he said he felt more "grown-up, not a kid" at the computer. Richard and Pam gave Alan a "V-Tech" computer that had a large screen and questions for young students in many subject areas. The difficulty level could be increased, so Alan used the V-Tech for years to practice spelling, sentence completion, synonyms, geography, and math. That computer was acceptable to him even though it was designed for children because it looked like a regular laptop computer. As long as the tool didn't look childish, Alan was amenable to giving it a try.

Alan could be remarkably sophisticated at describing his memory problems. After two months of cognitive rehab, he told me, "I remember when you tell me something (inconsistently), but I don't have my own feeling memory of things, like the feeling of my dog in my lap, the feel of my dog licking me."

Since we worked with whatever troubled or interested Alan most, we tried to build up a critical mass of tactile, feeling memory (somatosensory memory). We touched frequently; Alan ran his hands over the books and sniffed the bindings as he read; I described the source while he was enjoying a sensation to make a new link. I said, "Rub this fuzzy peach on your cheek. Smell how sweet it is before you eat it, Alan." The more senses we could involve, the better the chance of remembering.

In occupational therapy, Alan and Heather worked on building the concentration necessary to carry through a task such as writing a check. Every aspect of every session the therapists did was calculated as a step toward a goal that applied to real life. For example, Heather started by having Alan practice writing the check in a quiet room with no one else around. She worked up to holding their session in the dining room, with people coming and going, which required Alan to bring his attention back to the task repeatedly. Alan was humbled each time he realized he couldn't follow through on a basic procedure.

He started with "Why do I need to learn to write a check? I've been doing that all my life."

A few moments later he'd say, "Are you sure I used to do this? It's very confusing."

For the first month, I went to all of Alan's therapy sessions to keep his anxiety level from interfering with the tasks and to learn how to carry over the day's material. Over time, the focus changed to having Alan meet alone with the therapist so he could build trust and learn strategies to manage anxiety and frustration on his own. At first, I was apprehensive about leaving, but then I relished taking that time for a walk along the Charles River or sipping a cup of coffee while reading a good novel. I deliberately tried to not use that hour for business matters or insurance skirmishes.

Practicing the art of distracting myself from our problems and immersing myself briefly in something pleasurable turned out to be a survival skill. I learned to take brief respites throughout the day to let go of tension, take relaxed breaths, and focus on one need of my own that day.

I was also writing a logbook of my own. I soaked all the new information up like a sponge, but I also needed a place to capture my feelings about this new world. Over the years, I've found journaling to be a way of exploring, and chronicling how I came to be the person I am. Now I wrote in my constant companion, a small black notebook I bought in the Resurrection gift shop.

As time went on, I wrote on scraps of paper and tucked them into beautiful journals intending to go back and elaborate on the sentiment on the scrap of paper.

However, there was seldom time to do that and always something new to write about. When I came across the scraps and read them, I realized that they held the essence of what I wanted to say anyway. So I taped them on the journal pages and appreciated them as full-fledged entries. Better to write a furtive sentence in the moment than to wait for the "right" time to compose a full page.

Spaulding offered a weekly support and education group for family members. During the session, a physician explained some aspect of brain injury, how it would affect our loved one at home, and what we might do about the problem. There was also time to share our concerns and evolving coping strategies.

The single best piece of advice I took with me was offered by Val, an occupational therapist who facilitated the group.

"You will have to do whatever it takes to bring your best self to Alan every day," she told me. I interpreted that advice many different ways over the following years, but always came back to it.

I asked, "What do I need to come even close to being my best self today?" Then I'd try to take a step in that direction.

Every family member who is thrust into unanticipated caregiving carries all of who they are to the challenge. There were many skills I didn't know how to teach Alan, and I had so much to learn about brain injury. What I could offer was a certain skill and comfort level with understanding and communicating with people whose minds and brains work differently.

Years of working on inpatient units and in community settings with people who had major psychiatric illnesses prepared me to help Alan learn to perform basic life skills, manage some of his behaviors, think in more constructive ways, and enjoy life even with modifications. One of our differences would even come in handy. Alan thought in highly rational ways and sought a logical and swift solution to most problems. I had a higher tolerance for ambiguity and thought there was usually more than one fine way to approach a problem. I chose to work in specialties where many conditions were chronic, solutions took longer, and the relationship was part of the treatment. There is a lot of ambiguity in living with a brain injury.

The relevance of cognitive rehab to everything Alan was learning was readily apparent to me. So, I was aghast when the therapists explained that insurance companies will pay for a certain number of physical and occupational therapy sessions, but they will not pay for extensive cognitive rehabilitation, usually provided in the form of speech-language pathology sessions. Cognitive problems are harder to see, quantify, and explain than problems like not being able to walk or dress oneself. Not being able to cross the street safely, count to twenty-five, or tell someone you need help getting to the bathroom are harder to explain as disruptive to independent functioning.

This reimbursement issue quickly becomes a problem for the majority of patients who have to deal with cognitive and memory impairment after brain injury. As soon as someone can pass certain mobility and safety tests and do basic self-care tasks, the insurers want them to leave intensive rehabilitation. Never mind that the person can't read, write, or remember where he lives yet.

We too were caught in this conundrum because Alan's ability to walk and bathe progressed much faster than his memory, reading, and reasoning. At times, we backed off practicing self-care skills in service to more time for writing the alphabet. Alan's treatment team spent hours trying to educate the insurer about brain injury rehab and justify another week of inpatient rehabilitation. I also spent hours calling professional advocates in our healthcare network and campaigning for the treatment he needed most. In order for a brain injury survivor to have an optimal outcome no matter the extent of injury, cognitive rehab must become an integrated part of daily life for years to come.

7. THE SURGING TIDES OF EMOTIONS AND BEHAVIOR

When I stepped off the elevator in the morning, Alan would be waiting for me, wringing his hands and wailing, "Oh, there you are! I thought you were dead. What took you so long?" He wasn't just glad to see me; he acted as if I'd been gone for months instead of hours. He grabbed me in a crushing embrace and sobbed.

At night he cried, "Don't leave me here. When you're here everyone is nice, but when you're not here, they're all assholes." He hung on to my clothes and tried to squeeze into the elevator with me.

Then he cursed me, saying, "You're leaving me to be with another man."

Brain injury wreaks as much absolute havoc with the emotions and behavior as it does on memory and cognition. Like most people with a brain injury, Alan suffered from catastrophic emotional responses, in part from extensive damage to the frontal lobe of his brain. All of his internal controls and automatic responses were gone.

One contributing factor to the catastrophic reactions was that without working or short-term memory, Alan could not hold on to the image of me or anyone else when we weren't right in front of him. In his mind, I was dead, and he was alone and abandoned. He panicked when I went to the rest room for ten minutes. I can't imagine the terror of not having a picture of the person you trust most firmly planted in your mind. This played out many times when I went home at night.

Another contributor to his wild emotions was the stew of neurotransmitter chemicals coursing through Alan's brain. The brain injury disrupted the amounts, flow, and functions of all the chemicals we depend on to keep emotions manageable and predictable. Coupled with the inability to understand and interpret anything happening around him, Alan was in alien territory inside his body and in the outside world.

Alan also trusted his nephew Tom, so, bless his heart, Tom came in every night to sit with Alan until he fell asleep. Tom and Alan had their own way of bantering, watching TV, and telling stories. It also helped when Tom played my audiotaped messages for Alan.

"Hi Alan, this is your wife Janet. I'm at home, but will come see you at 8:00 AM tomorrow. You are safe, and now it's time to sleep ..."

When a new piece of information or a new experience worried Alan, he went into a full-blown panic. Panic escalated to rage and paranoia as he tried to understand what was happening. He shouted, "What's going on? Someone tell me what's going on!"

For a few weeks, Alan freaked out every time the nursing assistants approached with the blood pressure machine. As they tried to apply the cuff, Alan screamed, "What are you doing? I've never seen that thing, get it away from me!" I had to explain to the staff repeatedly that they needed to tell him what they were doing each time, even though he'd had his BP taken dozens of times.

When Alan thought something was funny, he laughed hysterically and ran down the hall shouting the joke to the nurses. He had no sense of judgment and was disinhibited about saying whatever came into his mind.

But worst of all were the rage attacks. Alan had no ability to modulate emotion, and anger is the most physically stimulating emotion for anyone. As soon as he felt humiliated, threatened, or confused, he lashed out, face red, eyes bulging, spit flying. He became stronger than his medical condition should allow and hit, pushed, and screamed. He tried to escape from the unit or beat off the staff who came to inject him with antipsychotic medication and place him in restraints one more time.

When I was there, he yelled at me, "I hate you! It's your fault I'm in this place." I dreaded these scenes. I got so churned up that later I vomited. I was terrified of Alan in a rage, yet hated the staff for not preventing more blow-ups and restraining my husband like a madman. I hated that his brain was like an easily tripped land mine in a field I would have to traverse every day.

Early in the Spaulding admission, the psychiatrist asked me many questions about my husband's personality before he became ill. Had he ever been depressed? Did he have a temper? How did he handle stress? On and on. I answered as honestly as I could. Later, though, I realized that it's hard to say anything bad about someone who is sick and suffering. Maybe I minimized some of my answers to the psychiatrist. Yes, in fact, Alan had been prone to angry outbursts before, but they came up suddenly for a realistic reason, he yelled and got it out of his system, then the outburst subsided. He turned toward finding a logical solution for the problem. Alan had never been violent.

Before the injury, Alan was an optimistic realist, as was I. Seasoned by life, he focused on the present and was full of ideas for future projects. He thrived on high levels of professional stress and could usually leave work problems at the office. He used his terrific wit and negotiation skills to put things in perspective and burned off aggravations by working out and jogging daily.

But now, post-brain injury, psychotic anger would be the toughest and most frightening problem we had to deal with going forward. Alan now had a pronounced psychiatric illness as a consequence of the brain injury.

The hardest thing about awareness after brain injury is that it is transient and precarious. As the weeks wore on, Alan became aware of his problems and pleasures. Sometimes, that was a consolation and spark; other times, it opened new realms of fear, despair, and anguish.

Alan knew his memory had been severely wiped out, and he had glimpses that he wasn't as smart as he used to be when he tried to do basic math.

Alan plunged into a wrenching and mournful agitated depression. Some days, he terrified me by saying, "Let me die, let me die, I'm worthless. I don't want to live…. You deserve a normal husband."

He was so impulsive that I feared he would hurt himself or escape from Spaulding. The nurses explained that depression is a common consequence of brain injury because of a combination of biological changes in the levels of neurotransmitters and growing awareness of one's losses and deficits. Alan's psychiatrist prescribed antidepressant medication and spent time talking when Alan could find the words. Memory impairment made it difficult to try the talk therapy usually helpful in depression.

I let Alan show me his genuine despair and anguish and consoled him about his suffering whenever possible.

"I might as well die … don't get any showness of better, just showness of stupid. I just want a little of my life with you back," he said. It helped when I pointed out the positive gains he was making but couldn't remember.

The staff assigned an aide to be a "sitter" to give Alan one-on-one attention and keep him safe. At night, he lashed out at the sitter, screaming racial epithets that the old Alan would have been mortified to hear. The worst part of the depression subsided in a few weeks, but Alan benefited from antidepressant meds for years.

When Alan was attuned to his situation, he let us know what mattered to him.

"This is extra hard for me because I've never been serious sick," he said. "I hope I get enough good life back after to make it worthwhile."

"Honey, what would good life be for you?" I asked.

"For me it's not to die too soon, to get more years," he said right away.

Alan was willing to keep going.

By the end of the day with Alan, I was exhausted from trying to calm him down, ease his sorrow, and defend my honor. I knew my stress level was sky high on the nights I drove home on Storrow Drive and had to hit the brakes as I took the wide curve near the Hatch Shell stage too fast.

Once at home, before tackling the pile of bills and legal papers to become his guardian, I sat at the kitchen counter with a bowl of popcorn and a glass of wine. I have since learned that this is the universal snack of family members after a rough day at the hospital. Crunching the popcorn gets out tension, while sipping one glass of wine (must be arousable for calls from the hospital) relaxes the muscles and makes sleep a possibility. Many nights, I swore I heard Alan's key unlocking the back door. My mind swung from thinking, "Oh, good, Alan's home" to "Oh, my God, he escaped from Spaulding!"

Most nights ended with a comforting ritual. I slumped to the floor and sat with my back against the wall to share a bowl of ice cream with our dog Molly. "Molly," I'd say, "you wouldn't believe what they told me today. I don't know what I'm going to do."

With Molly's tender attention, I managed to get to bed and be back at Spaulding by 8:00 AM.

Lack of insight is another major problem after brain injury, especially pertaining to limitations and deficits. Alan did not believe that he needed to be in the hospital, or that he couldn't just step out the door into his old life.

He said, "All these problems you say I have … it's a plot between you and the doctors. You just want to keep me in the hospital and give them all my money."

When we explained that his heart was weak, Alan grabbed a chair and hoisted it over his head, shouting, "See this? Does this look weak?"

The first time he did it, I almost fainted. Remembering his cardiac arrest and knowing what could come next, I got better at blocking future hoists.

One lazy afternoon, Alan awoke from our nap together. He smiled cherubically at me and said, "I had a dream that they poured all new memory into me." I swallowed the lump in my throat and said, "Wouldn't it be great if they could do that? But you'll get your memory back piece by piece."

In truth, I didn't understand that Alan couldn't distinguish between reality, memory, dreams, and hallucinations. With the magnitude of brain injury he'd sustained, the filters, boundaries, and compartments of his mind were all shattered and swirled together.

This strange problem became apparent when Charles, a young colleague from Northeastern University, came to visit. Alan didn't remember Charles, and my introduction was of no help. As Charles approached to shake Alan's hand, Alan sprung out of the chair and grabbed his arm, urgently asking, "Are you real, or a memory, or a dream? How am I supposed to tell?"

I was stunned at his brilliant question.

It is one thing to learn the alphabet or how to count money, but quite another to figure out what is real. I told Alan that if he could touch someone, they were real. I told visitors to expect to be squeezed. It might sound humorous, but it was very serious. Making the esoteric concrete was a daily battle.

Alan poked my arm and asked, "Are we here talking for real? I mean, so we're in your waking time and I'm in my waking time right now? Yes? Oh, good."

Alan's emotions and behavior were an ongoing focus of concern and intervention. Many of the problems he experienced were common manifestations of the early stages of recovery from brain injury. From the beginning, medications were used to help manage depression, anxiety, and physical and mental agitation. Even though I was a psychiatric nurse, I didn't realize how much Alan's brain required some amount of medication to make up for damage to the neurotransmitter system until the medication stopped working and his symptoms went out of control. I didn't like the idea of Alan being given strong antipsychotic and antianxiety meds. But without the meds, he couldn't think clearly, focus, pay attention, or listen to explanations. With the meds, he said, "I'm calmer today, let's try to read now."

Over time, I came to view the meds as performing the function that insulin serves for a person with diabetes: they substituted for something the body could not produce or use, and allowed the person to function more normally. Diabetes was a reasonable comparison because, as we learned, brain injury is also a chronic disease that requires long-term management and periodic adjustments in treatment. Like other chronic diseases, brain injury can also predispose patients to other diseases and be negatively impacted by other medical problems. It's all linked.

Effective and humane treatment always combines a behavioral approach with medications to help the patient and family understand what triggers the problem emotion, thought, and behavior, then trying ways to avoid or minimize the trigger and response. A lot of trial and error is mixed with new learning and faithful practice before the best approach is found and everyone is satisfied.

To that end, the team neuropsychologist Dr. C. and I devised a data collection system to track Alan's emotional responses and outbursts. Careful observation and tracking of patterns are important when trying to understand the cause of a problem, which interventions or medications made it better or worse, and what helps the person the most. The chart contained space for me to note the time and circumstances of the episode, for example anxiety or sadness, the behavior that followed, what seemed to help, and what made it worse.

After a few days of keeping these detailed hourly records, I insisted that we add columns to track Alan's good moods and positive statements, which were in evidence just as often as his anger and fear. Having information about what made Alan happy or reflective let us strive for balance in his moods and pleasures. Though tedious to keep, these charts gave us lots of valuable information to work with, even though there was no magic or quick solution. Patience is probably the first requirement for the person going through rehab, the family, and the treatment team.

One surprising finding was that boredom triggered Alan to become feisty and argumentative. So, when he was waiting for an appointment or was too tired to read, I suggested that he build a cabin with Lincoln Logs or water his plants.

Alan's anxiety scores went up as his spoken language skills improved. Analyzing the hourly data over days let us see that now that he could ask more questions about his medical, financial, and career status, he became more anxious about the answers. I gave him the same consistent answer in a reassuring tone and wrote the answer in a notebook for others to read to him. For the anxiety that so often triggered an explosion, we asked the staff to repeat an explanation a few times in a quiet tone, even if they'd done so ten times yesterday. If I was there, I guided Alan to practice relaxed breathing or tensing and relaxing the muscles of his hand, with me modeling the motion. It was too much to expect him to do these things just by saying, "Relax! Take a deep breath …"

Sometimes, Alan let us know exactly what he needed. The catastrophic reactions were often worse in the morning, and they wore Alan out. He said, "We've got to find a way for me not to be so messed up in the morning. Can't they take away people's bad dreams?" So we tried adding an early morning message to my tape, telling him which tasks to focus on first.

I said, "Alan, walk down to the dining room and get a glass of apple juice."

It also helped if a staff member brought him to the sunroom while they talked about something he could look forward to that day.

Dreams drove his overactive mind in both good and bad ways, so I even tried suggesting good things to dream about before I left. He liked to focus on great places we had vacationed, so we looked at travel photos while I described the setting. The night sitter repeated those cues when he awakened. I think Alan had an extremely good ability to "see" images while asleep.

Alan often became anxious while awaiting appointments. Priming him for the next activity just ten minutes in advance let him prepare for the next challenge and rehearse what to say so he had more control. "Heather will bring you to the kitchen in five minutes. What do you want to cook today?"

One of the subjects that's hard to bring up in brain injury rehab is the effect that patients can have on one another. Most patients on the brain injury unit were in early stages of recovery, just learning to figure out what's going on and to communicate in basic ways. During Alan's stay, the rooms were semi-private, so the two patients shared space but were seldom able to share a normal conversation or support each other in any way.

Too much stimulation in the environment is one of the guaranteed triggers for outbursts. There were many times when, through no fault of their own, they frightened or angered each other. Alan was fearful of the primitive sounds one roommate made while being turned or bathed by the nurses. He asked me, "What terrible thing are they doing to that guy? Will they hurt me?" On his worst nights, Alan terrified his roommate by ripping down the canvas curtains between their beds while in a rage.

I firmly believe that having private rooms on a brain injury unit could ultimately hasten progress in rehabilitation by making it easier to get more rest and use behavioral strategies to manage difficult emotional states.

Since Alan often lacked the ability to put his emotions into words, his behavior said it all. At Spaulding, we started the early steps of teaching Alan to recognize the first signs of anger, say he was mad, and get a grip on his response. This is a very difficult assignment after brain injury, but many survivors can build these skills with consistent practice, and we continued at home.

In many ways, Alan was easy to please. A phone call from a nephew, a bowl of ice cream, laughing at a TV show, walking outside instead of using the wheelchair, and a big noisy smooch all delighted him tremendously. We shared moments of contentment and happiness almost daily. On weekends, we took a break from rehab work and spent hours on the deck, watching the drawbridge go up and down over the lock between the Charles River and the Atlantic Ocean. As I watched the motor boats and canoes paddling along the Charles, I lamented to myself that our days of fun on the water were probably over, along with everything else. I appreciated the new navigational skills we were gaining at Spaulding, but I missed our old life as part of the fleet enjoying a summer cruise on the open waters more than I let on.

8. "Who Am I if I Am No Longer Myself?"

Our sense of ourselves, of our identity, is nebulous and fragile, yet taken for granted while we have it. Alan lost his entire sense of who he was as a unique person. He forgot who he was as a husband and uncle, professor, athlete, man in the world. As the weeks of evaluation and rehab at Spaulding mounted up, one image I had of Alan was as a collage: a pile of vibrant scraps from the past, present, and future all scattered around us, waiting to be pieced together into a unified being. A work woven with rich fibers and textures that told a story that made sense. One that has cohesion and can be held up at arm's length while you say, "Aha, now I see the pattern, the message, what was going on here."

I enjoyed making collages out of beautiful papers, scraps of material from old clothes, smatterings of appealing words clipped at random from magazines, and splashes of paint that matched the moods of the piece. *Webster's Dictionary* defines a collage as "the art of combining a variety of materials to form unique compositions." There was easily as much art as science involved in making Alan whole again.

Some of Alan's collage pieces had two sides. On one side, the major changes since the brain injury, and on the other side, some semblance of familiarity. For example, Alan loved nice clothes. He prided himself on always wearing a tie and tweed jacket to teach his physics classes. Many of the other professors wore casual clothes to class, but Alan said wearing professional attire was a mark of respect for his students and the material he was teaching. At Spaulding, he wore sweatpants and sweatshirts every day to make it easy to dress and do physical therapy. The new clothes hung loosely on his underweight frame, but we told him he looked like the jogger he'd always been. He and his roommate wore each other's clothes interchangeably since neither of them recognized particular items in the closet as their own.

After his morning shower, Alan still insisted on combing his hair forward for fullness before flipping it back and parting it on the right. How did he know he always did it that way? He couldn't say the words for comb, soap, or toothpaste, but he mimed their use effectively when he wanted to use them. Between his familiar mannerisms, bright blue eyes, and cheeks like polished apples, there was enough of Alan for me to recognize and hold on to.

And there was the huge collage piece of knowing and being known. Alan and I knew each other so well before he got sick.

After eleven years of marriage, I knew how Alan's razor sharp mind worked, always restlessly dissecting facts from falsehoods. I knew his mannerisms and what they meant. The way he nonchalantly hooked his right arm over the back of the kitchen chair after dinner, easing into his opinions on the news of the day. That when his lips got thin and his face got white, he was about to get mad. That he blushed when I teased him that the dimple in his right cheek was even deeper than the one on the left. I knew how to make him lighten up, to evoke gales of laughter. The areas we agreed to disagree on. He would only consider medical treatments that had been proven effective in scientific studies. I was very involved in integrative therapies that brought the mind, body, and spirit into the treatment equation. I knew that it made him feel loved when I cooked him lunch.

And my husband knew me so well too. He could usually read my moods and knew he could interrupt my worrying with a walk around

Jamaica Pond. He helped me put money into perspective and convinced me we could have a vacation house in Narragansett, where we biked and kayaked to our heart's content. He encouraged me to take the leap into private practice because he believed in my skills and talents. He knew that when we traveled, I felt secure roaming freely as long as I had a map somewhere in my purse. Alan's style was to stop at every intersection, pull out the map, and ask, "Where are we? Where do we go next?" He knew I felt cherished when he brought me a bouquet of freesia for no reason.

But now Alan could not remember basic things about himself. How could I expect him to know anything about me? His behavior and performance in therapy were wide-ranging and inconsistent. Some doctors addressed Alan as *Professor Cromer,* and then it seemed Alan tried even harder to answer their questions. Most of them called me *Mrs. Cromer,* and I didn't rush to say, "Call me Janet." I wanted it to be clear that I was Alan's wife, guardian, voice, and watch dog. I had not changed my name until five years after we married. I was independent, had my own professional reputation, and was the last McIsaac in my family. But as our love deepened and our bond as a two-person family became very solid, I'd wanted to share a name. So now I was Mrs. Cromer. Inwardly and outwardly, I was glad to claim the marital title.

I never sat around pondering what it means to *know* someone and to feel *known by* that person. Until brain injury. Now, by necessity, it was on my mind constantly. Alan usually recognized me by sight, had even held on to an innate sense that I was his wife. He'd wanted me by his side since he emerged from the coma.

One day when he woke up confused from a nap and saw me sitting by his bed, he said, "I think you are someone I used to know. I think you are someone familiar to me."

I said, "That's right, honey; I'm your wife, Janet. And I love you very much." He smiled. I smiled too. I took any recognition I could get.

There were several weeks when Alan called me Barbara, his sister's name. I didn't mind because Alan loved Barbara and had often considered her the most important woman in his life. But there is a difference between being recognized and feeling known.

Some parts of the Alan collage became more mysterious to me as I learned more about brain injury. I took in the facts and applied them intellectually. But the parts that bothered me most were those I found hardest to believe; for instance, his inability to remember the most essential information. I even resented that he wasn't trying harder to get a firmer grip on those particular memories instead of leaving me as the repository of all our shared experiences.

Big important memories were gone: How we met. The first time we said, "I love you." Why he decided to marry me instead of that other woman. How could you not remember that? But he didn't, and the shame and horror of not remembering engulfed him.

Some days when I talked about my sister Sherry in Maine, or our dog Molly, Alan drew a blank. "Who is that? Why are you telling me about that person?" he asked in an annoyed tone. Then I wanted to scream at him, "How could you not remember them?" as if he were faking.

I told him stories every day, like once-upon-a-time stories, only true.

When I recounted how we met at the Sunday Brunch Club, a singles organization, Alan hung his head and said, "You have to have memories for life. What will happen to me?"

Before answering, I tried to block out my own fears and lay the groundwork for the new attitude I was trying to adopt. Hugging him, I said with as much hope as I could muster, "You'll get your memories back. I'll help you. And now we have another chance to make new memories."

Brain injury can be surreal, like living in the Twilight Zone. I caught on to that early and tried to just go with it. For instance, Alan and I wanted some privacy. The noise and activity level on the brain injury unit got on my nerves and contributed to Alan's agitation level.

There were times we just wanted to be alone, to talk quietly, and to maybe even make love, to just be a normal couple. Hearing this, the neuropsychologist thought that having a sexual outlet might help reduce Alan's tension and reassure him that we were still a true couple.

So, after some campaigning, we got permission to spend occasional overnights in the living skills apartment down the hall from the brain injury unit. The apartment is set up so patients can practice doing all the normal bathing and cooking activities they have to learn before going home.

I felt both appreciative and apprehensive when, weeks into Alan's rehabilitation, we started the overnights. Appreciative because when we were in the apartment, we were both more relaxed and able to feel close. With the lights of the Cambridge skyline reflected in the Charles River, I almost convinced myself that we were on a romantic weekend in a lovely hotel. An active imagination is a plus when making a new life.

What could be more intimate for a couple than making love? But I was apprehensive because sex is risky business when you've had a heart attack and cardiac arrest. I was so happy to hold the full length of Alan's body against mine and to feel him hold me. But all of his ways of touching me and the rhythms we called our own were missing. For me, it was another discomforting reminder that we weren't the same couple anymore. As soon as we finished making love, I had to hop out of bed to check Alan's blood pressure and give him more nitroglycerine tablets for angina.

Alan, on the other hand, was elated. He exclaimed, "That was as good as it ever was!" I was glad that he was so happy and heard his relief that one core part of himself had not been damaged beyond repair. But lovemaking was a bittersweet experience for me. Over five weekends, we started to get to know each other's bodies again and to have fun in a new way.

One Sunday morning in the apartment, over the scrambled eggs that Alan had masterfully prepared, he looked at me with his most charming smile and said, "Tell me about yourself; I really don't know anything about you."

I thought, *Jeez, this is like a bad flashback to the 1970s, but I've been married to this guy for eleven years.*

So I answered his questions, tempted to throw in my horoscope sign. Intimacy can feel both tenuous and deep in the same morning.

Each time we spent a night in the apartment, disinhibited Alan blabbed about it to the whole dining room, including the kids from the pediatric unit. He crowed, "Did I tell you we had sex? It was as good as it ever was!"

I was mortified. "Alan, you can't say that," I growled under my breath.

He just looked baffled and shrugged his shoulders. "Why, isn't it the truth?" he asked.

I didn't mind imposing the plan that he had to eat in his room if he couldn't keep quiet. Alan told his doctors, "Conjugal visits should be part of every patient's therapy." He was right, and I agreed that couples need private time to practice being themselves, not just patient and caregiver.

Each overnight in the apartment was followed by questions from the team about how the weekend went for Alan. No one ever asked me, "And how was it for you? Being with your husband in such an intimate way? Was it as good as it ever was?" Professionals should be brave enough and caring enough to bring up sexuality with the caregiver as well as the patient. After all, giving us a few tools to begin rebuilding our bond should be an important goal of rehab.

I began to compose a mental collage of my own shifting identity. Alan wasn't the only one who didn't quite match internally and externally. I usually tried to act like a loving, competent, held-together person. I had even been made a member of Alan's treatment team with specific responsibilities and a voice at team meetings. This was an experiment in family involvement that later became routine.

But for months, I staggered around in a fog of bewilderment even as I functioned fairly normally, bewildered at all that had happened, at being forcibly ejected from the world I knew and sentenced to a horrifying new world where I had no control.

Bewildered at leaving behind my jobs without knowing that was my last day or saying good-bye.

Bewildered that I seemed to be married to a man I didn't know, while my real husband had disappeared. Bewildered that I had no idea what our future would look like, or if Alan even had a future.

Bewildered, angry, terrified, anguished, lonely, horrified, and grieving for two. Alan grieved globally for his profound losses. He didn't remember the specific losses, but I sure did, so I grieved for a catalogued list of all that had been taken from him.

Even stranger, there were many times I felt content, happy, grateful, blessed, proud, and hopeful.

I knew that I was going to need a lot of support and a safe place to say what was really on my mind when Alan was discharged from Spaulding. I thought about the kind of psychotherapist I would be comfortable with and chose Martha, a social worker who had been on my mother's hospice team and was now in private practice. Martha had the distinct advantage of knowing Alan and me before his brain injury, so she could appreciate the changes I described. I started therapy with Martha by telephone while Alan was at Spaulding and formed a relationship that helped me for years.

On the outside, I strived to look like the self I knew best. I dressed carefully in the comforting professional clothes I wore as a psychotherapist: long flowing skirts, soft sweaters, bright colors, and ethnic jewelry. I took the time to style my rapidly greying hair and apply plenty of blusher.

One fall day, the sale catalogue from JJill, my favorite store, arrived in the mail. I remember standing at Alan's bedside while he recited the days of the week, phoning in my order for a skirt with a crazy urgency. I knew I didn't need new clothes anymore, but I wanted the skirt to provide me with defiance to still be myself.

The one exception to my usual wardrobe was the blue chambray dress I had worn on the airplane and in the ICU in Chicago. The dress had been covered in Alan's blood the first night as I cradled him in my lap when the doctors told us he would probably die, so we should say our good-byes. To my astonishment, the blood washed out. I insisted on wearing that dress once or twice a week at Spaulding. I told myself it was comfortable, but the truth was that it was an emblem, an in-your-face reality check about what had actually happened. Months later, my friend Jane told me she shuddered every time she saw me in that dress.

I made a conscious choice to suspend all outside responsibilities in order to be an active part of Alan's rehabilitation. But I resisted full immersion in the caregiver identity that others were taking for granted I would assume without hesitation. When I passed a display of brochures for Well Spouse, a national support organization for spousal caregivers, I dropped the brochure into my bulging envelope of future reference materials, but didn't hurry to read it.

My resistance to the word made me curious, since I'd been a caregiver in my family all of my life and had chosen a career as a professional caregiver. In time, I understood that what I was resisting wasn't taking care of Alan. It was feeling squeezed into an all-consuming cookie-cutter caregiver identity and role. I wanted to find a way to have breathing space, to still nurture the parts of myself I treasured. That took some years, and eventually Well Spouse and support groups became part of finding the balance I needed.

Every family has other life obligations going on outside the doors of Spaulding. At the same time that Alan was undergoing brain injury rehabilitation, I was in the process of selling my mother's home. Mom died of metastatic colon cancer ten months before Alan's cardiac arrest. My mother and I had a close, loving relationship, and she had come to live with us during her horrendous illness. Alan and I cared for her together, and they developed their own sweet relationship for the first time.

Just before Alan and I left for that fateful weekend in Chicago, I had put Mom's house up for sale. While Alan was in the Resurrection ICU, I was on the phone with the Realtor, slashing the price as potential buyers found more major problems.

Now, two months later, the new buyers and I were on the verge of passing papers. Most of the house was cleared out, but I still had to let go of the tattered remnants of Mom's favorite chair. The chair was the one item I had begged Alan to dispose of to spare me the pain. Our plan was that Alan would stay at Mom's house on the day when the cleaning men made their final sweep.

But ... here he was at Spaulding. He didn't remember that I'd ever had a mother or that she had died.

At the last possible minute, I went to her house and hid upstairs while the cleaning men unceremoniously carried away her chair. In my mind, I kept accusing Alan, "You were supposed to do that for me.

You were supposed to take care of Mom's chair. You were supposed to help me."

At that moment, I was slammed with the reality that I had lost the husband I could count on to take care of me in any meaningful way. I cried for hours.

Alan was trying to puzzle out what it meant to be married too. For him, proof of marriage came through in actions. He made proclamations about what I should do to be a good wife. At dinner time, I usually set his tray up in the unit dining room and then went to the cafeteria to take a break.

One day Alan proclaimed, "Husbands and wives should eat the same food at the same time." So I started bringing my dinner upstairs so we could eat together. He still wasn't satisfied until I arranged the food to make the plates look similar. He couldn't understand why we had different entrees.

"Didn't you cook this food for us? That's what wives do."

His other definition was that "Husbands and wives should sleep in the same bed at night." He accused me of not loving him and having boyfriends on the side because I went home at night and left him alone at Spaulding. He did enjoy it when we had coffee dates in the cafeteria, where he could buy me a treat and practice making change.

But Alan was truly getting a grasp on who I was. He said, "You're 90 percent core [clear] to me now. No one else is near that. If you get less core [clear], we'll be in trouble."

We were both reassured when we could rest together on Alan's single bed at the end of his scheduled sessions. Alan turned to wrap me in a hug and said, "Let's do some of that holding around."

There is no accurate way to portray how much of himself Alan had lost. We have stacks of symptom lists, test scores, treatment plans, and dismal reports. There are anguished entries in my journal and shocked phone messages from family members after they visited him.

And yet ... so much of Alan survived. Over time, essential parts began to emerge. His lifelong determination to learn and persevere in breaking through new material were there in spades. He was motivated to keep improving his reading, writing, math, and walking.

Alan always had a keen curiosity about everything, and now he asked me questions constantly. We never had to deal with the apathy many brain injury survivors struggle with.

Alan wanted to think, even though the effort exhausted him. He wanted to know things again, even though he couldn't remember them. He wanted to talk about every observation. He wanted to be smart.

He even had a sense of humor that I recognized under the injury-induced disinhibition. He laughed at jokes and made some good ones. On the better days, we could use humor to connect and put things in perspective.

Alan had the capacity to love and, at least temporarily, to feel loved. He and I spent so many hours walking hospital corridors hand in hand that the nurses dubbed us "the lovebirds."

Shortly before discharge, Alan said, "I don't know what percent human being I can be, but I'll try to be as much human as I can."

From the time I first fell in love with Alan, I always told him, "I love you ferociously." I didn't know why I picked those words, but I trusted that I would figure it out in time. In the hospital, I began to grasp that it would take ferocious love to get to know this man all over again and keep coming back to each other, to piece together a new collage of our marriage and life.

9. "Listen to the Sun on My Face"

While the Spaulding staff prepared Alan for his long-awaited homecoming on October 28, I prepared our home. In the evening, I tended to safety features and made signs for the kitchen shelves. I drew pictures of sweaters and pajamas on the index cards to label Alan's bureau drawers, since the words alone wouldn't be sufficient. That part was fun. But there was one room I deliberately avoided until the last moment: Alan's study.

Alan's study was the most beautiful room in our home. Two walls were shaped by bookshelves full of antique science and literature books, political tomes, timelines of history, and his college textbooks. Antique microscopes, beakers, and balance scales held an exalted position at the top of the shelves. Mixed in with disarming informality were all the foreign translations of the books Alan wrote. His teak desk sat in the tall bay window, partnered with the club chair he received for teaching twenty-five years at Northeastern. He bragged that no one could tell the burgundy Oriental carpet came from the discount store Building 19. The walls were covered with masks from Papua New Guinea, aboriginal ancestors from Australia, and drums from Borneo, each one a memento of our travels.

Alan's heart attack and cardiac arrest struck on the day before he was to start teaching his summer program for middle school science teachers. So his desk was still littered with handouts and props for his trademark demonstrations. Now it was October, and I supposed the covering teacher had made his own handouts. Piles of research material and position papers spilled over the carpet. His beloved Macintosh computer was opened to book reviews he was writing for the journal *Science*.

My job was to make all of this disappear. The psychiatrist had explained that Alan was "visual stimulus bound" and would want to understand and try everything he saw. He would be devastated by so much incomprehensible evidence of who he used to be. Armed with trash bags and boxes, I spent a mournful Sunday sifting through Alan's life's work. I felt overwhelmed by the enormity of the task and stuffed armfuls of papers into boxes destined for the attic. I said tearfully, "I have no right to do this; don't make me do this; I'm sorry, Alan; I'm sorry, Alan." Sorry any of this happened to you, to us. I felt like I was building a funeral pyre out of the timbers of my husband's identify.

At that point, there was no room in my mind or heart to consider the corresponding changes in my life. My awareness was taken over by the visceral pain of confronting so many concrete memories of the husband I had lost: The brilliant professor with a fabulous sense of humor who taught me it wasn't necessary to have original ideas to write a book. The dashing visionary who told me to stop saying, "That trip was a once-in-a-lifetime experience." His attitude was, "No one goes around the world just once," so we went twice. The loving uncle who took the kids hiking and showed our four-year-old nieces how to look through a microscope in his home science lab. The guy eating a sesame bagel at Brueger's every morning as he read *The Boston Globe* comics and editorials—in that order.

I swept the graphic calculators, Rolodex of international contacts, and class notes off Alan's desk. In their place I put paper and pencils, a photograph of us, and a short list of family telephone numbers. I left the books and travel artifacts in place to recall some of our fondest memories.

As discharge approached, we reviewed Alan's remarkable progress over three months with his team. He was now able to speak in complete sentences that often made sense, especially when arguing to go home. He struggled to name objects, but was getting some of his fancy vocabulary back. His moods were more stable, and he could sometimes talk about being angry or frustrated without going wild. His short-term memory was severely impaired, but we used compensatory strategies with good results. Alan's ability to process incoming information was much delayed, as was his ability to relate information back out to the other person. He could shower and dress himself with cues, and he walked steadily for four blocks before angina made him stop. We knew this was just the beginning, but felt hopeful about his ability to keep improving.

On the day before discharge, Alan had special testing done by a neurologist who specialized in language problems. He struggled through the procedure and answered questions in much the same way as he did before three months of intensive rehab. The results were devastating. As I watched Alan becoming more agitated because he sensed his failures, I noted that in addition to having brain damage, Alan had turned into a poor test-taker. I thought that the way he did everyday ADLs, and his ability to communicate, read, and write at a rudimentary level, were quite a bit better than his test scores revealed.

Even so, we were all disheartened by the report's conclusion that Alan had extensive damage to many areas of his brain, especially those involved in memory and language. The report lowered the expectations for meaningful recovery in those areas.

That night, following a disagreement we had about something, Alan said bitterly, "From now on, you will always be right and I'll always be wrong because I have a brain injury."

I hastened to reassure him that we were equals. But I knew he was right that he would always have to prove himself much more than I did to be taken seriously in the world.

I was of two minds as Alan's discharge approached. I was extremely grateful to everyone at Spaulding and had now witnessed firsthand the miracles the admitting nurse had told me could happen there. I considered some of Alan's progress miraculous. I felt that Spaulding had given me back my husband—a very changed husband to be sure, but mine. They had prepared and empowered me to carry on a lot of the rehabilitation at home. At the same time, I was also sick of hearing about what I called Alan's diagnostic A-list: anoxia, amnesia, global anomia, apraxia, aphasia, etc. I just wanted us to go home. Together. Finally.

Before I brought Alan home, I set two guiding *intentions* for each of us. *Goals* were for therapy, and we did set those, but intentions implied my new humility about how much I could actually control going forward. For Alan, the first intention was to rebuild a sense of himself that he would be pleased to own. Second, that he always *feel* loved, and *believe* he was loved, especially by me. Memory impairment makes it very hard to hold on to reassurance that one is loved.

My intentions for myself were more practical than noble. The first was that I not become hardened and embittered from this experience. Over the years, I had seen that happen to several family caregivers for reasons inherent in their circumstances. My second intention was not to let my weight balloon up to two hundred pounds from eating under stress. For me, that would be a way of giving up on myself.

On October 28, Alan was discharged from Spaulding Rehab.

Four months after he left on a weekend trip, he was coming home. Naturally, we have a Polaroid photo of Alan and me waving good-bye to the Spaulding staff as we embark on our journey home. We are bundled into warm coats, bracing against the wind that whips off the Charles River as we get into our Honda. Alan wears his jaunty tweed cap and the red jacket with the emblem from his trip to the Arctic Circle two years earlier. He is still skinny and pale as a ghost, but he smiles broadly. I smile tentatively in my black leather jacket; my face and hunched shoulders sure look tense.

As soon as we pulled into the driveway, Alan rushed through the back door, buoyed by the "Welcome Home Alan" banners made by friends. "I'm home, I'm home," he crowed. When Molly bounded up to greet him, he said, "Daddy's home, Molly. Everything will be okay now. Don't worry." He rushed through the house, opening every door. One effect of the brain injury was difficulty sensing where his body was in space, so he tried out his favorite living room chair for a minute, then darted back into the hall to check where one room was in relation to the other rooms.

When he came to his study, Alan stopped and surveyed his domain with satisfaction. He moved his hands over every wooden surface—the bookcases, tables, file cabinet—feeling their solid reality. Next, he gravitated to his desk. "My desk, my chair," he said, stroking them affectionately. Finally, he sat still, exhaled a long sigh, and smiled. Now Alan was home and had an anchor to ground him. Over the next days, Alan sat at his desk for long stretches, fervently practicing his reading and writing.

As we tucked into bed on his first night home, Alan said, "My house is beautiful; my dog is beautiful; my couch is beautiful; my wife is beautiful; life is beautiful!"

Alan's first weeks at home were a combination of sheer magic, incredibly detailed instruction, tumultuous emotion, and the beginning of our "new normal" life. On his third day home, we took a walk along the Southwest Corridor urban parkland across from our house. Alan was jubilant. He lurched along the grassy slopes on unsteady legs, touching the vines and foliage, taste-testing the words *red berry, beech tree, chain link fence* for the first time.

Marching up a shallow slope, he threw back his head to bask in the full glory of the day. Alan flung his arms wide and proclaimed, "Listen to the sun on my face!"

His words became our slogan and our prevailing attitude.

Back in the living room, Alan took to his recliner with Molly on his lap. He stroked the pages of his history and science books with reverence, sounded out some words, and asked, "Will my reading ever be normal? I've got to keep practicing. I want to read Galileo." He piled stacks of books around his chair and seemed both fortified and soothed by their presence, even as he continued to read second grade books. We honored that corner of the living room as his fortress.

Alan and Molly read in their fortress, November, 1998.

I have a photograph of Alan balancing a volume of Galileo's writings on the back of a chair as his lips move to sound out the title. Wearing a handsome ski sweater, his shoulders are relaxed, although his brow is creased in concentration and his finger trails the words. He bites his upper lip as he always did and looks for all the world like a brilliant scientist who understands the brilliant tome, like nothing ever happened.

Alan received treatment from a physical therapist and occupational therapist for a few weeks at home. My concern was that Alan receive as much cognitive rehab as possible before surgery. That meant that I bargained with our health insurer to let me do the job they would pay a visiting nurse and home health aide to do, and put that money into the cognitive rehab pot. "I want you to put as much money as possible into the speech-language pathology visits Alan desperately needs," I said. When the representative explained that wasn't how resources were usually allocated, I replied, "Well, make it happen!" Eventually, they did.

Jennifer and I had campaigned for the insurance plan to find a speech-language pathologist who had extensive experience with brain injury, and Karen came with impeccable credentials.

Alan and Karen continued working on reading and writing skills. She also moved into the higher cognitive skills such as problem solving, abstract thinking, and reasoning: the executive function areas. Alan found these sessions grueling, but he thrived on the challenge. He liked the deductive reasoning puzzles that required him to go systematically through cues to make the proper conclusion. It appealed to him to do puzzles with logic involved. They also worked on attention by having him stay on a topic of conversation for lengthening periods.

As at Spaulding, Alan and I carried over the practice between sessions so he could sustain his gains. Alan became more adept at writing his daily log on the computer and got better at correcting mistakes on his own. One day he said to me, "I need a purpose in life. I want to write my autobiography and give it to the family." So he started by selecting a time from childhood that was still the most accessible time in his memory. "I'll write about Christmas in a Jewish family where the parents owned a toy factory," he said. First he wrote sentences on paper, with several misspelled words. Then he typed the story into the computer with Karen, while correcting the 50 percent of words he misspelled.

Alan had a new and unvarying way of speaking a sentence. He started out confidently, even if he needed a cue to a word. But he always paused right before the last word or two from the effort of sustaining a thought to the end and finding the words. I noticed that if anyone interrupted him during the pause or jumped in with the word, the thought was short-circuited and lost. He became justifiably angry when his thoughts and sentences evaporated. This was an issue when family visited from out of town, or friends thought they were being helpful by finishing Alan's sentences for him. So much about Alan being able to enjoy a conversation depended on the other person being willing to do their part in modifying the interaction. That meant waiting patiently for him to finish.

The biggest surprise was how much easier it was for Alan to sing than to speak sentences. Alan liked Broadway show tunes and could fluently sing long choruses of complicated Gilbert and Sullivan tunes. He didn't stop, search for words, or trip over the lyrics, even of songs I considered tongue-twisters. "I am the very model of a modern major general …," he sang. We sang together regularly for fun and as part of his speech therapy.

Just as he had before the brain injury, Alan thrived on making every experience a chance to learn. When we walked in the Arnold Arboretum, I told Alan the names of the trees. "Don't talk to me," he commanded. "Spell to me!"

So I said, "That's a silver m-a-p-l-e tree."

"Maple!" he yelled with pride that would outshine a second grader's.

One of Alan's permanent impairments was in remaining oriented to time and the passage of time. He took charge of the problem by saying, "We need a calendar in every room." He insisted that even the bathroom have a calendar. When people asked what gift they could bring Alan, I suggested a calendar of his favorite New England scenes, so he got the additional cue of seasonal photographs. Alan consulted his calendars many times a day for years. "Let me see where I am now," he'd say, looking at the calendar. He experienced time almost like a place and sought the date like an anchor to hold him steady. He liked to cross off the date on his bedside calendar each evening.

Yet time meant little to him. He wore a watch and looked at the daily schedule we wrote on the memo center whiteboard. He read the scheduled activities with interest, but had no sense of what time it was or how to plan his time. Mostly, he wanted to be left alone to read.

Alan decided on a few goals he would prioritize at home. His first goal was to learn to feed Molly her kibble twice a day. By having a purposeful activity, Alan also built independence and esteem, which

I hoped would help avoid depression. We started with an index card (always the index cards) with four steps:

- Go to kibble bin near stove. (He had to find it anew every morning.)
- Scoop out ½ cup.
- Put in Molly's dish.
- Replace scoop and close bin.

At first I read the steps, and we worked up to Alan being able to refer to the card and carry out the task. It took three weeks of daily practice, but feeding Molly became a source of purpose and pride. Weeks later, when we met Dr. N., the neurologist who would follow Alan as an outpatient, the doctor tried to get a handle on Alan's cognitive impairment level. He asked me to describe what we did at home.

When I told him the kibble training process, Dr. N. let out a low whistle under his breath and said, "Three weeks, huh? Well, that tells me a lot."

In subsequent visits, he always commented appreciatively that Alan brought so much more personhood into the room than one would expect from the hospital records detailing his disabilities.

Alan's second goal was to learn to walk around the neighborhood alone. To that end, we practiced walking to the baseball field diagonally across the street, with special emphasis on crossing safely in traffic. We lived on a very busy main street frequented by impatient drivers. Alan devised his own method of looking back over his shoulder every few feet so he wouldn't lose sight of the house. "I don't want to get lost and spend the night in a dark park," he said. The avid hiker who logged many miles in the White Mountains was now careful to respect his limitations.

Before Alan was discharged, I made a flier to distribute to our neighbors with a photo of Alan, Molly, and me on it. In a brief paragraph, I explained that Alan had suffered a brain injury that made it hard for him to remember people and directions. I asked that neighbors introduce themselves and show him the way home if he seemed confused. Several people thanked me for telling them how to talk with Alan, and they greeted him with friendly handshakes. "It's like I never left the block," said Alan.

My friend Mary described how Alan looked when he walked down the street: "Alan still looks as courtly as ever with his erect posture, even though his expression says he's not sure where he's going." Alan was indeed courtly.

We practiced one skill or another constantly, but built them into a new routine for the day. Alan did best when he had a predictable structure to follow. The plan from Spaulding was that we would build language and vocabulary as part of our daily activities. At breakfast, we used index cards to label the food we ate, and Alan had to say or sound out the words for cereal and juice. One strategy that helped with word finding when he was stymied was for me to offer the sound of the first letter or syllable, or say "Begins with t." He often jumped in with "toast." This technique is part of the errorless learning approach that helped Alan at Spaulding. The goal is to supply a cue to increase the chance of the person coming up with the right answer, instead of making several guesses that are only wrong answers. Errorless learning is the opposite of making a person come up with an answer on his own, especially a wrong answer. Wrong answers made Alan confused and might be remembered and repeated.

Food was also a tool for building awareness of wholes and parts. Alan could not grasp fractions or what the inside and outside of an object looked like at the same time. He liked to assemble and disassemble food like puzzle pieces. When I served him a juicy slice of cantaloupe, he said, "Wow, this is great but funny looking. What is it?"

Before I could retrieve the whole melon, he perked up with, "I know; this is how they make pumpkins!"

While the words were hard, the sensory pleasures were their own reward: Every bite was a luscious discovery. "Oh, this is wonderful food! What do they call it?" His ability to recognize food by taste was impaired, but that was one area where practice was effortless. He thought that grapes were the best food ever invented. He plied guests with the purple orbs, saying, "You've got to try these things. Have you ever had anything so delicious?"

Alan regarded his study as the epicenter of new learning, so we set up a learning lab for the new Alan. On his work table, we placed a few children's science picture books, a dictionary for kids, a magnifying glass, and an illustrated book about the presidents. Alan's brother sent him a Geo-Safari talking globe that included games we could play to locate countries or rivers. Alan always had an up-to-date globe in the living room, so he took to the Geo-Safari with pleasure.

Some of the activities Alan practiced in Spaulding occupational therapy sessions had to be modified at home. When we prepared dinner together, Alan liked to make a salad with lettuce and tomatoes while I cooked the main course. It quickly became apparent that he needed plenty of space for his prep work. If my hand crossed his field of vision while we shared the kitchen counter, it broke his concentration and resulted in an angry shout: "Don't do that, you messed me up!" It worked better when I left him the entire counter. In time, he was able to heat up a can of soup for lunch by himself. We placed his favorite foods at eye level on their own labeled shelf in the refrigerator, so he could choose and prepare a snack.

Grocery shopping was a travail for Alan. In therapy, he was taking steps toward shopping independently for his favorite cereal, but going to a supermarket was too visually stimulating. He came up with his own solution. While I loaded our cart quickly, he found the housewares display and glued himself in front of an eggbeater, trying to figure out its use. Knowing how to protect oneself from cognitive overload is also a survival skill. In time, Alan liked to shop at the small hardware store and to buy greeting cards at CVS. His plans could be a bit grandiose. One afternoon, he hurried back from the hardware store, demanding a credit card. "I'm going to buy us a Jacuzzi bathtub and install it with Tom," he announced. "I need $800 right now." He never did work up to carrying a credit card.

Alan's emotional responses required as much attention as his cognitive skills. One morning when he was upstairs in the bedroom getting dressed, I heard the thud of shoes being thrown against the wall. Alan raged, "I can't do this! This is crazy! I don't know what to do!" I ran upstairs to find him red-faced and panting, clothes strewn all over the room. There were a few pairs of shoes under the bed, so he couldn't decide which ones he needed to put on. He went wild. The main problem was that he was humiliated by not understanding something so basic. Humiliation was a surefire trigger for anger. From then on, we tried to keep the number of items he had to decide between down to two.

Alan had already gone through so many of the psychological manifestations of brain injury, but there were more to come. At Resurrection Medical Center, a pulmonary specialist told me that many people who've been on ventilators or in the ICU for a long time have a traumatic reaction later. I knew a lot about post-traumatic stress reactions from my professional work, and I might not have recognized Alan's night terrors as post-traumatic stress disorder (PTSD) if I had not had that experience.

For several nights over two weeks, Alan sat bolt upright in the bed, hyperventilating and screaming, "They're choking me, they're suffocating me, they're trying to kill me!" His eyes were as large as saucers. His heart pounded and sweat soaked his body as he tossed around in bed. Alan had been intubated, on a ventilator, and forcibly restrained many times. Now his body and mind were paying for those experiences.

Each time it happened, I put the lights on, sat him on the edge of the bed with his feet on the floor, and wrapped my arms around him. I said gently, "You're okay, Alan, you're safe in our home, I'm here with you. Take a breath. Nothing bad will happen to you." I stroked his back and talked softly until he became oriented and calmed down, which took about ten minutes. An extra dose of antianxiety medicine helped him get back to sleep.

The traumatic reactions were a serious problem. I could never tell for sure whether something I said registered with Alan until I heard him repeat it. Molly slept at the foot of our bed. One night, we were awakened by Molly yipping and flailing around in the middle of a dream.

I asked, "Alan, do you want me to put Molly on the floor so you can sleep?"

He said, "Oh, no! This is what I do for my dog. You watch." Alan pulled Molly into his lap, stroked her fur, and said, "You're okay, Molly, Daddy's here. Nothing bad is going to happen to you."

When she was alert and calm, Alan lifted her back to her spot on the bed. "See, that's how I take care of my dog," he said, pulling the blankets over his shoulder and dozing off. By soothing Molly in the same way I soothed him, Alan also learned how to soothe himself. Some part of his memory had been paying attention. The PTSD reactions decreased to being very occasional.

The most shocking agitation episodes always happened in the middle of the night. Our bedroom window looks out on Lamartine Street, with cars parked along the road. One night, Alan woke me up screaming, "I want my car! I'm going out right now. Give me the keys. You gave my car away to Tom. You had no right to give my car away. I don't have anything that's my own. You treat me like a dead man!" Over and over, escalating with every sentence.

My heart was in my throat. He had not been this agitated since we came home. Nothing I said made a difference for more than five minutes. He calmed down, then flared up again. The medications that usually took the edge off had no effect. Because Alan was not able to drive, I had told him that his nephew Tom needed to borrow his car for a while to get to his job. Alan bought it temporarily, but his car represented independence and everything he had lost control over. He screamed for the car keys.

I brought him to another room where he couldn't see the cars, and after about an hour, he fell into a fitful sleep while I stayed on guard. Alan's discharge plan included appointments with several specialists, including a psychiatrist. But the appointment was weeks away. I couldn't believe that we had come home without a plan for psychiatric emergencies. The next morning, we got an urgent appointment, new prescriptions, and a behavioral plan, and we began a long and fruitful relationship with Dr. P. Even so, I couldn't sleep for several nights. The loss of his ability to drive and ownership of his car was a mortal wound that was the focus of Alan's frustration, anger, and grief from then on.

Alan took written information seriously because it seemed more official and he could review it when needed. So I tried the first of several behavioral contracts that specified what Alan agreed to do and what I agreed to do to reach a common goal. It was important to include my responsibility to keep the contract from just seeming punitive to Alan.

Alan, Tom, and I drew up and signed a contract that included the following:

1. *Alan agrees to let Tom use his car for two months only to go to work.*
2. *Tom is very grateful to Alan and agrees to keep Alan's car clean and in good repair.*
3. *Tom agrees to drive Alan wherever he wants to go once a week.*
4. *Janet will arrange a driving test for Alan as soon as his doctor says that is safe.*
5. *We will all review this arrangement in January.*

Alan still had outbursts about not being able to drive, but he quieted down faster when I showed him the contract.

My race to improve Alan's thinking skills as much as possible before heart surgery was one of the reasons he became agitated. He was bombarded with more stimulation than his brain could process. He pointed out this problem by saying, "It's not that I can't remember, it's that I've got a hundred million things on my memory at once. Like where we've been, Tom's new girlfriend's name, what that lady who teaches me said to do. It makes me crazy." Alan's brain couldn't order or move some items to the background, so he was overwhelmed. One important change I had to make was to back off on so many lessons during the day and let Alan get more rest.

Alan had a new medical problem that disrupted his sleep terribly. During the night, his legs became cramped and very painful, jerked all over the bed, and often kicked me while he slept. He insisted on getting up to walk to relieve the restless sensation. Occasionally, I even saw his leg fly straight up off the couch while he napped. It took a few months to get the correct diagnosis of restless leg syndrome (RLS), a movement disorder characterized by sensory and motor abnormalities. We tried massage, warm baths, gentle stretching, and walking with varying degrees of benefit. RLS remained an ongoing problem in Alan's already overstimulated nights. Eventually, a neurologist prescribed medications that helped keep his legs still.

Now it was November and the holidays beckoned. We had often hosted our extended family for Thanksgiving dinners, and Alan insisted on doing so even though he'd been out of the hospital for only a month. On Thanksgiving Day, he presided proudly at the head of the table. "Welcome to my home," he said. "Thank you for helping me so much."

The impromptu blessings offered by Alan's nephews and my sister's family all included gratitude that Alan was with us and on the path to recovery.

That evening, Alan stretched out in his recliner, full of turkey and contentment. "I'm glad I lived to see this day," he said. My eyes filled with tears of relief. That was the first time since the cardiac arrest that he'd said he was glad he had survived.

I knew that it was just a matter of time before Alan would need cardiac bypass surgery. His angina increased by the week, and he was often uncomfortable. Understanding open heart surgery is a huge task for anyone, but Alan had no understanding of his body and little capacity to retain information. I was afraid he would suffer extreme mental anguish if he underwent surgery without comprehending what was being done to him. We found a transparent model of a man's body at the local toy store where Alan bought books and games. The model had removable body parts and a simple booklet about their functions. We began a very repetitive lesson plan to teach him that his heart pumped blood and oxygen to all his organs, that he had some blocked vessels, and how the bypass surgery would restore healthy circulation. Plumbing terminology made the most sense to Alan. Of course, we wrote the highlights in his trusty logbook.

We celebrated Christmas early since I could sense that Alan was getting sicker. In place of the eight-foot tree I usually insisted fill our living room window, we bought a small artificial tree and hung our favorite ornaments. Alan thought the tree, music, and cookies were nice, but the best part was exchanging presents with family and friends.

Alan beamed as he handed me my gift. "You get the first copy of *A Christmas Carol* by Alan Cromer," he said. Working steadily on revisions and edits, often independently, Alan produced an accurate three-page story for his autobiography.

"Thank you, Alan, I'll treasure this first edition," I said.

Later we mailed copies to his family, and he moved on to writing *Captain of the Milk Monitors* about a defining experience in sixth grade.

Alan liked my gift of a love letter detailing many of the reasons I loved the man he was now.

"Read that one again," he said.

So I read, "I love you for being so brave and fighting so hard to live. I love you for giving us your advice so willingly."

Sherry's family gave Alan a well-chosen gift that he couldn't wait to work with: a huge earth science set that included timelines of evolution with stickers for the life forms that evolved during each era, workbooks, and even a model volcano to erupt! We hung the timelines on his office wall and spent hours affixing the stickers as we read about the creatures together. The information was all new to Alan (and me), but he said, "I've always loved to study evolution," which was true.

In so many ways, Alan thrived during his first two months at home. He gained weight and strength, improved weekly in speech therapy, enjoyed many visits with family and friends, and met the goals he set. When his nephew Marty visited, he said, "It's strange … Alan's personality, affect, and the rhythm of his days are much like he was before he got sick. Alan always spent his days reading, talking on the phone, and working on his computer."

Alan had one relationship above others that gave him joy, purpose, and a sense of being needed. That was his love affair with Molly.

10. Molly the Rehab Dog

Molly was absolutely the best gift I ever gave my mother. A very lady-like mix of Maltese and poodle, Molly had a gentle disposition and mischievous puppy streak. She and Mom had two delightful years together before my eighty-year-old mother became very sick with metastatic cancer. Mom and Molly came to live with Alan and me for several months before she died. While I cared for Mom, Alan quietly took over caring for Molly.

The best gift Alan ever gave Mom was a videotape of their daily walks, filmed from Molly's perspective. Alan's camera captured all of Molly favorite routes and the neighbors who stopped to say, "What an adorable dog." Mom never tired of watching the video with Alan as a distraction from her pain.

When my mother died, we decided to adopt Molly and quickly became "dog people." I treasured Molly as a living link to my mother as well as being as source of unabashed joy.

From the moment Alan came home from Spaulding, he and Molly were inseparable companions. Molly even slept between us on the bed.

When Alan woke up from a bad dream, he called, "Where's my dog? Show me my dog." As soon as I placed his hand on Molly's warm apricot fur, he relaxed and fell fast asleep.

Alan talked to Molly all day long. As I flipped pancakes down in the kitchen, I smiled, listening to Alan upstairs with Molly.

"Molly, did you hear what Janet just told me to do?" he said. "Put on your shoes and socks and come downstairs for breakfast. Well, that's not easy, you know. First you have to find socks and make sure they match. You have to get your shoes on the right feet, but not till your pants are on. And hold the railing so you don't fall on the stairs."

On and on he went, as Molly sat attentively by with her head cocked to hear every word. He was right about the complexity of the task. Getting dressed activated several areas of his brain; the instruction was processed in the parietal lobe and sequenced in the temporal lobe. His working memory within the hippocampus kicked in to remember how to dress, and walking down stairs involved motor skills in the cerebellum. By talking to Molly, Alan worked through his apraxia problem and learned to cue himself. They both showed up for breakfast with brains in high gear.

When Alan was anxious, he talked it over with Molly. "Molly was worried," he told me. "But I wasn't. I told her you said you'd come back in twenty minutes. I told her we'd be safe."

Molly featured in most of Alan's chosen goals. "I want to be able to walk my dog by myself," he announced. So first we worked on the steps involved in crossing the street safely by himself and finding his way home from the park. Then he could walk Molly. Each time he knelt down to put on her harness, he asked, "Do you trust me, Molly? Do you feel safe with me?"

Her wagging tail signaled assent, so off they went.

In December, Alan's brother Richard and his wife Pam visited from California. Both brothers had been hit with devastating medical problems. Richard lost most of his vision from a rare condition and had recently begun training to walk independently with a white cane. He had only practiced with an official coach. Richard and Alan had serious conversations about what they had each lost and how they were coping. As the visit went on, they spoke of what remained that was still good in their lives.

Their conversations were private, but I overheard Alan say, "At least I can read like a kid, it's better than not reading, and I'll keep practicing."

Richard replied, "I can't model the fine sculptures I enjoyed so much, but I'm getting a freer, more abstract style now."

The brothers decided on a shared goal: Alan would guide Richard to the park, with Molly in tow, of course. We all talked though the steps, and Richard showed Alan how to guide him by holding his elbow. On a sunny morning, Pam and I stood on the porch, biting our nails while our husbands embarked on their milestone journey. Getting comfortable with Alan's growing independence was a learning curve for me.

Alan checked for traffic more carefully than when he walked alone, then guided Richard slowly across the street, pointing out the curbs and where to turn into the park. They circled the baseball field, and twenty minutes later, returned home triumphant.

"We did it, we did it!" Alan yelled.

"We're the Intrepids!" exclaimed Richard.

Richard praised Alan for guiding him with just enough instruction. Alan said, "I'm good at this because I had people telling me what to do all the time in the hospital. When they told me too much stuff, it got me more confused."

I took a photograph of the proud trio and had it printed on tee shirts with "The Intrepids" emblazoned across the chest. Whenever Pam and Richard visited, the brothers wore their prize tee shirts, and Alan was solicitous about guiding Richard on longer walks.

Alan loved the photographs of him and Molly, so we had another tee shirt made with a photo of Molly enthusiastically licking Alan's chin. We included Alan's slogan, "Tough Hombres," and when he wore the shirt, neighbors stopped to laugh and ask about the partners. Alan was usually uncomfortable talking without preparation, but talking about Molly was natural, and he reported enjoying the conversations with "my new friends."

I found out a lot about Alan's self-esteem level by eavesdropping on his conversations with Molly. "Molly, come here," he said. "I want to talk to you, man to dog." When Alan felt good about himself, he showered praise on Molly. But when he was down about his own abilities, he took it out on Molly:

"You've got a brain the size of a pea. You're stupid. What use are you to anybody?" he asked disdainfully. That's when I knew Alan needed extra affection and attention to whatever skill he was struggling to master.

When my presence became overbearing, Alan plotted his escape with Molly. "Molly, let's run away and join the circus. I know the train to take to get downtown to the place where the circus comes to town. I'll teach you to do tricks, and we'll get you a tutu to wear. I'll be the ringmaster and ride elephants. We'll get out from under her control and never come back. We'll be free."

I enjoyed his imagination, but worried once I found out he knew the train was right down the street.

Before long, Alan took on the responsibility for caring for Molly by feeding, brushing, and walking her. He said, "It feels good to be able to take care of somebody because I need so many people to take care of me."

Molly spent hours on Alan's lap in the recliner as he read aloud to her from *My Dog's the Best*. The best gift Molly ever gave Alan was her unconditional love and devotion.

11. MENDING BROKEN HEARTS

On December 22, Alan dropped his lunch fork, grabbed his chest, and cried out, "Oh, this pain is terrible … never this bad. Can't you do something, Janet?" As his color faded, and the pain increased despite the nitroglycerine tablets, I called his doctor. We agreed that surgery could no longer be postponed. An ambulance brought us to Brigham and Women's Hospital. Alan was admitted, but had to wait for an opening on the surgical schedule. Christmas week is a terrible time to need urgent surgery.

Alan's chest pain was so bad that he was treated with an intravenous morphine drip and Fentanyl patches: medications I associated with severe or end-stage pain. I was terrified he would have another heart attack while waiting. To the BWH staff, his condition was very serious, but their priority was with the patients in surrounding rooms who were receiving heart transplants. "We have to give top priority to the 'hearts,'" they said.

I grumbled, "What do you call Alan, a foot?"

We were old pros at personalizing hospital space. Days earlier, I'd packed a bag with the pre-op teaching materials, relaxation audiotape, and tape recorder and message tapes. We brought a poster made from a recent photograph of Alan sitting in his recliner reading his book *Uncommon Sense* with Molly on his lap. Hanging the poster at the foot of his bed reminded Alan of who he was and what he would return to. It showed the staff a fuller view of the person lying in the bed. Molly provided an instant opening for conversation.

We brought our trusty copy of *The Odyssey*, some word puzzle books, and photographs of family and friends. Most important, we had the Polaroid camera to document Alan's progress during each stage of recuperation so he would understand and later remember what he went through. I even packed the Christmas gifts we had already given to each other, so we could pretend to have Christmas on the 25th.

Alan was understandably frightened and worried about everything: being in the hospital again, the pain, and the surgery. I wondered if his mind could hold on to the weeks of explanations we'd drilled on and his own reasons for wanting to go through with the surgery. My jaw got tighter and my conversations got terser by the day. I prayed that Alan would live through surgery, that he wouldn't lose more memory or cognition.

We spent a quiet Christmas Day with a few dear friends and family. I read my Christmas gift love letter to Alan aloud:

I love your curiosity and exploring mind. I love the way we say, "Do I love you a little bit? No, I love you a lot. Do you love me a little bit? No, you love me a lot.

We hung the suncatcher heart Alan had made for me in the window and admired its warm red glow.

Alan's quadruple coronary artery bypass graft operation was scheduled for December 28. We met the surgeon, Dr. G., the night before surgery. I had selected Dr. G. because of his expertise with the most complicated patients. He understood our fears about Alan sustaining more brain damage during surgery. There were no guarantees, just the best that modern medicine had to offer. Alan listened to Dr. G.'s explanations and asked a few questions. Then he signed the consent form and said, "Well, let's get this over with so I can go home." My hand shook as I cosigned as his legal guardian.

Early the next morning, I tiptoed into Alan's room. Under glaring hospital lights, Alan sat naked on a chair, draped with towels while an orderly shaved his pale chest, arms, and legs before surgery. Alan turned to the door and smiled weakly at me. But his blue eyes lit up when he said, "Oh, good, here's my wife, my Loverlump." I wrapped my arms around him from behind and kissed his head, so he wouldn't see me cry. As much as I believed surgery was the right choice, I felt like I was sending a lamb off to slaughter.

I helped him get on the stretcher and walked beside him to the elevator. We shared an urgent, even passionate kiss.

"I love you forever," said Alan.

"I love you forever," I replied. Alan had started saying that only when he sensed the situation was most grave.

Nephew Tom and I kept company during the four-hour vigil. We told funny stories about Alan over the years and dared to touch briefly on our fears that he might die. Again it felt disloyal to let optimism lag for even a moment.

Then the receptionist called out, "Is Mrs. Cromer here?" and beckoned me to the direct telephone line to the operating room.

I heard Dr. G.'s strong and steady voice. "We're all done," he said. "Alan made it through without complications. We're bringing him to recovery now."

This time the cascade of telephone calls I made to family members conveyed good news: *Alan was alive. The surgery was successful.* Now all he had to do was recuperate, then we could get back to our new life without the frequent chest pain. He would feel much better. Maybe his brain could even get more oxygen. Of course, I understood that the bypass surgery couldn't cure Alan's extensive cardiovascular disease. He would still need cardiac medications and be at risk for another heart attack or stroke. Still, our fervent hope was that he could be active in the ways he enjoyed.

When the surgeon removed the endotracheal tube helping him breathe, Alan said, "Janet, Janet, everything hurts." But I was elated because he recognized me and could speak.

The next morning I brought in *The Boston Globe* and read him the headlines. He moved his eyebrows up and down to indicate interest. Later, to help distract him from the pain, I read the passage from *The Odyssey* that he had practically memorized:

> *Sing to me of the man, Muse, the man of twists and turns*
> *Driven time and again off course, once he had plundered*
> *The hallowed heights of Troy.*
> *Many cities of men he saw and learned their minds,*
> *Many pains he suffered, heartsick on the open sea,*
> *Fighting to save his life and bring his comrades home.*

Alan's nurse said, "Wow, I've seen a lot of things in the ICU, but never a patient who wanted the Greek classics right after surgery!"

I took a Polaroid photo every day to document Alan's progress as tubes, IV lines, and catheters disappeared, and I taped the photos in his logbook with a few sentences about positive changes. He was impressed with each small but significant step he read.

At first Alan's appraisal was, "I feel like my whole body got hit by a truck." Despite some complications, he was moved to a post-op floor after a few days and began to practice walking with a physical therapist. By the end of the week, Alan upgraded his appraisal to, "I feel like I got hit by a bicycle."

Alan hung on to the explanations that he would feel better over time. But his mind also wandered over all that had happened to him since July: How close he had come to dying. How sick he really had been. The progress he'd made in getting critical skills back.

One afternoon, he turned to me and said, "I had a too young wife who died. You had a too old husband who lived."

I was taken aback, but replied, "I'm so happy that you lived, Alan."

I was a bit worried about Alan's reaction to seeing the thick line of stitches that ran from the top of his breastbone down to his navel.

As he stood hanging onto the sink to brush his teeth in the mirror, Alan said, "Let me just look at what's under here." I carefully lowered his gown to expose the incision, several sticky discs attaching heart monitor leads, and a bulky bandage where the chest tube had been removed. "Wow!" he yelled. "They cut me open all the way through! Barbara's got to see this. Take a picture and send it to my sister!"

Alan ripped off his gown and thrust out his chest with a warrior's grin. The "zipper" incision was his hard-earned badge of honor. I mailed the photo to Alan's sister with a label on the envelope: "Warning: explicit contents."

Marty came from New York to spend New Year's Eve with us. We made a small but robust party with trays of hospital food. Raising glasses of apple juice, we toasted Alan and our hopes for the New Year.

"I wish for my driver's license back," said Alan for the hundredth time.

"I wish for some peace and healing in our life," I said for the hundredth time.

On the last night of the wildest year of our married life, a tired and sore Alan wrote his log entry in shaky script: "Janet says this is our best New Year's Eve ever. She is nuts."

On January 1, 1999, I greeted the New Year with a solo sunrise walk around Jamaica Pond. Under a crystalline blue sky, I took deep, full, grateful breaths of cold air and released the tension from my neck and shoulders. There was a mysterious clatter in the distance: a tinkling, tapping, lively sound. When I reached the far side of the pond, the tapping intensified and I could see sheets of ice that lined the shore dashing against each other, cracking, slithering, chiming. It was like applause filling the sparkling air.

"Oh," I said, "the universe is clapping for Alan! The universe is clapping for us!"

Alan was discharged on January 4. After his joyous reunion with Molly, she took up residence alongside Alan on the couch. She lined her fluffy body up along his ribs, while avoiding her usual cushions: his chest and legs. Alan proudly dubbed her his private duty nurse. "Nurse Molly, on the case!" he announced as she jumped up to assume her post. Alan often directed me, "Take a picture of me and my dog!" I have countless photographs of Alan and Molly on the couch, often looking like one seamless creature since it's hard to tell where one ends and the other begins.

A few days after discharge, Karen, the speech-language pathologist, did the assessment we were anxiously awaiting. She administered tests to check Alan's memory and survey the thinking skills they had worked so hard to master. Karen was very professional but I knew she shared our excitement as she held up her official conclusion, written on the medical record for me to see: **"There is no loss of memory or cognitive gains in the aftermath of surgery."** No loss of memory! No loss of progress! Even after four hours on the bypass pump and the trauma of surgery. No loss! The ambivalence I'd carried since deciding to delay surgery in favor of cognitive rehab vanished. The postponement had proved worthwhile. We had been granted everything we'd wished and worked and prayed for. Thank you, thank you.

On January 17, we celebrated our twelfth wedding anniversary. Our celebration included a short walk together at Jamaica Pond for the first time since Alan became ill. We walked hand in hand, our eyes crinkled in smiles above our snug fleece scarves. No anniversary could be sweeter.

Alan gradually grew stronger and more energetic. But then, three weeks after surgery, he complained of worsening chest pain while we were eating breakfast. Another ambulance ride back to Brigham and Women's ED, another admission, another angiogram. The test showed that a blood clot had formed in the new graft that bypassed the diseased portion of Alan's right coronary artery. The graft was ruined. Reduced blood flow to the area was causing Alan's pain. The cardiologists performed an angioplasty to open up the blockage by inserting a catheter with a balloon tip through his groin and up into the blood vessels of his heart. When the balloon was inflated, it compressed the blockage against the artery wall to open up blood flow.

I paced the waiting room, furious, distrustful, and disgusted. Furious that not one part of treatment could go the standard way and that Alan had to suffer in new ways. Distrustful of the doctors, not knowing if they could have prevented or detected the clot earlier. Wondering if they were giving him the same amount of attention they'd give someone who didn't have a brain injury and had a better prognosis. Disgusted with it all: illness, uncertainty, setbacks. Alan, terribly shaken by the setback, turned somber. After a few days, we went home again, humbled but determined to keep going.

One week later, he had more chest pain late at night. This time, the angiogram revealed that the angioplasty had not held, so the artery was blocked off again. The cardiologist inserted a stent: a small mesh tube to prop the artery wall open. It sounds so routine, but every time Alan had an angiogram, he developed complications that required emergency treatment. Every time the doctor came out to the waiting area and said to me, "Well, it was touch and go for a while ..." Every time my heart sank as my sense of being powerless escalated.

I became adept at summarizing Alan's medical, neuropsych, and emotional history in several sentences spoken in rapid medicalese with just enough drama to ensure the staff took me seriously. Every admission gave me a better understanding of how fragmented and pressured the healthcare system really was. Staff who didn't have access to a unified electronic medical record would read the summary I carried and say, "I had no idea of all he's been through and how many problems he has." I was appalled by how much noncritical treatment is done with little history or communication among providers.

In the elevator I rode up to Alan's room after the stent was placed, a weary intern juggled a stack of medical records in his arms. Gesturing to the manila-clad volumes with his chin, he said to his fellow intern, "These all belong to my new admit. I'll be up all night reviewing them, and I still might not figure out what's wrong with this woman."

I nodded to myself. I knew this scenario well from being a medical nurse: The patient comes back again and again, treatments are tried, each time less successfully. The patient and family are miserable, and the nurses whisper, "Why don't they just give up and let him die with dignity?" I got off on Alan's floor musing that, like the intern's patient, my husband's medical record was already a young doctor's nightmare.

I drove home at 5:00 that morning, exhausted and angry. Crawling out of my car in the back yard, I shook my fist up at the stars. "Why do I bother talking to you?" I yelled. "Why do I bother hoping and praying that Alan will be shown some mercy, that things will just go okay for a while? If he's going to die anyway, just take him now instead of torturing him like this. Instead of torturing me." In the house, the living room still looked like the scene of an emergency it had been when I called 911 for the paramedics. I bent over and picked up the paper backings from the ECG leads, mopped up the spilled IV fluid, and pushed the furniture back into place. This time, I was too numb to cry. I thought we were doomed to more emergencies, and then Alan would die anyway.

We never had to bear these emergencies alone. Each time Alan was rushed to the hospital, I called Tom and my friend Jane and asked them to come. They were there in an instant with their arms wrapped around me. Each time, Alan looked up from the stretcher and said, "Thanks for being here Tom, Jane. It really helps a lot." I couldn't agree more.

Finally, after one more emergency admission for chest pain in March and another angiogram, we learned that the stent was holding, the remaining grafts were functioning, and the latest pain was caused by circulation pulsing through the narrow new collateral blood vessels that were growing around the bypassed areas. That was what was supposed to happen after a bypass. We had good news for a change.

After spending the better part of seven months in hospitals, Alan never needed to be hospitalized again. I was wrong about my projected scenarios. It took a long time for me to believe his progress was going forward, but I don't mind being disproven when my assumptions are wrong.

12. LURCHING TOWARD EQUILIBRIUM

During the spring of 1999, after Alan's four hospitalizations, we tried to find a semblance of equilibrium that would break the pattern of lurching from crisis to crisis. Alan's cardiologist told me that Alan's frequent angina episodes made him ineligible for a standard cardiac rehab program. He added, "You should design a cardiac rehab program for Alan to do at home." Sure, what's one more treatment to add to our already full day? So we bought a treadmill, and by walking slowly on it every day, Alan gradually began to regain strength.

Alan chose to apply his limited energy to studying, and he wanted some new subjects to learn about. He liked to read the top news stories over breakfast, so we labeled folders with the hot news topics and he cut out articles to talk to friends about. As I asked him questions about the article to build comprehension, he wrote the answer in his logbook. Later that day, he could telephone his nephew and say, "Did you hear about this? Let me tell you my opinion." We set aside a small table in the kitchen for Alan's folders and supplies, and hung a sign over it, marking it as "Alan's Project Space." Having his work space so close to where he read the paper let him transition smoothly through the steps without going down the hall to his office, where he might forget what he intended to do.

Alan came up with topics to investigate in depth. I don't remember what started it, but Alan became obsessed with learning about gypsies. We looked up the origin of gypsy tribes in his beloved *Encyclopedia Britannica* and on the Internet. Friends brought him articles and told him stories about their encounters with modern urban gypsies. Our friend Ginny's stock went up appreciably with Alan when she told him she had gypsy blood in her heritage. He repeated these stories to me and patted his thick file of gypsy information with satisfaction. These fascinations would last for weeks and provide boundless ways to engage Alan's thinking, writing, and memory skills.

After a drop in performance from post-surgery fatigue and worry, Alan started making more progress in cognitive rehab with Karen. Steady progress in rehab doesn't necessarily mean fast progress. Most gains are slow and incremental and take enormous effort, even long after the brain injury.

One day when he was depressed about progressing slowly, Alan said, "Am I ever going to be smart like I was? I get discouraged."

Karen replied, "Alan, you are still very intelligent. It's the access route that's detoured. Your intelligence is absolutely helping your brain's healing process." She continued, "You delve into things very completely, and that helps open up your memory about that whole subject matter. It's an amazing strategy you have used systematically."

On another day, Karen watched Alan talk himself through a deductive reasoning puzzle and said to me, "I can practically see how Alan's brain is struggling to make new pathways around the damaged ones."

I think some of those new pathways got where they were going.

Karen was referring to neural plasticity, a branch of brain science that has exploded with useful information in the years since Alan's injury. Not long ago, doctors would tell families that patients who had a traumatic brain injury would probably recover as much as possible in the first year or two, then plateau at that level. Now doctors point to research that shows that our brains have an innate ability to heal, repair some connections between neurons, and reroute the neural pathways so necessary for thinking, memory, emotions, communication, and movement to a greater extent than previously believed. While the study of how to best apply discoveries about plasticity is in the early stages, exciting programs are being developed to customize treatment for people with brain injuries.

Alan's treatment team told us early in rehab that it would help him if he could *think* through the steps of what he was learning when he was able, not just repeat it or imitate me. This process takes more time and concentration, but I believe it was an important part of the reorganization that seemed to be ongoing in his very damaged brain.

Another critical aspect of brain plasticity is that the best results happen when the patient has the benefit of an expert therapist, the right kinds of stimulation, and carry-over by the family in the home situation. I would add that family members need extensive training before we are able to coach our loved ones in these sophisticated strategies. I was fortunate to learn some principles and techniques from the best therapists early in Alan's rehabilitation. However, as the months and years went on, it became harder to find individualized resources or coaching. I could be reasonably creative and resourceful, but having more ongoing training available would have saved us some trial-and-error approaches.

Alan's efforts in therapy paid off in an improved ability to formulate and share thoughts. One night, he pondered awhile, then said, "The difference in higher level thinking is you can hold three points in your head at one time and remember them. Right now, I can only hold one, but I can see what I can't do.

This from a man who six months earlier couldn't say the months of the year in order; he probably still couldn't, yet he had this capacity to watch his brain at work.

Alan thought I was getting smarter too. "Wow! How did you ever remember where you put the car?" he asked in awe each time I led him back to our car in a dark, multilevel parking lot. When we went to appointments, I had to coax him out of the garage since he feared never finding the car again.

One night at dinner, our friend Kathy asked, "Alan, how do you keep going? Where do you get the perseverance to keep practicing and learning again?"

His reply surprised us both in its complexity.

Alan said, "I studied hard subjects all my life. This would be even harder if I had not studied science. I know that when I studied chemistry or physics, I always hit a wall where it seemed impossible. But if I kept studying, I'd break through and understand. If I hadn't studied physics, I might have given up on learning to read."

I marveled that long before Alan could describe that experience, he was able to make it the engine driving his determination.

That spring, Alan felt as if he lived on a Metro-Goldwyn-Mayer movie lot. Chunks of music loosened up in his memory and tumbled out all day. Alan had always loved music, but I had no idea he knew so many Broadway musical tunes and camp songs. Sometimes, the entertainment annoyed him.

"Why am I remembering that movie about the priest who ran an orphanage for boys?" he asked. "I hated that movie!"

Karen explained that when memory chunks like movies return, we don't get a choice about whether we liked them or not.

But from that time on, Alan was never without a song. Before he became ill, Alan's wit often included song references. In the middle of a discussion about a topic, Alan would pipe up, "Oh, there's a song about that ...," and launch into a tune that captured the topic.

Then he'd say, "What? You don't know that song?" Now he started being able to associate songs with topics in the news again.

Many of the songs Alan remembered came from musical parodies, folk songs, and protest music from the 1960s. When he remembered a singer he liked, we quickly ordered the CD on Amazon. We spent hours singing along with Tom Lehrer's songs that poked fun at academics and politicians, and Alan grinned at the sly humor.

We even made up songs to help him remember the steps of an activity by setting the words to a familiar tune.

In March, Alan was deemed well enough to leave home for therapy, so we said a grateful farewell to Karen. Alan began several sessions of outpatient cognitive rehab therapy at Spaulding Rehab with Jennifer, his speech pathologist from the inpatient brain injury unit. Alan didn't recognize the hospital at all after a gap of five months.

"What is this place, why are you taking me here?" he asked in the parking lot. None of the staff, who were excited by his progress, looked familiar to him.

But when we walked by the adaptive living apartment, Alan perked up and said, "Look, that's our apartment! Can we go in?" One more validation of the importance of conjugal visits!

Alan made strides in conceiving and writing descriptive language, reading comprehension, grasping abstract concepts, and writing stories for his autobiography on the computer. His favorite exercise worked on his ability to describe the action in a picture in writing. That meant he was to glue a photograph on paper, then write a paragraph about the photo. His sense of humor came through when he wrote multiple-choice answers to the question "What's going on in this picture?" Ever on the lookout for good photo ops, he got a lot of mileage from photos we took at the zoo. On the sheet containing a photo of him mimicking a peacock spreading its wings, he wrote, "What is this man doing?" The choices were a.) Become a tai chi master; b.) Learn to fly, and c.) The dance of the fanning feathers.

He came up with difficult questions and puzzles to stump Jennifer and me, and started saying, "I'm a pretty smart guy," for the first time since his brain injury.

Jennifer also taught Alan to use more associative memory strategies, where he linked a new piece of information to something he already knew. Alan knew the names of several presidents, so he chose that association. "You say his name is Calvanio? I'll remember it by Calvin Coolidge."

At home, we shifted our focus away from only didactic lessons at the kitchen table to a few activities in the community. We took drawing and tai chi classes at our local adult education program. "These are the normal things couples do," Alan said. His problems with visual perception came through in his tiny drawings with missing areas crammed into the corner of the paper. He found it hard to draw from his imagination, but liked copying animals from a magazine in watercolor. Alan enjoyed showing off our masterpieces on the refrigerator gallery.

The tai chi classes challenged Alan's ability to mirror movements and move his body in flowing motions. However, he focused intently on the instructor and reminded me to practice together between sessions. At first, I tried to help him move like the rest of the class. But when I noticed that the instructor relaxed in Alan's presence without making corrections, I did likewise and focused instead on forming the soothing motions with my body.

Tai chi taught me to let go of my belief that if Alan didn't do everything the "right" way, his rehabilitation would be doomed.

Alan persisted in insisting he could drive. I didn't think he had enough memory or judgment to drive safely, but I agreed to help him review the driver's education manual he picked up at a local driving school. Spaulding Rehab offered a driving readiness evaluation performed by an occupational therapist, so we made an appointment and agreed to go by her neutral decision. I tried hard to prepare Alan for the likelihood that he would not pass the test, but he couldn't hear it. He was sure he would pass and be back behind the wheel tomorrow.

Alan did well on concentrating and completing all the required tests. He scored well on the rules of the road, but practice on the simulator showed that his cognitive processing time was only fifty- percent of normal, so he took in and interpreted information too slowly to react quickly and safely.

Alan was stunned when the OT went over his results. On the trip home, he alternated between weeping and yelling in anger. He never gave up hope of driving again and asked everyone he rode with to give him pointers.

Alan often asked, "Aren't there any movies about people like me?" When I thought we were both ready, we watched the movie *Regarding Henry* starring Harrison Ford as a tough lawyer who suffers a brain injury in a robbery and has to learn to read and relate to his family again. The movie simplified the recovery process, but I gave the film makers credit for tackling such a difficult subject. Alan kept saying, "That was a very scary movie. Scary because you can lose your memory so fast ... have your life change so much. You have to learn to do everything again." I wasn't sure how much Alan related the movie to himself, until three days later when he said, "That was a very scary movie. But everyone should see it. That guy was a lot like me."

Another spring highlight was Alan's visit to his Northeastern University office. Dressed in a nubby tweed jacket and red tapestry tie, he presented himself very well to nervous colleagues who had not seen him since the early days at Spaulding. Most of the faculty didn't bother to introduce themselves, even though I had explained to them that memory loss meant that he wouldn't remember their names.

Easing back in his desk chair, Alan sighed with contentment and said, "I got my biggest wish: to come back to my office." He was unfazed by all the projects he no longer understood cluttering his desk. "I just want to sit in my chair like old times."

I pretended to celebrate with him, but I couldn't banish the pain and anger I felt at all that had been taken away from him by the brain injury. We went to the Northeastern library and located all of the textbooks Alan had written, then loaded up on NU mugs and souvenir tee shirts in the student union. Alan was very satisfied with the day's accomplishments.

A few months later, Alan set a goal of taking the MBTA train to Northeastern University. He wanted to accept his friend Christos's invitation to sit in on the teacher training classes they used to teach together. This idea petrified me at first, but we practiced the steps together and used written instructions. Northeastern was only four subway stops from our home, and a colleague agreed to meet Alan at the destination subway stop and walk with him to the classroom. She would also see that Alan got on the right train for the return trip. Alan proved to me that he could sustain his concentration enough to check off the names of the four stops, a major accomplishment with his distractibility problem. He also knew how to call me on a cell phone to keep in touch by that point.

Alan met his goal once again and made the trip a few times. He became discouraged when he couldn't follow any of the content discussed in class and soon lost interest. "Mostly I wanted to be independent again, and I did that," he said. That journey was the absolute height of adventurous independence for Alan.

❦

I, on the other hand, was sinking as fast as Alan rose. After each of his hospitalizations, I took longer to rebound. I tried to articulate for myself what the latest medical problem meant for the future since his doctors couldn't predict which way his heart would go.

I asked myself, "What am I running here, all within our home? Is it supposed to be a hospice or a rehab?"

I decided I didn't have to choose because we were already integrating the best elements of both into our daily life. We included hours of cognitive rehab and physical therapy into our daily routine and applauded every step forward. At the same time, we made the most of our time together and filled our days with the people and activities that meant the most to Alan.

Overwhelmed by myriad responsibilities and negotiations with the insurance company to continue outpatient cognitive rehab, I had a dream that I was running on a treadmill as fast as I could go but not as fast as the treadmill belt. On the ground along the right side of the treadmill were strewn a few novels and watercolor paints, which were my favorite ways of relaxing. On the left side was a wide swath of insurance papers, medication records, and must-do lists pertaining to Alan's care. When I bent down to the left to pick up something up, I almost lost my balance. I was moving too fast to even look at what I was leaving behind on the right side.

My own professional life felt like it was disappearing, and with it my network and friends. I had resumed my private therapy practice part-time from my home office, but after taking long leaves of absence from my jobs in organizations, I reluctantly resigned. One day a friend brought home brown paper bags containing the contents of my desk at the cancer support program.

Suddenly, I couldn't avoid feeling all the lost and changed relationships that were tugging at my heart. Relationships with colleagues, clients, and myself as a therapist. Not being able to go out to dinner or a concert at night with my closest friends. When friends visited, Alan's illness was most often the topic of conversation instead of their interests and problems. It was hard enough to lose the mutuality in our marriage, but now I felt I was losing the mutuality that keeps friendships alive. The absence of my mother's sustaining love also left me feeling alone.

Reminiscing about the good times with Alan only made me feel worse. After my mother died, I learned that before a memory of a shared good time could become a cherished source of consolation, I had to face the stark realization that we would never do that together again. One day I saw a poster for the Massachusetts Horticultural Society's annual spring flower show and automatically thought, *Oh, I'll get tickets. Mom and I love going every year.* Within seconds my body buckled and fell forward as I groaned, "But we'll never be able to do that again."

Now I was having those realizations about Alan every week.

I didn't know it at the time, but I was in the throes of ambiguous loss. Also called chronic sorrow or "the loss that keeps on giving," ambiguous loss covers all the losses that aren't acknowledged in our culture by rituals or condolences from others. They always involve a lot of uncertainty and instability, and often go on for a long time. Chronic illness is a minefield of ambiguous loss. Alan and I were both deeply affected. We had been focused on the multiple losses and changes Alan underwent, but now my losses were demanding equal time. The loss of husband, chosen work, personal freedom, routines, people, and roles at home and in the community, as well as financial troubles. Ambiguous loss isn't the same as depression, but it is often a big contributor.

I felt worse as the weeks went on. Some days, I couldn't control when or how much I cried. I was convinced that Alan would die that year, so I got our legal affairs in order and bought a burial plot. I was irritable and impatient with Alan's perseverative questions like, "Why can't I go see my brother in California?"

Among my worries was my own brain. I had trouble concentrating and did not have enough mental energy to follow through on the multiple steps that each responsibility required. I ruminated over decisions I needed to make without reaching a conclusion. I had trouble falling asleep and woke up on high alert whenever Alan stirred. I envied my friends who had "normal" marriages and what I called "standard issue husbands." As in "I can't figure out how to refinance the mortgage. This would be a good time to have a standard issue husband." I knew I was in trouble when not even a walk around beautiful Jamaica Pond could lift my spirits. I had wonderful support from my friends, and continued to talk with my therapist on the phone, but that wasn't enough.

Being a psychotherapist both helped and hindered. I could recognize that I was depressed and tracked my cognitive and emotional symptoms. Despite the explanations that I gave my therapy clients about the value of medication in tough circumstances, I still thought that I should be able to cure myself. And I was embarrassed to admit that I couldn't.

The tricky part of depression in caregivers is that we usually keep plowing ahead and doing what needs to be done every day. In contrast to many people who practically stop functioning when depressed, we keep moving, so we look better off to observers than we feel.

Finally, my better judgment prevailed and a referral led me to make the acquaintance of Dr. A., a psychiatrist whose creative ways of framing challenges resonated with me. After I recounted the experiences that led to my depression, Dr. A. said, "No wonder you're depressed. You've labored many months to give birth to this new person, and his problems never end. We could look at this as a sort of post-partum depression." I agreed to try an antidepressant and started to feel the benefits within a month.

Martha, my therapist, was concerned about how much Alan and I practiced, read, did his homework, and worked on rehab every day. She asked me, "Can you consider letting go of the pressure to work on rehab on Friday at 5:00 PM? Give Alan and yourself a Sabbath to just be?" Her permission and encouragement helped me to lighten up on some self-expectations and appreciate how much progress we had already made.

In addition to talking about all the problems on my mind, I continued to sort through my emotions and changes by writing and drawing in my journal. I also found it helpful to keep a gratitude journal to provide some balance. Every day, I wrote a few things that I was grateful for that day:

The first snowdrops sprouting in the front yard.

Watching Alan, his face turned up to the full moon, singing the song from The Mikado *about the sun and moon.*

Seeing my neighbor's light come on at 1 AM because she sees the ambulance pull up to our door.

I started making more time for the activities that I needed and craved time for: sitting meditation, exercise to restore some physical strength, and thinking about my own hopes and dreams apart from Alan's needs. I was rebuilding my private therapy practice in my home office and enjoyed working with clients again. I discovered that as I felt better, I was able to rejoin Alan in the intense renewal our relationship was going through that spring. As we rolled out pizza dough one night, Alan interrupted his mushroom distribution to say, "Do you know what love is like? It's when everything you do together is fun and exciting."

We became adept at keeping an attitude of adult playfulness in the house to combat the infantilization that can creep into a relationship where disability is involved. Instead of helping Alan with his bath, we took on geisha and patron roles while I scrubbed his back. Bored by common vocabulary lists, we made lists of the body parts involved in sex. As he struggled to spell the words, his face lit up as I dictated my favorite parts of his body: muscular thighs, furry chest. Alan said, "You're a woman. You're made differently. You have nice breasts and a tush I love to push."

Alan loved choosing movies in the video store, and we had movie dates to watch his favorite movies over and over. *Casablanca, Arsenic and Old Lace, Chaplin, Around the World in Eighty Days*. I was amazed that he remembered themes and endings of several movies.

We brought pond water from the Arboretum and looked at the drops under a wide-screen children's microscope. We were students together, matching the squiggly creatures in the water to the illustrations in his natural history books. It worked particularly well when Alan was the teacher and I was the student for a change.

One of the cruelest parts of memory impairment became part of our intimate experiences. Alan looked forward to making love, enjoyed playfully planning our afternoon rendezvous, and relished the afterglow. I loved it when he was manly, when he leaned up on one elbow in bed and bent down to kiss my lips. We sang our theme song, "Sky rockets in flight, afternoon de-light." A few hours later, he couldn't remember.

"We made love? Today?" he asked.

I felt angry that he was cheated of pleasurable memories, and I felt cheated to be left alone with experiences that a couple should share.

Even so, we kept making new rituals to express our love. Every night I said, "Alan, the joy of my life is going to sleep with you every night and waking up with you every morning."

He unfailingly replied, "Uh-huh," and closed his eyes.

I thought my ritual only mattered to me, until one night when I crept into bed after midnight, being careful not to awaken him. From the mound of blankets in the dark room, I heard a voice say, "Aren't you going to say it?"

"Say what?" I asked.

"You know. About me."

I recited, "Alan, the joy of my life ..."

"Uh-huh. That's right," said the voice as it drifted off to sleep.

Alan took charge of organizing our home in ways that worked for him. His most demanding job was emptying the dishwasher and putting the dishes where they belonged on the shelves because he still had trouble with naming objects. Alan recited the index card labels over and over to learn the shelves' mysterious contents: *bowls, plates, saucers.* After awhile, he became exasperated by the sentimental collection of mismatched dishes we used every day. To him, the shelf looked like a jigsaw puzzle without a space for the piece in his hand.

"We need to throw all these dishes in the trash and start over with everything the same!" he proclaimed.

So off we went on a shopping expedition to Bradlees. Prior to his brain injury, Alan the physics professor rarely bothered with the minutia of home décor. Discount department stores were foreign territory best left to the wife. But now Bradlees' home furnishings department looked like the Promised Land to Alan: everything in matching sets wrapped in neat, white boxes. He swooned over china patterns with judicious deliberation.

"Whoever heard of black plates?" he said. He picked up one plate, then another. "This one's too busy, too much stuff on it. Now this one is sooo beautiful. This one is just perfect!" He stroked the cream-colored plate with a bright mosaic rim.

Alan lovingly placed the service for eight in the shopping cart and moved on to silverware. Each pattern evoked comments usually reserved for sculpture. At the end of the aisle, the sale on drinking glasses caught his eye. "We don't really need these," he teased, "but they're too gorgeous to leave behind." Talk about role reversal; that used to be my line.

As we steered toward the check-out counter, I said, "Alan, this overflowing cart makes us look like newlyweds setting up a home."

"Yeah, we're newlyweds. Newlyweds," he repeated with a satisfied grin. We referred to that trip as our most romantic date ever. Yes, we had managed to fall in love again and become newlyweds in this post-brain injury life.

Wonderful escapades like Bradlees and moments of closeness made it even harder to believe and live with the remnant of brain injury, which was also an intruder in our midst. Alan was prone to abrupt shifts into episodes of wild rage and delusional beliefs that were ferocious in intensity. They took hours or days to completely manage with medications and behavioral approaches. The outburst often came from the frustration, humiliation, or misinterpretations arising from Alan's limitations.

We had some success using an emotions intensity scale that ranged from 1 to 5. Alan could point at the scale and estimate the strength of his anxiety or anger. Then I could offer a suggestion aimed at whatever upset him. The scale worked well up until the middle range, but after that, I had to take responsibility for reducing the intense feeling. We even made lists of things he could try to calm down or refocus.

For example, Alan's reactions often started with anxiety. If he could say or show that he was anxious about company coming for dinner, I asked what made him nervous and offered a suggestion to handle it. One night he said, "I don't know these people; they're your friends. I don't have anything to talk to them about."

I said, "How about showing them the crafts you've been building? They like art and will be interested in how you choose projects. What do you want to say? We'll write down your talking points."

But if the stages accelerated quickly, he became agitated and lost track of his original reason. At the upper-level intensity "Jekyll and Hyde" mode, he swore at me, threw newspapers on the floor, and tried to run away. He yelled, "You stole all my money and gave it to your boyfriends." Or "You ruined my life and I hate you." He ran to his office and raced through the Yellow Pages in search of a lawyer's telephone number so he could divorce me.

I kept my distance while saying, "Stop. You're out of control. We can figure this out."

Sometimes, an explanation registered and he was willing to sit down and have a glass of juice until he calmed down. Other times, his distrust escalated along with his voice. Most times, he responded to my suggestion that he go into his office for a "time out." Once at his desk, he found a book to look at that distracted him until he forgot what he was angry about. Alan found it disquieting that the bodily sense of the emotion persisted long after he forgot what made him angry or anxious.

When Alan couldn't distract himself or regain control, I pulled out the hardware drawer. Alan used to like tinkering with home repairs, so he had quite a collection of small tools and widgets in the hall closet. On bad days, I brought the drawer to the table and engaged him in organizing the contents and figuring out their uses. He could spend a half hour engrossed in making up uses, since he forgot them all. I would never have provided him with the tools if they were sharp or large enough to use as weapons. That's always a consideration with an agitated person. By the time he'd had enough, the medication kicked in and he wanted to take a nap. His memory impairment was an advantage when I could use the hardware drawer every few weeks without him remembering doing it before.

At the end of an outburst, he often fell asleep and awakened oblivious to the havoc he had wreaked. Meanwhile, I was still shaken and angry. If I thought the situation was workable, we sat down when he was calm to talk over the incident and make a plan to minimize a reoccurrence. Occasionally, Alan became shocked and apologetic when I described the horrible things he'd said. But at other times, he restated his justification: "I yell at you because you control my whole life and took away my car. You deserve it."

Alan's craziness cast a pall over the trust and predictability I was struggling to rebuild. We swung on the arm of a pendulum between genuine love and distrustful unpredictability. I wanted to trust my husband, but knew that whatever Alan said in the moment was what he believed. My prayer was often, "Please keep us safe." I meant safe from more medical problems, but sometimes I meant safe from Alan's anger and confusion.

13. NARRAGANSETT HOMECOMING

More than anything, Alan and I longed to return to our vacation home in Narragansett. The Narragansett house had always been our retreat, our "love nest," the place where we gave each other our full attention. After our wedding in 1987, we spent our January honeymoon beside the wood stove, daydreaming about our adventures to come. Here we had walked miles on the beach on blustery winter weekends and kayaked down the river all summer.

Alan campaigned for his doctors' permission to travel the seventy-five miles away from Boston hospitals, and eventually they granted his request. I wasn't as brave, but because Narragansett's local emergency services were satisfactory, I agreed to pack our bags.

On Memorial Day weekend of 1999, we returned to a house frozen in time. My muddy garden clogs rested at the top of the basement steps, where I had kicked them off last June. The coffee table was strewn with 1998 tourist information and a list of art festivals to attend. Paintings by Rhode Island artists we'd met at past festivals adorned the walls. Our swimsuits hung on the shower rod, ready for the next dip.

For years, we'd had a routine of paddling down Narrow River to the mouth of the ocean, where we spread our blankets on the sand and relaxed all day. The late afternoon currents ensured that we got a workout paddling home. Then we fired up the grill, and Alan prepared his signature swordfish steaks, which we savored on the back deck as the sun set on another perfect day.

Now the house looked as if we had just left, not like we had been in a foreign land for eleven months. Alan's eyes were pink-rimmed and teary for the first hour. "I can't believe I'm here!" he cried. "I can't believe I'm back."

When he grasped that I was as disoriented as he was, he exclaimed, "So we're equal here! Because you haven't been here for as long as I haven't been here. Now you know how I felt when I came home from the hospital."

For the first two days, I veered between giddiness at being back and the sinking recognition that our usual ways of doing things in Narragansett would need to change. Fueled by my yearning to see favorite places, I made the mistake of dragging Alan with me into overload and exhaustion.

Driving along Ocean Road, I pointed excitedly and said, "Alan, look at the view of the ocean behind that house!"

He cringed and framed his hands into blinders at the sides of his head. "No, no, I'm trying *not* to take in so much. Not to look!" he implored.

Even though I had adjusted every aspect of our life in Boston to Alan's disabilities, some part of my mind magically believed that we would be our old selves in Narragansett and thereby resisted changing.

We renewed acquaintances with welcoming neighbors and explored the local children's beach on the shores of Narrow River. In the past, we frequented the town beach on the Atlantic, but going there now was out of the question. The children's beach, with its roped-off swim area, diving raft, and sandy space for a few lounge chairs, was far safer for Alan. He declared it his private beach and swam daily. Alan had always been a strong and stylish swimmer. I'm not much of a swimmer, so the first time he entered the water, I stood by nervously with a neighbor I'd enlisted in case he needed help. Fortunately, Alan's procedural memory took over and he glided through the water with the agility of a dolphin. Taking nitroglycerine tablets before swimming delayed the angina his exertion brought on. Before long, he had the stamina to swim twenty feet to the raft, dive off, and swim back to shore.

He came ashore sporting a victory grin, which quickly screwed up in befuddlement. Even when there were only three or four people on the small beach, Alan couldn't pick me out until I stood up to wave and meet him.

"Thank goodness you found me, wife," he said each time. "I was lost."

Alan was desperate for a role and a skill that was uniquely his, something he did best and could teach others. Swimming and diving provided continuity in his identity and turned out to be his forté. Over the course of the summer, we hosted several nephews and nieces in Narragansett, and Alan was appointed Director of Waterfront Recreation. He taught the youngest children how to put their faces in the water and how to dog paddle. Being able to teach the younger generation a valued skill meant the world to Alan. He even coached me: "Janet, turn your head from side to side as you stroke for a better breath." His older nephews reminisced with Alan about how he had taught them to swim at the Chicago YMCA or in the lake near his first vacation home in New Hampshire. As everyone in the family acknowledged his superior form and power as a diver, Alan's pride and esteem swelled.

Our other favorite routine was riding our bikes out to breakfast at the local pancake house and to the lighthouse at the Coast Guard station at the tip of Point Judith. Alan wanted to do that again, so he set the goal of relearning to ride his bicycle. Whenever Alan insisted on trying an activity that I didn't have the guts to teach him, I turned the project over to Tom. One Saturday, I returned from the farmer's market to find Alan and Tom pedaling toward me. Alan's balance was shaky so the bike wobbled a bit. But once again, the procedural memory honed by a lifetime of riding enabled him to stay upright and gain momentum.

Alan's face lit up like a Christmas tree: "Look at me; I'm back in the saddle!"

His ability was limited only by the angina that made him stop after pedaling two blocks. Alan checked off another crucial accomplishment on his list.

One balmy afternoon, we walked along the sea wall on Narragansett Bay, listening to the incoming tide crash on the rocks and the squawk of seagulls diving for clams. We sat on the stone wall, savoring the salt air and holding hands, our faces turned up to the sun.

Alan perked up: "I know what would be good for relaxing. Someone should make a tape of the ocean wave sounds! Has anyone ever thought of that?"

Alan loved to invent things he didn't know were already in common use, so I applauded his idea. The next time we went shopping, we found a CD of Pachelbel's *Canon in D Major* with a background of ocean sounds. Alan pronounced it the best music he had ever heard but said, "I should get royalties on this idea."

Time and again, I learned that yes, there were parts of our lives that were gone forever. Yet still other parts that I had mourned as impossible turned out to be quite doable in modified ways. And sometimes what most needed to be modified were my assumptions and expectations. For example, I thought that we would not be able to enjoy live theater performances because Alan had difficulty tracking the plot and processing the dialogue of TV shows. When we watched a movie at home, we paused the action at frequent intervals so Alan could review the plot and ask me questions. But that summer, we were even able to indulge our shared love of theater by returning to Theatre by the Sea, a classic red barn where national and regional actors staged fabulous performances.

To Kill a Mockingbird was in production, and Alan wanted to see the play. We prepared by watching the movie video a few times and talking about the characters and plot. We even wrote the summary in his logbook. On the day of the performance, Alan refrained from reading and enjoyed an afternoon nap to keep his mind sharp. We had a great time at the theater, and Alan managed to stay through both acts, with some whispered clarifications. He was so profoundly moved by *Mockingbird* that he remembered the inherent moral issues, later asked me to read him the book, and brought up the story years later whenever racial injustice was in the news.

Returning to the Coast Guard House restaurant overlooking the Atlantic Ocean was its own momentous homecoming. For many years, we had explored major decisions, including moving in together a few months after meeting, over romantic dinners here. Now we were celebrating the first anniversary of Alan's resuscitation after cardiac arrest.

Alan said, "I'm celebrating being alive and being back at the Coast Guard House, so I'm having the baked stuffed lobster."

As he plunged into the lobster with gusto, I sat back and shook my head in awe at this resilient man. Last year at this time, Alan was on the brain injury unit eating pureed food with his knife, stumbling to walk, unable to write his name or say the word "lobster."

I reached over to stroke his strong, tanned arm. "Alan, I feel like we're on our second honeymoon," I said. "I love you so much."

He laughed, "We should have honeymoons more often, not wait so long in between."

I also reflected that at the one-year mark, I was the other survivor in this couple. I appreciated the progress we had made as individuals and as partners. I could exhale and be proud of us. I was less vigilant and more trusting in several areas. I trusted others to teach Alan what he wanted to learn because I didn't obsess about protecting him constantly. I had more trust in Alan's capacity for regeneration and didn't consider him to be on the verge of another heart attack. Perhaps I was better at living with uncertainty and paradox. We had even found aspects of each other to love and were building a new marriage. That night, we made love with moonlight and a sweet summer breeze gracing our bodies.

We feasted at the Coast Guard House several times that summer. Each time, Alan looked up with butter dripping off his chin and said, "This is as happy as it gets!" I agreed completely.

The problems Alan experienced in Boston with cognition, behavior, and judgment came with us on Narragansett weekends. There are some problems from which there is no vacation. We experienced many adjustments, trade-offs, and mixed emotions in Narragansett. Yet, the overarching message was that we had reclaimed one of the best parts of our life and made it work.

Alan and Janet on their wedding day, January 17, 1987.

14. Ceremony for a Second Marriage

One year after Alan's cardiac arrest, I wrote a letter to Dr. S., the director of the Resurrection ICU, to detail Alan's progress. In part, the letter said:

"Alan reads well and comprehends about 70 percent. He struggles with spelling accuracy of 50 percent. He is writing his memoirs on the computer. He has been able to learn some new material and routines with much training. He remembers a lot of facts from history, geography, and politics, but still cannot access much science knowledge or retain what he studies. This causes him enormous pain and periods of despair. He mourns his ability to be a professor after a distinguished thirty-five-year career.

"Alan has mild receptive aphasia, but communicates well when the other person uses correct strategies. He has word-finding problems and gropes for the word to finish his sentences. He speaks and understands a sophisticated vocabulary, and says, 'Ooh, that's a good word; say it again.' Just as before the cardiac arrest, he loves to give opinions and make speeches. He has long conversations with good friends, but doesn't remember them unless he takes notes. A major challenge has been to walk the line between

stimulation/challenge and frustration/cognitive overload. When he crosses that line, he becomes angry, agitated, and self-deprecating. We have learned to take just a nibble of a favorite activity.

"Alan's short-term memory is severely impaired, and he now accepts the use of memory aids and lists. He can safely walk four blocks to Centre Street and buy a snack. We even trained so he could take the train to Northeastern University, find his office, and return home. His neuropsychologist considered that miraculous!

"Alan has been very prone to depression, and medication helps. A small dose of antipsychotic decreases preoccupation, ruminating, and agitation. I stopped being attached to specific outcomes early on, when experience taught me that I had to match my expectations and wishes to the healing capacity and timing of Alan's body. The rehab staff tell us that Alan has surpassed the outcomes they expect from anoxia survivors. They attribute that to his innate intelligence, motivation, much social support, and my involvement. Alan still has his tremendous zest for life and sense of humor. We appreciate all the small things even more, and consider this year a bonus for which we will always be grateful."

And yet, even Alan's progress didn't take away my sense of restlessness, of something left undone. On the surface, Alan looked like nothing ever happened. He walked the same, dressed the same, even made the same facial expressions. But in truth, he was a man with an injured brain, whose every physical action and cognitive effort took enormous concentration and coaching. Parts of Alan's personality had survived, and the newer parts were becoming familiar. We were reconstructing our life together, learning to take small steps forward when every part of our world was drastically changed.

And yet, I was aware, in ways that others could not be, that he was totally changed as my husband. So much of the mutuality was gone from our marriage. We were partners in healing Alan, but not in many other ways. He knew me in relation to how I cared for him and how we had fun together, but he really didn't know me as a person.

My soul howled with loss. Alan could not understand it and would be terribly hurt if I told him about his absence in my life. I needed to do something to heal myself and live fully in our present life.

What I needed was a bridge between what I now experienced as my first marriage and second marriage to the same man. I needed to say good-bye to *My Alan*, to set his spirit free from any hold my yearnings and false hopes might have on him. I sensed that an act of deliberate letting go would free me to fully embrace and commit to my love for this new man I called *Another Alan*. I needed to open up to receive his love in different ways. I was ready to move into a new phase of life.

I have always loved to create rituals for myself, friends, and therapy clients, special ceremonies to mark transitions, life events, personal milestones, and the endings that precede each new beginning. So I created a ritual to simultaneously commemorate my first marriage to Alan and mark the death of that marriage and the husband I knew best. I also wanted the ritual to bless the beginning of my second marriage to Alan as he was now.

On a sunny August morning, my sisterly friends Gail and Marla joined me in Marla's beautifully landscaped garden as witnesses and participants in my ritual. I sprinkled the space with ocean water and made offerings to the Divine and to the earth: offerings of flowers and fruit for the beauty, juiciness, and zest of life. I offered cake to the birds, my companions and connection between heaven and earth.

I dressed in layers of garments topped with the blue chambray dress I'd worn on the day of Alan's cardiac arrest. Under that dress was the regal purple dress I'd chosen to recently celebrate my fiftieth birthday and to salute the core parts of myself that were still alive and dancing within me.

On a small table, I set up an altar adorned with precious objects from our first marriage: photographs, gifts, and a new plant. And the airline tickets I'd kept from our fateful trip to Chicago. On a second table, I made an altar to represent our new marriage and the life we shared now. On it, I placed photographs of Alan and me laughing and hugging on our front porch. And the bracelet Alan gave me for my birthday with handcrafted links that were inscribed *"Words of wisdom: be good to yourself; be kind to others, get a dog!"* When we came across the bracelet in a craft gallery, Alan had roared with delight to find jewelry that shared our philosophy for a happy life.

Wearing the blue chambray dress, I bent down and lit an entwined ivory candle to start the ceremony. Two candles started off side by side, then braided together as they reached their full height. I stated my intention: "I want to remember, give thanks for, and then let go of my first marriage, which began on January 17, 1987." Although Alan remained at home, I invited him into the space by showing Gail and Marla his photograph in the double-sided antique locket he had given me years earlier. Alan's face beamed with joy right after saying "I do" at our wedding. Looking at that treasured photograph, I said to Alan, "I will always feel gratitude and wonder at your ability to open your heart and let me in when you lost Margie after fourteen years together. Knowing how much I love you now and can't imagine loving anyone else, I am in awe that you took that risk. I have such gratitude for the life we have shared all these years. I give thanks for who we were as very separate individuals who had many complementary interests. But we always knew what we valued in our marriage and brought it to fruition."

I continued, "We certainly challenged each other, had plenty of times when jealousy and anger reared up. Times when we accidentally hurt each other. But I think we made up for those times and went on to thrive. We listened to each other hatch new ideas and later encouraged the endeavors those ideas became—for me, new specialties and my own business; for you, a new path of educating teachers instead of students."

Now I was in a trance of reverie and oblivious to the cars passing by on the other side of the hedges.

"You were always more of a visionary than I; you were never afraid to look far down the road. When we met in 1985, you were planning a trip around the world for the following summer. I had no idea I would be going with you to Thailand and Borneo, but I did and we became ardent travelers. You taught me that anything is possible if you want it and are willing to work hard for it … and willing to have fun right now."

Gail and Marla sat in lawn chairs close by, emotions crossing their faces like shadows. Their presence gave me the strength to continue.

I wept as I confessed my terrible fear that I would forget Alan, forget myself, or forget us as we were for eleven years. In the hospital,

I'd been obliged to shut the door on those memories so I could get to know Alan all over again, without the expectation that he would ever be the same.

Standing at the altar commemorating our first marriage, I tore the airline tickets into jagged pieces that drifted into a ceramic bowl. I said, "By destroying these tickets, I give up the fantasy I entertain late at night that *My Alan* got on the wrong flight. I give up the fantasy that he is wandering around some distant airport looking for *His Janet*. Now his spirit is free to go where he needs to go."

I set a flame to the tickets and watched as they burned to ashes.

I acknowledged that there were many bridges between my first and second marriages, and a strong foundation. I shared a story that would extend across marriages: "One blustery winter day when we'd been married only a year, Alan and I walked on the beach in Narragansett hand in hand. All of a sudden, I was filled with a sensation of light and awareness, a sense of sublime union and timelessness. I felt that there had never been a time when Alan was not in my life. No past or future, just always there. It was the most peaceful, loving feeling I've ever had. I invoke that felt sense often and can still find it in my heart."

I read from the vows Alan had written for our first wedding:

"There is yet another deep and personal meaning that this marriage has for Janet and Alan. It is the honor that each shows the other in becoming husband and wife. It is this sense of honor that ennobles their love and life together."

I pledged to thread that honor through our current and future life together. Then I sealed the first part of the ritual by saying, "My first marriage ended at 5:00 PM on July 5, 1998, when Alan's heart stopped and his life as we knew it ended."

When I was ready to transition to the second altar, I lit the other entwined candle. Slipping the blue dress off my shoulders, I let it fall to the ground. Underneath, I wore its replacement, the beautiful purple "Birthday Queen" dress I had worn to celebrate attaining the age of fifty with wisdom, grace, and resilience (at least some of the time). My heart melted as I picked up a tiny photo of Alan taken at Spaulding Rehab, kissed him, and tucked it into the other half of my locket. Alan's face was thin and pale, but his life force shone though his blue eyes. I fastened the delicate chain around my neck and pressed both husbands to my heart. "I've been very fortunate to have two perfect husbands."

This new marriage required a different set of vows to honor the changes we had been through. In a clear voice, I recited new vows to Alan: "Alan, I vow to love you with the fullness of my being every day for the rest of our lives. I will help you recover in any way I can. I will make sure you feel my love in every tangible way. I will see all of who you can be with my eyes wide open. I will celebrate our interdependence, our mutual need for each other. I will be your memory and continue to weave stories of our past life together, as well as what we did ten minutes ago. I will not let you or others forget how unique and phenomenal you are as a person right now. I will treasure you, adore you, laugh and make love with you. Together, we will create many sources of joy and fun."

And this time, I made vows to myself as well: "Janet, I vow to love you in all your frailty, vulnerability, mistakes, and courage. I vow to forgive myself for the mistakes I will make in this new terrain, and to ask others for their forgiveness. I will try to give myself the time and space to reflect, understand, integrate changes, and feel love. I will do whatever it takes to keep myself whole. I will now put aside the constant apprehension of this past year and give myself over to the fun and joy that Alan and I often share. Someday I will write a book about our journey to give hope and sustenance to others on this path."

> I read from a poem by Jean Giorno called "Fullness of Days":
> *We have forgotten that our goal is to live*
> *And that we live each day in the very hours of that day.*
> *We are reaching our true goal if we are living.*
> *These days are fruits and our goal is to eat them.*

I plunged my hands into a bag of rich soil and scooped soil into the indigo pottery vessel that has been my favorite planter since 1970. The chiseled inscription "This good old pot is made with hope for the future" dances around the lip of the pot. I gently placed a small, lacey Aurelia tree in the pot and patted soil around the roots. I treasured the continuity my planter provided by gracing every home I'd lived in for twenty-nine years. Now I hoped the tree would flourish and the pot would continue to ground me in this new phase of life. I also knew that this pot would come with me even after Alan had passed on.

In halting voices, Gail and Marla generously shared their own stories of loss, love, and regeneration. We wept, smiled, and expressed appreciation for our honesty and resilience.

We ended the ceremony by blowing out the candles and standing in a circle with our arms around each other. My friends held me up as I sobbed my grief for a long time.

Later in the afternoon, as we slowly recovered from the intensity of the ritual, we shared tea and cake and celebrated our powerful bonds of friendship. We laughed as Marla's four-year-old daughter Hannah danced around the garden like a nature sprite.

As the sun set, I drove home to my groom, Alan, convinced that I had cared for myself and our marriage in an elemental way. I doubt that I could have given myself freely to Alan and his ongoing needs if I had not taken the time to commemorate all that we had lost and embraced the wonders that remained and flourished. Over the next few months, my restlessness settled and my commitment deepened. Perhaps Alan's second marriage ritual had taken place earlier in Bradlees housewares department when we purchased new dishes.

Whether our rituals are consciously planned or serendipitous, we deserve to find ways to honor and make real such monumental transformations.

15. CRAFTING A NEW RETIREMENT

Alan had always been a persuasive debater, prone to making pronouncements about our future. Before he became ill, he announced, "This twelve-room house is too big for us now. We should sell it and move to a condominium. I'm going to call a Realtor tomorrow."

I was always a few beats behind him, bleating, "Wait, I have a stake in this decision too! I'm not ready."

Now Alan began to adamantly campaign to go on a "real vacation far away."

He said, "I deserve a vacation after all I've been through. You do too. I want to go to Florida where it's warm and I can swim. People our age go to Florida in the winter. They don't stay here where it snows and you can't walk your dog."

My first response to his idea was to sarcastically think, "Yeah, I might get on an airplane with you again after what you pulled last time." However, Alan stayed on the subject, and his doctors even agreed his heart was stable enough to handle the trip. What about my heart?

We consulted a travel agent and decided to go to the Sundial Resort on Sanibel Island on the west coast of Florida. In our former life, we always stayed in budget accommodations and spent our time taking in all the sights. Now I knew we would need an all-inclusive facility where we could go to the beach, eat our meals, and keep the surroundings within Alan's stimulation level.

We spent weeks preparing for the trip: poring over the glossy Sundial brochures, investigating nearby hospitals, describing the flight and hotel room to Alan, and packing his familiar clothes and toiletries to balance out the new summer clothes he ordered from LL Bean. We rehearsed so much that Alan said, "I don't know if it's possible, but I have completely pre-remembered our whole vacation!" He had aced anticipatory planning.

Alan was also wise enough to say, "You know, getting on that plane might bring back some bad memories."

I agreed that we might feel anxious, so we practiced the relaxed breathing from tai chi class and relaxing every muscle in his right hand. He also chose word puzzle books to focus on during the flight.

The flight went smoothly, but Alan disliked the long rental car ride from Fort Myers to Sanibel. Our luxurious suite, decorated in lively tropical pastels that mirrored the blue sky and pink sunsets, made up for his displeasure. While Alan napped, I labeled his bureau and posted direction arrows to the bathroom with my trusty pack of index cards. When Alan awoke, he said, "Wow, this place is very deluxe. Look how easy they make it to find all your stuff."

That night as he savored a prime rib dinner and virgin strawberry daiquiri in the oceanfront restaurant, Alan said, "This is a miracle. I never thought I'd be well enough to travel again."

I smiled in agreement and felt myself open up to new possibilities with Alan. We both reveled in walking on the beach composed of seashell fragments, bending over in the position known as the "Sanibel stoop" to claim even more varieties of exotic shells, and swimming in the turquoise waters of the pool. As always, nature was a reliable source of replenishment for our spirits.

Alan often used the strategy of finding similarities to feel comfortable in a new environment, and he practiced often in Sanibel.

"This restaurant is just like our breakfast place in Jamaica Plain," he said as he surveyed the bustling coffee shop. "I should try something different, but I always get blueberry pancakes."

Later it was, "That lady looks just like the lady who taught me to read in the hospital, so I guess the people here are friendly and won't hurt me."

Without the strain from competing pressures at home, I could enjoy Alan's company and see things through his eyes. He bent his face low over our patio table, heaped with dozens of seashells we'd collected to send back to my nieces in Maine. "Just look at these," he said. "It's like a million diamonds glittering in the sun." We spent a few afternoons in bed, taking time to make love in the playful way that we'd been missing for a while.

One morning, I studied my reflection in the bathroom mirror as we dressed for a swim. I had been going to yoga and Pilates classes, and managed to lose the ten pounds gained during the first year of Alan's illness. I'd rewarded myself with a new blue bikini from the Land's End catalogue—a daring move for any fifty-year-old woman. As I checked out my firmer abs and more relaxed face, I felt a new sense of hope for my own resilience. I liked this woman I saw and wanted to offer her more of what she enjoyed.

So I set a goal of attending a writer's workshop at the Fine Arts Work Center (FAWC) in Provincetown, Massachusetts, during the summer. I wanted to study writing, and my friend Gail, an artist as well as psychiatric nurse, raved about her experience taking painting classes at FAWC. She had convinced me that even a beginning writer could take classes there, and I fantasized about spending a whole week learning to write a memoir and exploring the beaches of outer Cape Cod. In the past, the amount of work involved in finding and training the right person to stay with Alan had discouraged me from leaving. But now I was on a mission.

Waiting in line at the grocery store and frequent traffic jams on the island's main road triggered Alan's low frustration tolerance. One afternoon, we finally drove back into the Sundial complex after Alan had been rude to the retired gentleman bagging our groceries, then threatened to get out and walk home as we sat in traffic. He was still yelling as we passed the tennis courts. I'd had it.

"Alan," I snarled, "do you know what happens to husbands who drive their wives crazy? They get dumped on the tennis courts and have to find their own way home, that's what."

Alan shrunk down in his seat, momentarily chastened. Then his whispered retort, "Well, it's still all your fault you know."

Alan had an unusual incident as we walked on the beach one evening. "My legs don't work. I can't walk," he said, stumbling sideways in the deep sand. "If I sit down, I won't be able to get up. Let me lean on you." I was terrified that he was having a stroke and had all I could do to support his trembling weight back to our room. His blood pressure and heart rate were normal when I checked them, and he walked normally after resting for a short time. But the episode stayed with me.

After our uneventful flight home, we made an album of our panoramic Sanibel pictures of the ocean, beach, pelicans, and breeching dolphins. Alan carried the album to his appointments for a few months and told everyone we'd return to Sanibel next winter. This time I agreed that it might just happen.

While the vacation helped, it couldn't cancel out some travails at home. I had been imploring Alan's nephews Marty and Larry, both businessmen, to give me specific advice about managing our retirement account investments. Alan had researched and changed investments monthly when he was well. Now I paid for an advisory team at Fidelity to make those decisions, but I had the unrealistic expectation that Marty should just know the right answer. After some general discussions, I felt angry and dissatisfied with his opinion.

When I complained to my therapist, she said, "You want to hear Alan's voice coming out of Marty's mouth. That's the only voice that will satisfy you." Her comment hit a nerve and I cried bitterly.

Later I wrote in my journal:

"I need Alan to come back for fifteen minutes to make this huge decision. Alan will never come back for fifteen minutes no matter how long he lives, not even in my dreams. I worry I'll forget the Before us because I'm so entangled with Alan as he is now. I have a crack down the center of my heart tonight."

I had these reckonings I called reality slams over and over. Just when I thought I accepted this new man, another reality slam. I wrote about a few times when I had a thirty-minute crying jag to the litany of, "My husband died; my husband died; I can't save him; my husband died." The problem wasn't that my antidepressant medication wasn't working. It worked fine. I just had to spiral back into grief over and over. Grief unfolds in stages and layers. As another change in Alan disclosed itself or finally bothered me, I grieved again.

Alan had recently started to not be able to find me in the house. I mean in an adjacent room. Sometimes, when he napped in bed before dinner, I took the chance to curl up on the couch. One evening, I fell asleep and didn't hear Alan calling me from the bedroom. Finally, he stumbled into the living room, short of breath. "I've been looking all over for you," he said. "Where were you?" As he lost me more often, I missed him more.

That winter, Alan grappled with his growing awareness that he wouldn't be able to teach college physics again. While facts about history and literature were readily accessible, his knowledge of science and math proved very hard to unlock and never really returned. He struggled to understand basic concepts from the study guides and while calculating money. He asked me, "Was I a good teacher? Did I ever amount to anything?" It broke my heart that this accomplished man couldn't embrace the memories of his career.

Alan concluded to his psychiatrist, "This is probably as good as I'm going to get physically and in my mind."

Coming to this conclusion had been a long and painful process for Alan. He told me, "I never thought I'd be like this: a sick guy who isn't as smart as he was. I thought I could outrun a heart attack. Or at least it would be the kind you could recover from. I don't think I can be a physics professor anymore. I guess I should retire and find an easier job; maybe teaching young kids."

Once Alan accepted that he would not return to Northeastern, he agreed to plan the swankiest retirement party that the physics department had ever seen.

The tradition in the department was that when a colleague retired, the whole group went to Joyce Chen's Chinese restaurant for a laid-back meal punctuated by spontaneous speeches and toasts honoring that person's career. Inevitably there would be jokes about who forgot to buy the gift, and a lot of good-humored remembrances about the professor's foibles.

While this tradition suited most retirees, I wanted Alan to be feted in a more dignified way. I wanted his career to be honored and remembered. To that end, we reserved Northeastern's elegant Faculty Club, catered a fancy dinner, and ordered lavish floral arrangements.

In preparation for the party, I visited Alan's colleagues in the physics department. Many of them did not know me well, but I spoke to them frankly: "I want you to come to the party and say whatever you would have said at Alan's memorial service if he had died after the cardiac arrest." A few of the professors were taken aback by my directness, but they got my message.

Alan decided he deserved a new suit for his retirement party. At Filene's, he picked out a dapper charcoal pinstriped suit. He topped off his look with a new red silk tie and pocket square, and stood at attention during the alterations.

Alan labored over his retirement speech for weeks.

He told me, "I don't want anyone to say anything about me being sick or brain injured in their speeches. I want to talk only about my career and what I accomplished."

His speech included vocabulary he had not used in quite some time, so he spent many evenings rehearsing.

On the April night of Alan's party, a gala atmosphere emanated from the Faculty Club. His family members came from around the country, and many professors and their wives attended from across the university. I got all dressed up in a new blue silk suit and played the gracious hostess, greeting each guest as they entered. It was important to me that the party reflect Alan's dignity, intelligence, humanity, and social nature. The event exceeded my intentions.

I had one jarring moment while telling a faculty wife that Alan had learned to read and write again as part of his arduous recovery.

This woman, who held a Ph.D., said, "He needed months of rehabilitation to learn to read? I thought the brain just healed itself."

I almost shouted at her, but said emphatically, "Even a broken leg doesn't just heal itself, and a brain injury is a thousand times more complicated than that. Recovery goes on for years." I was aghast at her lack of understanding, but our exchange made me realize how little even educated people know about brain injury and sharpened my resolve to raise public awareness.

In our favorite photograph from that evening, Alan stands in the center of a circle of colleagues. He raises his glass of ginger ale in a toast and regales them with stories from the founding years of the physics department in the 1960s. He looks hale, hearty, and resplendent in his new suit. His colleagues seem relieved and relaxed to be in his presence. His appearance and way of communicating far surpassed their expectations and memories from the early days at Spaulding. This is how I wanted my husband to be remembered.

Following a fabulous dinner, Alan's friends and colleagues treated us to an hour of speeches. Each person talked about a different aspect of his long and distinguished career. I found out much more about Alan's legacy than I ever knew. The president of Northeastern and his colleagues praised his early research in nuclear physics, his collaborations across departments, and his scholarly publications over thirty years. The speakers didn't hold back on the funny stories and references to Alan's stubbornness or political battles.

Then Alan took the podium. Straightening his posture and adopting the scholarly tone that launched thousands of lectures, he began:

"I was born to be a scientist. I have been fascinated with science and nature since early childhood. As a youngster, my family doctor was my idol. He took me into his lab and introduced me to the microscope and Bunsen burner.... I grew up in the era of the atomic bomb. Nuclear physics was talked about everywhere, and I wanted to contribute to the field. I have been at Northeastern University since 1961. I did research in theoretical nuclear physics as well as teaching for many years. In 1974, my all-time best seller Physics for the Life Sciences was published. However, the Indonesian version really took off in 1994.... I was never a teacher who could repeat the same class over and over for twenty-five years. Part of my interest was always outside the physics classroom.

"By 1980 I was deep into computers and convinced of their value in science education. For four years I had everyone's dream of a summer job. I taught Using Computers to Teach Science workshops on Martha's Vineyard. I remain convinced that the teachers came as much for the classes as for the lobster bakes and beach parties.

"In my continuous attempt to be a Renaissance man, I was even an entrepreneur. I founded EDUTECH, a software company to publish educational science software for the Apple.... Writing has always been my great passion. After publishing three textbooks and several lab manuals, I went public with two books for the educated layperson. I wish I had discovered years earlier that you can publish your opinions and advice and have people pay to read them!

"In retirement, I plan to continue writing. I have completed volume one of my autobiography. There will be more tell-all volumes to come. I'm looking forward to spending more time with my family and traveling to exotic places. I have some advice for the younger faculty: Stay curious and keep learning something new all the time. Don't be afraid to venture into new areas of interest. Thank you for joining my family and me this evening. Most of all, thank you for thirty-seven wonderful years at Northeastern University."

By the end of his speech, Alan was exhausted but exuberant. He needed to sit down while accepting the faculty's gift of a ship's captain's clock. But the genuine love and admiration that rang out in the standing ovation filled the room with energy.

The next morning, Alan said to me, "Alan the super-normal is up. Thank you for that wonderful party. Now let me talk to my dog. Molly, I am officially retired now so I'll have time to take you on nice walks. I used to ask my doctors if I would ever be normal again. Now I think I'm pretty normal. I felt the same as all the other guys at my party."

In June, I mentioned to Alan that the second anniversary of his resuscitation was approaching. As we washed dishes, a funny conversation followed.

Alan asked, "Did Christ come back to life or did he just fly up, fly away?"

"After he was resurrected, he rose up to Heaven, as the story goes," I said. "No, he didn't come back to live on Earth."

"So Christ didn't come back to real life, huh? But I did come back to life, right?"

"Yes Alan, you did something Christ couldn't do," I laughed.

"Wow. So why is he so famous?" he said with a straight face.

Since he had touched on religion, I ventured into an area I hadn't dared to bring up until now.

"Alan, you know a lot of our friends ask me if you remember what it was like while your heart was stopped," I said.

In the sarcastic tone I recognized well, Alan said, "Oh, I know what they mean. They want to know if I saw a white light. Or if little angels in robes came to meet me. If I heard heavenly music."

"Well, yes, that sort of thing. Did that happen?"

"No, I didn't see anything. I was just gone. Just gone," he said resolutely. "That was all there was to it."

Alan seemed matter of fact about "just being gone," so I let it be.

Being officially retired seemed to give Alan a more acceptable way of looking at himself.

He said, "I need a hobby and more work to do now that I'm retired. Let's go get some more craft kits so I can make stuff for people."

Alan had enjoyed the process of assembling projects from structured kits for awhile, but crafts became his new occupation. We hung a sign that said "Alan's Craft Projects" above his kitchen work space. He announced his new career to friends and soon had a request list hanging above the table.

"Let me see now, how many new orders do I have?" he said. "Wow, I'd better get to work."

We shopped at a toy store, but the kit manufacturer's slogan was "Ages 9–97!" which made them acceptable. At first I steered him toward the simpler kits by suggesting that he make gifts for our nieces. As his skills improved, Alan selected kits with moving parts or smaller pieces. A kit that an eight-year-old girl could complete in an hour took Alan many hours of effort. But he didn't mind. We spread the pieces on the table, and I wrote each step of the instructions on a fresh sheet of paper.

I sat quietly by, just answering questions or switching the direction steps when he was ready. He needed breaks and seldom stayed with a project for more than an hour. Critical of his results, he thought of how to paint the next lobster boat more neatly. I so wanted him to have an activity he considered worthwhile that I was usually patient while waiting to turn the pages. I could surreptitiously practice meditation or read a magazine if I wasn't obvious about it.

If Alan thought I wasn't paying attention, he lost his concentration: "Stay with me on this now, this is an important step."

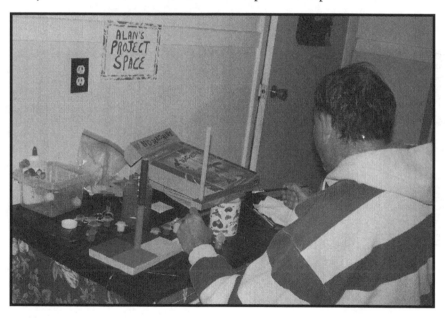

Alan builds a wind machine at his crafts table (2000).

Painting suncatchers that looked like stained glass became Alan's specialty. We found a great kit that contained a pattern book and plastic sheets to lay over the pattern while applying special paint from tubes. When the fish or cat dried, the suncatchers peeled off ready to stick to a window surface. I watched as Alan deliberated over which animal to make, how to apply the colors, and his color scheme. The same concentration and creativity that he used to channel into devising science experiments now went into suncatchers. If I didn't know what his current end product was, I would have expected an easy yet elegant experiment to emerge.

Alan got enormous satisfaction from giving suncatchers to his former therapists and doctors when we visited.

Jennifer, his speech-language pathologist, said, "Alan, I'm going to hang this beautiful fish in my office window and tell new patients that a man who had to learn everything again got well enough to make this."

Alan felt his most worthwhile contribution was inspiring another patient. "I should do more for the guys who have to stay in the hospital," he said.

The approval of his endeavors by his high-achieving family always mattered to Alan. They responded by showing interest in the process, and Pam turned her colorful photographs of his exotic fish into note cards Alan could use to write letters.

Alan explained to them, "Craft kits help me work every part of my brain. I have to plan the steps, organize the parts, hold a thin brush, decide on colors, and figure out the problems that come up." He understood more about his brain than I sometimes gave him credit for.

Alan's carpenter nephew Tom precut wood to make key holders. He and Alan spent an afternoon sanding, painting, and twisting in screws for the keys. Even though Alan hung his finished key holder by the door, he didn't finish the extra key holders Tom left.

"I feel more organized when I have a kit with the directions on paper and a picture of what it will look like," he explained. Starting a project from scratch was too vague and unorganized unless a companion worked alongside him. When Tom bundled the pieces for one holder into a plastic bag and wrote out the directions, Alan approved and took orders for key holders.

A few months later, Alan told his artist brother Richard, "I'm getting pretty advanced now, but I started with kid's kits. The terrible thing with drawing is there's no right or wrong. Everyone will say it's pretty no matter what you draw. With these kits, you have to do right or what you're making won't work. I get a lot of satisfaction when it's done."

In 2000, I was invited to resume being a guest lecturer at area colleges and hospitals on subjects that comprised my clinical specialties. Now when I spoke about the stages of adjustment in severe chronic illness, I used our experience to illustrate the didactic material. I enjoyed engaging with students and workshop participants and wanted to get involved with educating people about brain injury. I also wanted to give back to the community that had helped us so much.

The Brain Injury Association of Massachusetts had an Ambassador Program that sent volunteer speakers to organizations and civic groups to talk about brain injury prevention and treatment. I trained to be a speaker and gave talks to Rotary and Kiwanis clubs. Sometimes, Alan accompanied me and critiqued my performance. On a number of occasions, a former student of Alan's was in the audience and came forward with tears in his eyes to tell him how much Professor Cromer taught him at Northeastern, and how much he learned from Alan's story that night.

So much of our life was going forward that second year, but there was also the harder part I summarized as "All of the above is true."

16. "ALL OF THE ABOVE IS TRUE"

Alan was now a man of sharp contradictions. His family was puzzled by the discrepancy between how smart he sounded during their scheduled Sunday phone conversations and how confused and irritable he could be in person. While visiting us, Barbara said, "Last week he told me about how the Israelis and Palestinians were fighting and compared it to World War II. But today he yelled at the dog, buttoned his shirt wrong, and doesn't remember the headlines we read aloud at breakfast."

The main difference was that before Alan made the Sunday call, I propped his logbook in place and reviewed his week to prime the conversation. When Richard asked if Alan had eaten at the Chinese restaurant, Alan said, "Let me consult my notes here ... oh yes, we ate mu shoo shrimp on Tuesday," before answering. If he was in a bad mood or tired, we postponed the call.

But being around Alan all day showed how complicated our life really was. When people asked which was the real Alan, I shrugged my shoulders and gave my standard answer: "All of the above is true." Alan had many facets, and brain injury and dementia shaped some more than others.

Alan and his sister, Barbara Kahn, stroll our neighborhood in 2000.

Alan could be flirtatious and fun. One spring afternoon as we walked around Jamaica Pond, he spontaneously pretended to pick me up: "Do you come here often?" he asked slyly.

"Oh, yes, three times a week," I said, batting my eyelashes. "How about you?"

"I'm retired from my first job, but work full time at my new career."

"What's your new career?" I asked.

Flashing a big grin, Alan replied, "Staying alive!"

"Where would you take me on a first date?"

"Do you like seafood?" he asked. "I know two great places, but one is in Rhode Island, so I'll take you to Legal Sea Foods."

"Do you kiss good night on the first date?" I asked coyly.

"This is how I kiss good night," he said as he wrapped me in a romantic embrace, gave me a light kiss, and waltzed away.

"Wait, I want more, more!" I called.

The next day, Alan might be tired or overloaded from reading his college text on ancient Greece that he couldn't comprehend. That activated what I called his "default button," and he brooded that he'd recently argued with a colleague.

"I had a big fight with Steve," he told me glumly.

Each time I reality tested by saying, "Alan, you had a good conversation with Steve when he visited on Wednesday. You didn't fight at all. That's a false belief that your mind gets stuck on when you're tired." He was frustrated by his thinking, but usually believed me and let it go.

Sometimes, when Alan was angry at me, he could heed the reality testing of trusted family. He said, "I told my sister and brother that you were controlling my life, and I was yelling at you because you won't let me drive."

Then he reflected, "My entire family said I was wrong, I was lucky to have you, and I should stop what I'm doing and do the opposite. I guess my entire family can't be wrong."

At other times when his agitation persisted, we called Tom, who confronted Alan in no uncertain terms about being verbally abusive to me. When Alan wouldn't respond to my limits about yelling, he seemed to hear Tom's directions—to lower his voice, take a short walk, and then read a book—from a *man* he respected.

Or it might help for Alan to just vent to Tom, who would commiserate about Alan's losses. Then Tom could crack a joke that got them both laughing and off the hot topic. We needed a repertoire of ways to help Alan manage emotions because one approach might stop working, or something might be bothering Alan that he had not yet found words to explain.

Sometimes, I wanted to have a good argument with Alan, the normal kind couples have to clear the air and resolve a problem. I knew that wasn't possible and had seen that arguing back just escalated his anger. When Alan got angry, his emotions overruled his ability to think logically, problem solve, and tune down his response. I got mad that we couldn't fight, but tried telling myself he couldn't help being this way because of frontal lobe damage. But more often, I resented that he expressed his anger and frustration freely while I had to be in control and therapeutic.

I wanted to have a loud tantrum too. On those days, I went into the bathroom and tensed every muscle of my body as I crouched into a curl. Then I let out a "silent scream" and shook my every limb free while yelling soundlessly. That felt better. I also saved up old crockery and then whacked it with a hammer. The shards provided drainage for my flower pots. If I could pull weeds for thirty minutes, the reward was an immaculate garden and lower blood pressure. Only physical release could ease my anger.

Just because I didn't argue doesn't mean I didn't confront Alan. I confronted him when he was mean or disrespectful by saying, "Alan, I don't yell at you and I won't stand for you yelling at me. When you don't like something, please ask me to sit down at the table so we can discuss it. I'll do that too instead of yelling at you." Sometimes, he was quite capable of using the approach I told him was acceptable.

Years earlier, I worked in a psychiatric day hospital where a lot of the treatment focused on teaching people skills to communicate better and manage their symptoms in public. One slogan we used was "Mental illness is not an excuse for bad behavior."

Now I said to Alan, "Brain injury is not an excuse for bad behavior." He got the point when I offered him an alternative way to respond.

When we went back to our Narragansett house in May, Alan couldn't learn to walk to the neighborhood beach alone. He was easily confused walking around the block. One day, I drove to the store on a fifteen-minute dinner run. Alan was happily watching a video and promised to stay inside. As I returned to our neighborhood, I thought, "That's the color of Alan's orange shirt." He had walked around the corner, became lost, and fell into the weeds by the side of the road. It was a scorching day, and he was sick from the heat.

I dragged him into the car, berating myself for leaving him. It took a long time to cool him down and get his blood pressure back to normal. He dozed off, but when he woke up he belligerently insisted he was going out again. He had no memory of being so sick or lost. I never left him alone in that house again.

Back home in Jamaica Plain, Alan was more easily oriented and able to follow his routine. But that was soon affected as well. Late one Friday afternoon, I drove four blocks to the post office to mail an important document. Ten minutes later, I arrived back at our house just as a Boston Police Department car pulled away. I ran in breathlessly to find Alan standing in his undershorts and "Tough Hombres" tee shirt.

"Where did you go?" he asked indignantly. "I filed a missing persons report on you and sent the police to find you. I thought you had an accident or got kidnapped. Or maybe I did something terrible and you left me."

I showed him the large note I'd left beside him on the couch that detailed my errand and return, signed with our trademark two entwined hearts.

"Alan, my note explains that I'll be right back," I said with a hint of exasperation in my voice.

"Oh, I didn't see that," he said.

I called the police to report myself found but they weren't concerned. But I knew we were moving into dangerous territory.

When Alan had a new or worsening symptom, I always looked for a medical cause first, because so many medical conditions led to temporary setbacks in mental status. A bad cold or bladder infection left Alan confused and weak for two weeks. When his doctor couldn't find any infection or medication imbalance, I had to admit Alan's dementia was making it harder to remember things he knew only months ago.

Ever since the brain injury, Alan had two simultaneous processes dueling in his head. One was the ongoing improvement in cognitive functioning in some areas, and the other was worsening memory impairment from vascular dementia. It's hard to understand how they could coexist, but I saw the evidence. Vascular dementia involves much more than memory. It results when critical cells are deprived of food and oxygen due to impaired blood flow. The symptoms overlap with those of brain injury's aftereffects and can include confusion and difficulty concentrating, planning, carrying out responsibilities, and communicating.

There were times when Alan was doing well with some forms of thinking and keeping busy with activities he enjoyed. But at the same time he was more forgetful and confused. Then I thought the dementia might be to blame.

I saw Alan's use of language improving steadily, even with the pause to find the last words of a sentence. His vocabulary was superb, and he was back to correcting my grammatical errors like an English professor. Late one night, I was in the usual struggle to get him to drink enough fluids to prevent dehydration.

"Just finish this glass and then you can sleep," I said.

Alan drew himself up tall and held the glass to the light. "This glass was finished years ago when it rolled off the assembly line," he said. "However, I will consider drinking the juice."

Another day he read a humanities article comparing ancient and modern tragedies and said, "My recollection of what I've been taught is that the character has to have a flaw that leads to tragedy. Disaster is caused by something a person has done; that's a Greek tragedy."

That week, Alan was entranced by the Madonna movie *Evita*, based on the life of Eva Peron. After seeing the movie a few times, he said, "I figured out why I like *Evita* so much. It has a Greek chorus that tells what's going on and what might happen. That goes back two thousand years. We've gotten away from it but it's a great device."

He didn't care that he buttoned his shirts in a crooked alignment, and when I pointed it out, he told me, "You don't really care that I look stupid on the street when I dress funny for my sake. You just don't want the neighbors to think you don't take good care of me." I had to agree there was some truth to that.

He was smart enough to quote Shakespeare's *Macbeth* at length, and he enjoyed the video biography of Sir Isaac Newton. When we had a busy day or unexpected guests, he said, "Too much tumult, too much tumult around here, it's like Shakespeare's scene in the forest."

All this in the same week when he couldn't find me in the living room. All of the above is true.

My frustration always peaked around the little things that Alan couldn't do to help me. When friends were coming to dinner, I wanted to say to him, "Can you clean the bathroom, vacuum the hall rug, and turn down the stove before the soup burns?" I wanted him to do it in ten minutes, all without direction, to just do it like a regular husband working as a couple.

But that was asking too much. If Alan hurried to do anything, his angina kicked in and he had to lie down. He couldn't do two tasks in a row without a break to clear his head and review the directions.

I didn't know the term at the time, but I was feeling "caregiver burden," which refers to the cumulative effects of unremitting responsibilities and relationship changes that wear caregivers down. Family caregiver organizations now educate caregivers about managing the effects of such stress. I could handle all the emergencies, new learning, financial responsibilities, and house repairs. But when Alan couldn't set the table fast enough, it was the straw that broke this camel's back. I poured my frustrated lamentations into a poem titled "Can You?" but then felt guilty for being mad at Alan for what he couldn't do.

…No, you can't.
It's too much to process. Overload will overcome.
You will throw up your hands;
We'll both know you can't think right now.
You will need to lie down.

We look at each other in frustration and sorrow.
I need you back.
Eventually my anger smolders then cools.
Hot tears from the blistered heart of missing you.
We need to lie down.

At least my poetry was published in the Well Spouse newsletter, *Mainstay*, where I found an empathic audience.

We were often rescued by Alan's intense curiosity about the natural world, which deepened every year. One drizzly morning, I noticed several snails clinging to my flower pots on the porch. I arranged the snails in a row on the top ledge and called Alan. In the photograph he instructed me to take, Alan smiles at the snail inching its way along his hand. He studied every detail of the snails intently with his magnifying glass, before looking up snails in his multivolume encyclopedia of animals. Over his lifetime, Alan collected every kind of reference book, so we had a research library in the living room.

Eventually, he wrote information about snails in his log, but declined escargot for lunch. His curiosity was a saving grace for both of us because we shared a love of nature, and I could always come up with something new to entice him. Curiosity was one of the qualities I liked to be reminded that I loved most about my husband.

In the world of catastrophic illness, people become adept at "living in the paradox." The paradox that your life has completely changed but you've made a new life that works a lot of the time. The paradox that chronic illness doesn't mean problems stay stable. Medical problems flare up and need treatment adjustments all the time; Alan needed his cardiac or psychiatric medications adjusted every few months as his problems got better or worse. The paradox that the person you love can be so changed in some ways, so recognizable in others.

One night, Alan remembered being in Spaulding and said, "I was lucky to have you. I knew you were my wife, and when I saw you, I knew I had a life. I knew I had a life if I could just get back to it." Now we were living that life, with all its contradictions.

I knew that we would need to attend to both Alan's brain injury and dementia if he was going to enjoy life and use his skills to his fullest potential. But I also knew I would need more help and guidance as we moved into this newer territory.

And I had concluded long ago that it takes a village to keep a person's mind active.

17. The Quest for Upwardness

(Please note: the names of the program, participants, and staff have been changed for privacy.)

By the summer of 2000, we were in the middle of the dilemma that confronts everyone who has a brain injury severe enough to prevent their returning to paid employment: How to find meaningful engagement, be a respected and contributing person, and feel productive and valued? Even though Alan responded well to stimulation and new projects, he was totally dependent on me to come up with the projects and then do them with him step-by-step.

He did short-term volunteer projects such as reading to the children who attended the preschool near our home and handing out campaign flyers for our state representative. Alan was lonely and liked talking with people, but had only a few friends who visited regularly. Sometimes, he confided to our dog Molly that he was a worthless old man. While he could still learn new material that interested him and held onto his skills with much practice, the vascular dementia caused by his cardiac arrest was making his memory problems noticeably worse. I knew we needed to try a new approach to filling Alan's days with interesting, maybe even meaningful, activities.

And there was this, too: I needed more time to relax and pursue my own interests.

It took weeks before I could bring myself to schedule a visit to the highly recommended, private-pay center I'll call the Alzheimer's Day Program. On three occasions in the week before the appointment, I circled the stately Georgian building, crying each time. After all the progress Alan had made in two years, part of me felt like I was giving up on him by enrolling him in anything with the word "Alzheimer's" in the title.

I was relieved to meet Clarice, the director, a warm and extremely skilled woman who understood my ambivalence. She explained all the ways they could personalize Alan's treatment plan. Up until now, we'd been devoted to a rehabilitation model that aimed to help Alan regain and hold on to as much of his previous functioning as possible. But the day program was based on a "habilitation" model. Habilitation emphasized helping participants achieve small successes throughout the day. The intensively trained staff worked on maximizing current abilities and self-esteem rather than trying to regain abilities lost to dementia. This approach was new to me, but I knew we could continue working at home on cognitive rehab for the areas Alan was still capable of improving. I was all for blending approaches I thought would benefit him. The day program offered a lively group schedule including exercise, creative arts, current events discussion, community outings, ancient Greek trivia, and barbecues in the landscaped gardens.

Alan had many concerns about trying something this different away from home. "I don't know if I have the personality to be in a group program," he told Clarice. "I don't always get along with people, and they don't always get along with me." He did like Clarice because she met his criteria for any leader being "smart and nice." After Alan and I visited for a few days, he agreed to try the program three days a week for six hours.

On program mornings, Alan chose his outfit with care, preferring a dress shirt instead of a casual golf shirt, and red suspenders to ornament his new summer trousers. He topped off the look with his signature brown felt explorer's hat that we brought back from Australia. He checked himself out in the mirror and angled the wide brim just right to channel Indiana Jones heading out on his latest adventure. We walked the mile to the day program together holding hands.

Still, it was a difficult adjustment. Half the days, I would just be settling in at the nearby café with my cappuccino and poetry in progress when Clarice called me to say, "Alan is too agitated to stay at the program. We've tried several things but nothing is working. You'll have to come get him."

Gathering up my journal and fine-point pens, I'd think, "A group of trained professionals can't calm Alan down, so I have to be alone at home with him? Does that make sense?"

I stuffed my blank pages into a tote bag and went to meet Alan.

In fairness, we all tried many sophisticated ways of understanding what made Alan anxious or angry. When the trigger was identified, the staff gave him a break from the situation or helped him to handle it better. The customized plans often worked well. Overstimulation was a frequent problem that stemmed from his brain injury. The sights and sounds of up to twenty people in a room was more than he could process. So, he was encouraged to rest in a soothing room with a bed any time he wanted to. Although many participants do well with the schedule of group activities that change subject hourly, because they like the variety, Alan did better with long breaks between a few groups of his choice. During the breaks, he enjoyed reading, helping the staff set the table for lunch, or a one-to-one conversation.

He wanted to make friends, and the staff deliberately sat people with similar backgrounds together at meals and facilitated the conversation. I wondered how they could make friends when they couldn't remember who they liked or what they had talked about yesterday. Gentle prompting helped: "Eric is a retired history professor. You both know a lot about ancient Rome." The focus was on the present moment, and everyone made a valiant effort.

Alan's worst frustration was his awareness that the program had locked doors to keep participants safe and prevent wandering. When he couldn't leave on his own accord, he screamed, "I'm a prisoner here. I have my rights and demand to be set free." Since he was more physically fit than many of the other participants and exercise was his proven strategy to reduce tension, a plan was devised that Alan could ask to go out in the locked garden for a walk on the circular paths when he felt pressured. The only requirement was that a staff member accompany him, wait unobtrusively, and escort him back indoors. When Alan remembered the plan, he liked the "special privilege" and used the walk to calm down. Other times, he forgot to ask or refused to have anyone supervise him. That meant he couldn't go out, and he yelled instead.

One afternoon while Alan and I were preparing to go home, Priscilla, a diminutive older lady, had an agitated outburst. Pummeling her devoted husband's chest with her tiny fists, she shrieked, "You stole all my money, took it all away!" As the staff moved in to calm Priscilla and console her husband, Alan noticed how tense and frightened the other participants looked.

"Is that me yelling?" he asked me. "Sounds like me, but doesn't look like me ... you call that agitation?"

"Yes, that's how you sound when you get agitated," I said.

The incident stayed with him. As we walked home, he said, "That lady sounded like me when I get agitated. That's not a good way to behave at the program."

The next time he raised his voice, I reminded him, "Do you remember when Priscilla got agitated and yelled? You said it was scary and unfair to the other people."

He recalled his words but said, "Well, she didn't have a good excuse. I do. They won't let me go outside by myself whenever I want to."

All the participants were given as much control as possible over their schedules and preferences. But some things set Alan's agitation off unexpectedly. One Tuesday, he stormed out of his favorite music group. It wasn't until Thursday morning, when he sat stewing about something at our kitchen table, that he could finally explain what had upset him.

"Those people have no respect for music," he said. "And they don't even know the words to songs. You know what they sang?" He launched into the lyrics we all heard as kids: "On top of spaghetti, all covered with cheese, I lost my poor meatball when somebody sneezed ..."

He crossed his arms and looked indignant.

I was incredulous that this was what miffed him.

I said, "Alan, that's just the funny camp version; you probably sang it at Camp Martin Johnson."

He sniffed, "Songs should be sung the right way."

But he agreed to return to the program as a model of proper decorum.

I was so relieved and appreciative to have very experienced nurses, a social worker, activity therapists, and program assistants giving me their impressions of Alan and suggestions to make things better for both of us. The nurses monitored his cardiac problems carefully so I never worried when he enjoyed a trip to the Museum of Science on a hot summer day. They made great suggestions about fine-tuning his psychiatric meds to help keep his thoughts clearer for longer periods and reduce his anxiety. The activity therapists shared ideas for craft projects and types of exercises Alan liked. The program assistants and other staff modeled unfailing patience and kindness while never coming across as patronizing to a participant.

The best benefit for both of us was the opportunity to work with Dr. B., a neuropsychologist who specialized in dementias. Alan had individual counseling, and we shared marriage counseling. Alan liked the chance to talk with "a very smart young guy who gets what I'm saying."

Alan always chose what he wanted to talk about with Dr. B. One day he asked, "How can I learn to hold two thoughts in my head at once, especially when I'm angry?"

Dr. B. was masterful at ways to make such higher level brain functions concrete. He said to Alan, "You're a scientist; you know what a balance scale looks like, right?"

Alan immediately recalled the antique balance scale on his bookcase and nodded.

"On one side is your anger at the moment. On the other side are the good experiences and successes you've had at the program." Dr. B. reminded Alan of the museum trips and a visit by a historical re-enactment troop that he'd enjoyed.

Alan got the idea, so that night at home, he and I sat down to draw a "mixed feelings" balance scale with positive and negative sides. We made photocopies of the diagram so Alan could label each side when he was starting to get angry about a situation.

He needed help to sort out his thoughts and feelings, but came up with negatives, including "I feel like I am in a hospital." His counterbalance was "I have a purpose: to be out of the house and of service to myself and others." Some days it was just "I feel like I'm in prison" and "The food here is good." The balance scale technique served us well for a long time.

Dr. B. thought one reason Alan yelled was that he felt deprived of the boisterous interactions that characterize academic life. He missed that part of his identity and was trying to keep it alive. It had always been Alan's style to speak loudly and emphatically. He loved to argue just for its own sake. Dr. B. understood what I was too close to see: that arguing was the official language of academic scientists, who loved to debate ideas and fight for their wedge of the research money pie.

I laughed as I described the parties we attended when I first met Alan. "Alan and his Northeastern friends stood in a circle yelling, jabbing their fingers in each other's faces, and occasionally spraying spit as they interrupted each other. I found it intimidating and hard to join, but those guys looked forward to those gatherings. It was their idea of fun," I said.

I admitted that now, any time Alan yelled, I was so afraid that he'd have a heart attack or hurt me that I tried to make him stop. Dr. B. recommended that we find people Alan could have lively discussions with on the topics of his choice. They even used part of their sessions to debate. Marlene, one of the nurses, offered to be Alan's debating partner during his breaks. Alan loved that plan, and it took the pressure off me to argue about a topic I didn't care about.

I found that having more time to myself, along with sharing responsibility for Alan's care, made me more receptive to listening to Alan. One day in our marriage counseling session, Alan expressed what it meant to him to be in a place that had "Alzheimer's" in the title.

"People here are at all different levels like a one-room schoolhouse." With tears in his eyes, he went on, "I want to be praised for working so hard to get back my reading and writing. I don't want to be sent to a program for not being smart enough. I don't want you to forget how hard I worked."

I leaned across and embraced him. "Alan, I promise you I'll always remember how hard you worked to get your alphabet back. I know how hard you work every single day to be as smart as you are."

He nodded, and we closed in for a mushy hug.

Another day, Dr. B. asked us to say one thing that we needed from each other.

Alan said, "I need some power back. My wife has all the power in the house. She won't let me drive. She makes all the decisions."

He was right. I'd been running our lives for so long that I didn't think he noticed. Alan said he wanted to know more about our money. "Tell me how much we have and where it is," he said.

We agreed that I would find better ways of explaining our finances to him. We did write out checks together, but he found the process so confusing that he quickly abandoned the task. So every week, I gave him a two-sentence "executive summary" written on plain white paper. The memo contained a total money figure and the names of two retirement funds.

Alan reported to Dr. B., "It makes a man feel powerful to know he earned good money and can provide for his wife."

When it was my turn to tell Alan what I needed, I decided to go all the way. I said, "Alan, I need you to try to remember that my sister Sherry is very sick. I am very worried and sad about her. I need you to be kind to me when I'm upset."

Alan looked concerned and said, "Oh, my goodness, I didn't know that. Should I give you hugs or cook you dinner?"

We agreed that I would write a reminder that Sherry was sick in his logbook (minus the details). He would read it to help remember. When I felt sad, I could ask Alan for a hug.

Sherry had been extremely ill and hospitalized all summer. We had made a few arduous trips to Maine to visit Sherry in the hospital, but Alan found her condition horrifying and tried to push it out of his mind. He hadn't been able to even make me a cup of tea in years, but I appreciated his new gesture. This plan worked well. Alan took my request seriously and said, "A man should always try to cheer his wife up by kissing her." When he embraced me, I felt like I had a caring husband.

The program Alan went to specialized in providing services for people with early onset Alzheimer's who were in their fifties, or those in the early stages of the disease. Most people had lives that included professional careers with substantial achievements. Everyone was still able to live at home with family members. Even so, Alan intuited the range of cognitive abilities and memory deterioration among the participants. One day when he resisted going to the program, he explained his position to me. "Janet, a good program has to have upwardness to it," he said. "It wouldn't help me to always be the smartest person in the program. I need upwardness."

I understood "upwardness" to mean hope and new accomplishments, so the director and I asked Alan to set a goal for something he'd like to dare to try. Alan decided he wanted to give his first lecture since the brain injury. He chose as his subject "How Craft Kits Help the Brain" and prepared in earnest for a few weeks.

Alan could generate what he wanted to say, but couldn't spell well enough to write down sentences legibly. So while he paced across the kitchen floor working out his thoughts, I wrote down everything he said verbatim. Later I ordered his words and typed them up for him. Alan edited his speech and wrote brief notes to himself in the margin: "look up, show wind machine," etc. He practiced delivering it many times. The language was simple and direct, yet the neuroscience behind his ideas was accurate.

When I look at the photographs I took that breezy summer day, I am transported back to the group of ten people in their fifties and sixties seated around an umbrella table. Most are actively listening to the speaker, a distinguished man in a white, button-down shirt and khaki trousers who focuses intently on reading his lecture notes. A few participants drift off, head in hand. Alan's sleeves are rolled up so he can pass around the objects he's demonstrating: a wooden key holder and a brightly painted wind machine. The wind machine is modeled on a simple helicopter with a pilot seated between two propellers. One man turns the key holder over in his hands, strokes the rounded edges, admiring the sanded corners. A woman laughs as she playfully sets the wind machine's propeller in motion with her finger and feels the breeze on her face.

"It is important," Alan said, "to pick a very simple project to start. I chose this kit so we could find our keys. You start with a pile of small pieces and have to follow step-by-step directions. I decided what colors to use and practiced painting on paper before painting the wood.

"With kits I use several parts of my brain at once. The directions can look too complicated, so Janet helps me write out one step at a time on a separate piece of paper to stay focused. Kits help my coordination because you have to move your hand in different directions. Kits teach me to stay with a task and work through the problems."

Alan went on to explain the challenge of building the wind machine, his first kit with moving pieces. His face is intent and his voice is authoritative. He concluded:

"In summary, I have found that craft kits help my coordination, motor skills, planning, and patience. I am unhappy about the parts that aren't right when I complete a project. However, I learn and move on. My advice is to be patient, have fun picking out a kit that matches your ability, and be proud!"

Alan looked up with a beaming smile to receive the group's warm applause. He couldn't wait to rush home and phone his brother and sister, who were awaiting his update.

"Barbara, I did it! I gave my first lecture in two years! I must still be a real professor! The people were quite congenial. It's starting to feel like my place now. I felt respected because they were willing to accept a participant leading something."

His other triumphs included co-facilitating the current events discussion and starting "Alan's Craft Club." Clarice asked Alan to choose a craft kit he thought he could teach interested members to build. After deliberation, he chose wooden boat kits. He got a lot of satisfaction out of demonstrating how to assemble the little sailboats while the activity therapist helped the men gathered around the table.

Although the many times Alan got agitated stick in my mind, my notes from those months reveal that he actually had long periods where he was content in the program and considered it his "club for retired professionals." He took pride in his ability to co-facilitate groups and demonstrate the yoga poses he and I did at home in exercise class. He announced to Molly, "I am officially high functioning, Molly, so show some respect!"

Alan and I joined with his nephew Tom and a few friends to form "Alan's Team" and participate in the Alzheimer's Association Memory Walk. We sent a fund-raising letter to everyone we knew, and our team raised almost $1,200. On the day of the walk, we proudly donned our blue "Alan's Team" tee shirts and marched along the Charles River. Alan walked two miles, his longest distance since learning to walk again.

It took me weeks to adjust to what Alan being in the program represented to me. When I walked through the door, my stomach flipped and a clot of tears formed in my throat. I understood that many participants found a sense of belonging and esteem through the activities. But I got snagged on the sorrow, diminishment, and humiliation of these accomplished people now laid low by dementia and Alzheimer's, including my husband. At the social worker's suggestion, I joined a support group sponsored by the Alzheimer's Association that met at the day program. The facilitator was a seasoned Alzheimer's professional and compassionate woman. At first I felt like Alan. I didn't want to admit how much I had in common with my fellow group members. It was easier to focus on the problems related to brain injury that made Alan unique and less hopeless. But before long, I shared our problems and welcomed their emotional support and experience.

I was hungry for practical information about understanding and managing problem behaviors and boosting memory, not to mention more ways to take care of my own health and get more family members involved in respite coverage. I scooped up armfuls of excellent handouts and applied them right away. My favorite was the business card printed with "I have a memory problem; please be patient with me." When Alan and I went to a store or to JP Licks, ice cream shop, I slid the card across the counter to the waitperson while Alan decided what to order. People always responded patiently.

It turned out that most members were years ahead of me on the dementia trajectory, and I cringed when those who had placed a loved one in an Alzheimer's nursing home cried and shared their guilt week after week. I knew I would feel the same way and couldn't handle thinking about my worst case scenario for Alan so often. After about four months, I left the group, as members do, but took their stories and wisdom with me.

In August, my nieces Sammie and Cassie came to visit for a few days so I could introduce them to a treasured family tradition. Before my mother died, she had asked me for only one final wish: "Promise me you'll take Cassie and Sammie on the Swan Boats for me," she said.

"Bringing the girls to our Swan Boats will be my privilege. We'll think of you and make believe you are with us," I said.

Every summer when we were kids, she took Sherry and me on the Swan Boats that gracefully glide on the Boston Public Garden Lagoon. She loved bringing Sherry's sons for their first rides on the boats, powered by a strong young man pedaling the foot-propelled paddle wheel.

The girls bounced around in anticipation as we prepared for our adventure. Alan resented going to the day program instead of coming with us. I explained that it would be too much effort for his heart to take the train ride downtown and then walk several blocks. True, but mostly I was desperate for my nieces and me to have a day to ourselves. I needed to not divide my attention between playing with my nieces and taking care of Alan. This trip was also intended to be a respite for Cassie and Sammie, who visited their desperately ill mother in the hospital almost daily.

Just as we scrunched together laughing on the Swan Boat bench and waved to the tourists taking our picture from the bridge above, my cell phone rang. I tried to ignore it, but recognized the day program number. It was the director.

"I'm so sorry, but Alan is in a rage," she said. "He's kicking the door demanding to be freed to go with you and your nieces. We've tried everything, but nothing is helping. He remembers where you are and can't understand why you didn't take him along."

I fought my urge to scream at her, "I'm on the Swan Boats fulfilling my dead mother's last request. Is that too much to ask? Can't I have this much?"

"You must come get Alan. He's putting the safety of participants and staff at risk," she announced.

Of course I knew why they had those policies, but I tried to bargain, to beg for more time with my girls. It didn't work. Sammie and Cassie had already witnessed a few of Alan's Jekyll and Hyde swings and were apprehensive around him. I didn't want to upset them more.

Clenching my jaw to the breaking point, I said, "I'll be there in an hour."

I struggled to hide my fury and extreme disappointment as I explained to my nieces that we had to leave right away instead of enjoying a few more rides. On the way back to the subway, I hustled the twins into Burger King for a quick lunch instead of the formal tea at the Four Seasons Hotel I'd been promising them for weeks.

I hated Alan and never wanted to see him again. When I picked him up, his fury couldn't top mine. I wanted to provoke him into a screaming, knock-down, drag-out fight. But I knew it wouldn't change his damaged brain or the day that was thoroughly ruined.

Instead, I glared and refused to speak to him all evening. Alan quickly became subdued and watched me cautiously. He knew I was mad when I slept with Cassie and Sammie that night. As usual, he forgot the whole incident by morning, so he took no responsibility for his disruptive actions. I was still too angry to guide him through our usual post-hash of the incident.

I never forgot or forgave him for ruining the ritual my mother had entrusted to me.

In the fall, a new man whose presence was upsetting to Alan joined the program. Edward had a sweet nature complicated by advanced Parkinson's disease and dementia. He wanted so much to engage with Alan that he shuffled up to him and stuttered out a sentence with great difficulty. Alan tried very hard to understand Edward and felt terrible that he couldn't. Edward embodied Alan's fears of losing his hard-won ability to walk and talk. He whispered to me, "I can't do anything to help that guy. Why can't they do anything to make him better?"

As Alan's anxiety and powerlessness increased, so did his agitation episodes. One day in November, he kicked the heavy metal door of the program with such force that the staff worried he'd fractured his leg.

We had yet another meeting with the director. She voiced her concern that Alan was now a safety risk to the participants and staff.

He complained that he had done everything interesting that the day program had to offer and now wanted to be at home. We all agreed that Alan's involvement had been beneficial, but now it was time for him to leave. Alan was ready, but I wasn't. I missed the staff and Dr. B. for a long time. We incorporated many therapeutic aspects of the program into our routine but, once again, Alan was all mine.

I was more than ready for some upwardness of my own.

18. Baptism in Provincetown

During the same summer that Alan participated in the day program, I found upwardness at the Fine Arts Work Center in Provincetown. By August, I was holding myself together with string and tape, but I was able to fulfill the goal I set in February of taking a writing workshop through a lot of preparation, negotiation, cooperation, and determination.

Alan would only stay overnight with a family member he knew well, someone who was comfortable handling his ten medications, three glaucoma eyedrops, communication strategies, and behavioral plans. Fortunately, Alan's nephews Marty and Larry rose to the occasion and gave me my first week-long respite in two years. I spent weeks putting together a loose-leaf book of Alan's routines, exercises, schedules, emergency contacts, strategies, and my standard answers to his perseverative questions. Alan didn't like the idea of me going away, but since I was going to a writing class, he relented. Then I was free. Well, except for a number of daily phone calls and problem reports from home.

Provincetown is situated on the tip of Cape Cod, as far out to sea as land can be in New England. Long revered as an artist colony as well as an active fishing port, Provincetown strums with creative energy day and night. The bicycle-jammed narrow streets are lined with art galleries representing some of the most talented artists in the United States. The Fine Arts Work Center is the hub of a dozen art and writing classes every week. Hundreds of students travel to FAWC in the summer to study with nationally known faculty in a setting of incredible natural beauty.

I dived in to a week-long "Memoirs of Crisis" workshop taught by Kathryn Rhett. Although intimidated by my novice status, I brought the journals, poetry, and essays I wrote late at night while Alan slept. We were a mixed group of students both in our experience as writers and the crises that formed us. Everyone had a reason to be there, and listening to the first round of introductions confirmed that this would be an intense way to spend my vacation week. However, Kathryn set a standard as a teacher and facilitator that I looked for in writing classes thereafter. She gave us guidelines that emphasized that the best way to support each writer was to give her/his work respectful, honest, and sensitive attention. Her approach kept the emotionally charged writing as the central focus, rather than turning the class into a support group for the writer's situation.

I stayed in an old guest house run by a former mariner and joined my friend Gail for dinner when she took a break from her painting class. Being away from Alan made the enormous weight of our daily life settle in my bones. I'd been away for a few overnights, and the combination of loneliness, love, sorrow, fear, and utter exhaustion I'd felt at those times seeped in again like the morning tide. I soothed myself with slow walks to look at the tidy gardens of bright rose bushes and voluptuous blue hydrangeas that craned over the fences. I couldn't take in the enormity of the ocean, even though it beckoned from every view. Small and enclosed worked better at first.

I inhaled new energy from the salty ocean air and felt it start to dislodge the mental fatigue from my brain. Being accepted into a community of writers and artists where each individual was taken seriously and listened to was a new and affirming experience. I felt another facet of my identity beginning to seek light. During the day, writers wandered in to the artists' classrooms to watch their colors turn to forms, and artists sat in the courtyard discussing contemporary novelists with the writers. Creativity was all that required tending at FAWC. I missed this kind of intellectual stimulation and discussion so much. Now I realized how many books about brain injury, caregiving, and heart disease snuck onto my bedside pile of recreational reading. Many weeks they shoved aside the books of poetry and natural history I intended to read.

The class format included four hours of writing, listening, and giving feedback on the strengths and areas for development in each other's work. There were assignments and personal projects in the evening, but I didn't tackle them until after my favorite part of the day, which was the nightly presentations by that week's faculty. These sessions were a banquet for my soul because the artists gave a slide talk about their work in progress, and the writers read from a fresh work and discussed the craft issues they were wrestling with. I was mesmerized by the curtain parting to reveal their artistic struggles.

Thursday night was the highlight of every week. After a cookout, where we mingled with newfound friends, the studio doors were thrown open to exhibits of experimental paintings and etchings by the art students. Then the thirty writing students who had the nerve read one page of their polished drafts from the same stage that regularly hosted Pulitzer Prize winners and Nobel laureates. Three of the writers I held in high esteem—Robert Pinsky, Michael Cunningham, and Mark Doty—gave readings there often.

When I gave my first public reading from the FAWC stage, I chose an essay that much later led to this book you, dear reader, are holding. Waiting for my turn, I applauded my classmates and tried to get the saliva flowing in my mouth. When I get nervous or excited, a bright red rash spreads from my chest to cheeks, and now I felt the heat rising.

Finally, I stood at the tall podium and heard my voice rise up clear and slow, as I read from an essay about the first anniversary of Alan's cardiac arrest:

"On July 4th weekend, 1998, my husband Alan and I went to a family reunion in Chicago. A happy couple on a weekend jaunt, quick trip, two changes of clothes.... I felt his heart stop. ... never said good-bye to my husband.... My Alan was gone, and in his place Another Alan.... I needed a bridge between my first and second marriage to this man.... I took off the blue chambray dress and gave it away.... That dress is still in the Chadwick's catalogue every summer. I'm drawn to it as if for the first time. Hmm, nice dress, my style, think I'll buy it, until I shriek to a halt and recognize the dress. Even after all my adjustments to our new life, I hear a tantalizing whisper, 'Maybe I could start that summer of 1998 again. Undo the summer that was. Give the dress a different set of adventures. Nice ordinary dress. Nice ordinary life.'"

A classmate flashed my picture, and I broke into a huge smile at the applause. I caught Gail, who inspired me to come to FAWC, giving me the "thumbs up" from the back of the crowded room. A very heady debut and hard act to follow! I had been bitten by the urge to tell our story and there was no turning back. Many detours, but no turning back. I returned to the Fine Arts Work Center several times, always on respite breaks that left no time for just snoozing on the beach. But I returned home with an essential part of my non-caregiver self enlivened in my passion and nurtured by all I'd learned.

On the night I reluctantly turned into our driveway, Alan greeted me with, "Janet, Janet, Janet. I would like you to come upstairs right now to go to bed with me. I need you for everything. Well, mostly for eyedrops and hugs."

Yes, Alan did need me for all but the handful of things he could do independently. I was discovering that caregivers need respite breaks the way we need oxygen. We've all heard of the "oxygen mask principle" on airlines for a good reason. The flight attendant always instructs, "Place the oxygen mask on your face first, then place the mask on your child's face." Similarly, if the caregiver doesn't meet her own health needs first, she won't be able to take care of her sick loved one. We need to safeguard our own health by having time to relax and let go of some stress, to sleep through the night uninterrupted. We need the chance to rebalance our emotional equanimity, sense of humor, and physical energy at regular intervals.

I came to believe that only a respite could offer me the geographical and emotional distance necessary to take an honest look at our home situation. When away, I could think about what was working and what needed to change. Most of all, I had to go away to make the conscious decision to return to Alan.

That first year at FAWC, I even missed Alan and wanted to return to him, but I knew we needed much more help to make this work. The day program was not ideal, but it helped a lot. In September, I wrote a letter to Alan's family, outlining our situation and my need for more time away. I said I wanted to spend time with my sister Sherry and her family in Maine and hated choosing between the two people I loved best when they were both seriously ill. What I needed from them was respite time to look forward to.

My letter led to discussions about what each person could realistically offer, considering their family and professional obligations. I had to adjust my expectations and acknowledge that the time was coming when I'd have to hire a home health aide for Alan. The letter did ultimately lead to a few more respite breaks for me.

After Alan stopped going to the Alzheimer's day program in November, Tom stepped in to do structured activities with Alan every week. They began swimming in the Curtis Hall Community Center pool and browsing in the old-fashioned library next to the center. Alan enjoyed both activities. He thrust his chlorine enhanced arm under my nose and boasted, "Know what that smell is? I've been swimming with Tom!" The one-room library was peaceful and just right for exploring, so Alan checked out every video in the collection and many biographies.

I called on Alan's best friends to spend more time with him, and they came up with ideas that I worried would overstimulate him. But I was wrong. Jack and Alan went to the IMAX theater at the Museum of Science. The IMAX was renowned for its projection capability that makes your body feel like you're driving a careening race car around a Grand Prix track. I usually had to close my eyes to avoid fright or dizziness at the shows. Not Alan. He took the sensory assault in stride and enjoyed the movies about the ancient Egyptians and Lewis and

Clark's expedition. He and Jack also went to the Harvard Museum of Natural History and discussed the dioramas and fine mineral specimens at length.

Alan's friends Sue and George were constant supports. Sue had a jewelry business, so she brought over compartmentalized trays of beads, and she and Alan designed and strung earrings. George communicated with Alan better than anyone in our circle. He spoke slowly and proposed topics based on his career as an electrical engineer, politics, and history to discuss over a lunch of Thai food.

I wanted to join a women's group that some of my friends were starting, but needed evening coverage for Alan so I could go to the meetings. Alan decided to start a men's discussion group, so he invited Tom and George to join him. They met several times at George's house to enjoy dinner and talk about boxing, politics, and retirement. Throughout Alan's illness, each family member and friend contributed something unique from their past knowledge of Alan or their personal skills. We were enormously grateful for every visit and suggestion.

In November, Alan had a terrible accident. He'd exercised on the treadmill since the bypass surgery, but the arrangement was that someone should be with him to double-check the settings and be sure he stopped before the angina got bad. One Saturday, I was deep into tea and conversation with Holly in the kitchen when Alan decided to go up and exercise.

All of a sudden, we heard a loud crash, followed by a sickening thud. The motor raced on at high speed, but Alan made no sound. I flew up the stairs and found him crumbled at the foot of the treadmill, which had flipped straight up in the air and came to rest where it crashed into the broken wall. Alan had neglected to attach the safety cord for automatic shut-off, pushed the speed to maximum, and started to jog. He'd been thrown off the back of the accelerating belt, hit the wall behind him, and then landed on the rear of the belt, which caused the heavy machine to rise into the air like a bucking bronco.

As I yelled for Holly to call 911, Alan swore and fought to get up before I could check him for injuries. Being frightened always made him belligerent, and I worried about a concussion if he'd hit his head. "Leave me alone, I'm fine," he yelled, batting my hands away. The

EMTs arrived and agreed that Alan would have some bruises, but had no serious injuries.

I watched him closely for a few days, but he returned to normal and couldn't understand why the treadmill key had been hidden. That was the first of several accidents that would have challenged a professional accident reconstruction team and almost give me a heart attack.

I always had to remember that even when Alan was doing well, he had absolutely no ability to keep himself safe. This was an enormous and constant impediment.

By the end of 2000, Alan was functioning at the highest level he'd been at in months. His mood was even; he was able to think clearly and remember his daily routine. He was sociable and controlled his temper with minimal prompting. He followed the presidential campaigns of George W. Bush and Al Gore, and marched proudly to the polls to vote. We even made love twice a week after a dry spell of five months.

What made the difference? Part of the equation was the right combination of psychiatric medications that helped with mood, ruminations, and anger without causing side effects like drowsiness or confusion. His heart was pumping along on several medications, but the doses were small enough now that side effects weren't a problem. Alan attributed the improvements to being happy and enjoying his freedom from the day program while getting more attention from family and friends.

For Christmas, I found one of the best gifts I ever gave Alan. He loved the book *Reading Lyrics,* which contained more than a thousand song lyrics spanning seventy-five years. We wore out the binding reading some songs aloud for the sheer poetry of the lyrics, and singing the full lyrics to every song Alan remembered by the first line. Broadway musicals were well represented, so he referred to the book while singing along with videos of *My Fair Lady* and *The Music Man*. Alan memorized many of the songs and tested his memory against the book.

19. Descent into Parkinson's Disease

In late 2000, Jennifer invited Alan and I to join a planning committee to form the first brain injury support group in Boston, for survivors who lived in the community and their family members. I was eager to connect with others in similar situations and to contribute my skills. The Boston Acquired Brain Injury Support (BABIS) Group was launched in January 2001 and immediately drew sixty to seventy members to the monthly meetings held at Spaulding. BABIS was a unique collaboration between rehabilitation staff from Spaulding and the community rehab programs MENTOR and Community Rehab Care (CRC).

Once a person leaves formal rehab treatment, there are few options for finding ongoing support and information that help build skills and coping strategies. The expert speakers who presented workshops on memory strategies, relationship issues, and managing emotions gave us valuable information. BABIS also provided opportunities to socialize and try new activities. I made wonderful friends with whom I could share my feelings and needs, and compare ways to lighten the caregiver load.

At one early session, Alan and I spoke on a panel about making a new life after brain injury. Alan was eloquent as he described his impairments and attitude:

"My wife was a nurse for people with serious mental or physical problems. I used to tell her not to tell me about them because it was too scary. But now I know that brain injury, like those problems, can happen to anyone, people like us in this room today.... Let me tell you how I learned the alphabet and how to read again.... I was a professor for thirty-seven years, but I never understood how it felt to be a 'C' student and have to work extra hard. My experience has made me more patient and understanding with other people."

Now in its eighth year, BABIS is still going strong, and our annual "Heads Held High" Brain Injury Awareness Walk draws hundreds of people with brain injuries, families, and friends every October. The proceeds from walk pledges and the bountiful raffle are used for social activities chosen by the members, and donations are made to brain injury prevention programs and organizations providing rehabilitation and education.

One outgrowth of our BABIS involvement was that we were invited to speak to rehab professionals, students, patients, and families. Alan was thrilled to be a "real professor" again. The catalyst for our growing involvement was Marilyn Spivak, the mother of a woman with a severe brain injury and co-founder of what is now the Brain Injury Association of America. Marilyn became our dear friend and mentor, and encouraged us to share many aspects of our experience to receptive audiences.

We started a post-retirement resume for Alan titled "Brain Injury Education and Advocacy Activities" and updated the entries after every presentation he gave. His self-esteem grew with each entry on the list, and he compared it favorably to his professional curriculum vitae (CV). "How many retired guys have a whole new career?" he boasted.

During the winter, Alan started having more neurological problems. He dragged his feet in a trudging gait that caused him to fall a few times. His elbows and wrists became stiff, which made it hard to bend his arms. He spoke slower and in a softer voice. When we went to Dr. N., Alan's neurologist, he pointed out that Alan was having a Parkinsonian reaction to the antipsychotic meds that had been so helpful for the last few months. He added Cogentin, a medication to counteract the effects, and reduced the antipsychotic dose. This always happened. A medication regime would work well for weeks or months, then Alan's symptoms would break through or side effects would appear. The Parkinsonian reaction was serious, but not uncommon when someone had been taking these medications for a few years.

Alan was looking forward to our planned trip back to Sanibel Island in February. The week before our departure, Alan spiked a fever of 103 degrees and had trouble breathing. All of the Parkinsonian symptoms got worse, and he could hardly walk. Dr. F. diagnosed pneumonia and gave Alan antibiotics, which quickly eased his breathing as they fought the infection.

Alan was wiped out, so we considered cancelling our vacation. At the same time, I had bronchitis and a bad asthma flare-up. After talking it over with Dr. F., we decided that we would both be better off recuperating on a sunny beach in Florida than lying in bed in barren Boston. So off we went to Sundial Resort. Alan remembered the buildings on sight and started describing where to find the restaurant and swimming pool. This year, I'd reserved an ocean-front room, which had healing properties for us both.

Alan had trouble trudging through the deep sand, so we used the wheelchair to get to the edge of the beach. One afternoon, he agreed to wait on his chaise lounge, sipping a virgin pina colada smothered in whipped cream, while I walked five minutes in one direction down the beach, then returned. That was a mistake. I found him wandering around the maze of buildings, looking for me.

Why did I keep trying to do things when his memory had proven incapable of holding on to them? Sometimes, I craved doing the normal activities I loved so much that my willfulness elbowed my judgment aside. There was an air of rebellion to it too. This was my vacation, not just Alan's. I wanted to walk for hours and forget I had to come back, the way I always did at the ocean. Now I couldn't even get ten minutes.

On afternoons when Alan took a rest, I read on the couch lulled by the rhythm of ocean waves ten feet from the patio. Without fail, as soon as I drifted into a nap, Alan awoke and headed for the door, announcing, "I'm going for a walk alone. I want some privacy." Since he couldn't even find the elevator, I jumped up and asked him to let me come along. We got into a struggle as he denied needing a companion, and I ended up tagging along behind him until his legs gave out.

I resolved to bring another person with us if we came to Sundial next year.

As we crossed the lobby after breakfast one morning, a display of formal portraits of families posed on the beach caught Alan's eye.

"Hey, let's have our picture taken together, Loverlump," he said.

We'd never had a professional portrait taken, since even our wedding pictures were done by an amateur photographer. So we made an appointment.

The next day, the photographer waited until almost sunset before leading us into the deep marsh grass to an opening where high tide would soon peak. Alan could barely walk there, but he posed gallantly. The portrait is beautiful. Alan sits in the sand with his shoulders hunched forward, but a broad smile carves dimples into his tanned face. He looks broad shouldered and hearty, like a man born to wear tropical print shirts, smoke cigars, and spend his days reeling in swordfish on an expedition boat. The pneumonia and Parkinsonian reaction have vanished from sight.

I kneel in the sand with my arm around my husband's shoulder, my body contours melding into his. My smile isn't as wide as Alan's, but my face looks relaxed and pretty, years younger than I usually feel. I'm wearing a soft yellow dress trimmed with eyelet, which I bought in Sanibel so I could take home a tangible connection to this boundless sea and sky. Peach and violet streaks of clouds backlight our faces with a rosy glow.

When Alan saw the portrait, he said, "Look at us. We look like a happy couple who loves each other."

I said, "That's how I see us too."

Our portrait became a cherished keepsake housed center stage on Alan's bureau.

When we came home, Alan said, "I want to go to a gym and work out. I need more exercise." His combination of problems made that unrealistic, but we searched for a personal trainer who could work with Alan at home. Our friend Ginny, who directed eldercare programs, introduced us to Jeff, a certified trainer who specialized in working with the elderly.

It was a match made in heaven. Jeff skillfully designed a program that combined stretching, weight training, balance, and meditation. Jeff was a martial artist, and he incorporated tai chi into the warm-up. He was open to my suggestions about communicating with Alan, so their conversation flowed freely. Jeff and Alan exercised in the kitchen for an hour once a week, then Alan and I practiced some of the exercises on other days.

Over a few months, Alan became much better at mirroring Jeff's movements. His balance improved, and he proudly flexed his strong biceps and displayed his muscular thighs. Alan said the bonus benefit was having a new male friend to talk to. I sometimes underestimated how much my husband craved male companionship, surrounded as he was by the loving/smothering attention provided by me and my women friends.

From January until May, Alan's psychiatrist and neurologist conferred on medication adjustments as his moods and neurological problems went up and down. They were trying to figure out if Alan's Parkinsonian symptoms were caused by the meds or by actually having Parkinson's disease. It was a process of elimination trial. We had to reduce all the medications very slowly to prevent other problems, so the process took weeks.

Even when Alan was off the antidepressant and antipsychotic meds, he continued to shuffle when he walked (festination), move very slowly (bradykinesia), fall over when his legs stiffened like tree trunks (rigidity and freezing), and write in a tiny, cramped script (micrographia). Some nights, he walked in his sleep and later said, "I must be someone else at night; that feels awful." There were times when his upper back muscles twisted and turned in as he walked, and then his lower back twisted to the opposite side and arched outward (dystonia). All of these symptoms were very frightening to both of us.

One night in May, we were going upstairs to bed. Alan started up, holding on to the railing with both hands. I stood two steps behind him, bracing his hips as he carefully lifted one foot in front of the other. As he reached the fourth or fifth step, Alan's body jack-knifed and he fell sideways to his left and *over* the railing to the hall floor below. As he fell, his feet kicked me, and I fell backward and landed hard on the foyer floor.

I scrambled over to where he was already struggling to get up even though he couldn't bear weight on his legs. We had an arrangement with Juliane, a neighbor who offered to come help me lift Alan when he fell, so I quickly called her and ran back to examine Alan. He hit me and swore while using all of his strength to push up and stand. My heart raced as Juliane and I managed to seat Alan on a chair.

Miraculously, he escaped with bruises, but no fractures. When I tried to describe the fall to his doctors, they said, "Alan fell down the stairs?"

I had to repeat, "No, no, he fell *over* the stairs."

The next morning, Tom and his work crew moved our bed down to the dining room on the first floor and moved that furniture upstairs. It took constant vigilance to prevent Alan from going upstairs to bed, since that had been his habit for years. When I put a child's safety gate and sign on the staircase, he tried to climb over it. "Nobody tells me what to do in my own house," he announced.

Alan's combination of leg weakness, lack of awareness, and memory loss was dangerous. Time and again, he stood up from the table to walk as I called from across the room, "Wait for me, you'll fall."

He insisted, "Nothing's wrong with me," as he fell to the floor. Falling was an ongoing issue for years. I accumulated my own muscle strains and bruises helping him up. Sometimes, he got up from the recliner without lowering the footrest and fell onto his knees and face. He never learned.

Then Alan started to spit anywhere and anytime. As we planted pansies in the front porch window boxes, he pointed urgently to his puffed-out cheeks, saying, "Mmmmph, mmmmph, mmmph …"

Then he spit. Onto my shoes, on the car seat, into the paper cup he insisted on carrying at all times. This was a related symptom. Alan's involuntary reflex to swallow was impaired and, combined with his memory, he couldn't think of how to swallow fast enough to do it normally. While that lasted, I had to coach him by pointing to my mouth and throat as I demonstrated, "Swallow. Gulp. Down the hatch," all through dinner.

Jeff could also track Alan's symptoms by monitoring his stiffness and difficulty mirroring movements during their workouts. Alan was very upset when he couldn't walk and said, "My legs forget how to walk; I have to teach them all over again every day." We were both afraid his walking would continue to deteriorate.

One more way I monitored his symptom severity was in his artwork. Alan and I often drew together. Sometimes, we alternated adding a drawing of a flower to a still life of a vase of daisies. When we drew together, he tried to copy what I had drawn, but his tiny flowers were missing half their shakily sketched petals. When Alan tried to copy the fish he often used as a pattern for suncatchers, the poor fish looked shriveled and on the verge of death with closed eyes and a sick expression. The colored pencils barely grazed the page enough to leave pigment.

When Alan's symptoms were less intense, he was able to draw a jolly fish with bright stripes and round eyes.

In June, Dr. N. surveyed the copious records I'd kept tracking Alan's intermittent symptoms. He reviewed all the medication changes, then said, "I'm afraid Alan really has Parkinson's disease."

Alan hung his head and asked, "Isn't it enough that I had to get a brain injury? One bad disease should be enough for a person."

Dr. N. agreed that Alan had been dealt more than his share. He prescribed Sinemet, the medication most commonly used to manage Parkinson's.

He added, "You can get plenty of good information about Parkinson's on the Internet now."

I didn't think Alan understood most of what had been discussed in medicalese. But when Dr. N. asked if he had any questions, Alan responded, "I just have one question. Are we still married? Am I too sick for you to take care of me?"

I quickly said, "Alan, we're still married and always will be. You're going to feel better, and I'll still take care of you."

That night, I wrote in my journal:

"I am mute tonight. Only my bones are talking. My bones shout in outrage and agony. Too cruel. Too excessive. He already has three progressive, destructive diseases. Parkinson's threatens our life together, raises nursing home prospects. I need a few days to take in this new diagnosis before I start explaining and being the case manager. I need time to mourn before I have to adjust and guide and love a new version of Alan. I'm going on strike against having to learn all about a new disease. I've spent three years learning all I can about brain injury. Now I have to become a Parkinson's expert. I refuse."

For a few days, I held my outrage close while reassuring Alan that in a few weeks the new medicine would start making it easier to walk.

I finally went to Brookline Booksmith and dutifully bought a stack of books about PD. The selection of PD books available made me realize how many people are affected. I also ordered a set of comprehensive booklets from the National Parkinson Foundation, Inc. and started to study.

I found out that Parkinson's disease is a chronic neurodegenerative disorder that happens when certain neurons in the substantia nigra stop working or die. Healthy neurons in this area produce the chemical messenger dopamine, which is responsible for transmitting signals between the substantia nigra and the corpus striatum to allow smooth, coordinated function of our muscles and movement. More than 1 million people in the United States have Parkinson's, but there can be a range of symptoms and degrees of impairment. Alan had all four of the cardinal features: tremor at rest, bradykinesia, rigidity, and impaired balance. A person might have a few or many of the secondary symptoms such as decreased facial expression (hypomimia), muffled speech (dysarthria), and sleep disturbances. Sometimes, Alan had the "masked face" that made him look expressionless and stern.

There are many medications available to treat Parkinson's. Carbidopa/ Levadopa (brand name Sinemet) is the oldest and most effective med to manage symptoms. Levadopa is converted into dopamine in the brain and stored in the neurons until needed for movement. Carbidopa blocks an enzyme that prematurely converts levadopa to dopamine before it gets to the brain and can cause side effects. Combining levadopa and carbidopa in one pill reduces the rate of side effects.

We quickly made a series of changes to our house to make it safer for Alan. Tom mounted handrails along the walls of the entire first floor. We'd had bathtub grab bars since Alan came home from Spaulding, but we added a shower chair with a sturdy back and hand grips. Out went the throw rugs that might trip him. Side rails on the bed allowed Alan to pull himself into a seated position and hold on getting into bed. We replaced our drinking glasses with cups that had easy-to-hold handles. Alan conceded to using a wheelchair outside, but groped along with the handrail in the house. Many changes, and they all helped Alan function more safely.

The biggest change was having a wheelchair ramp installed on the house so Alan would not have to walk down the steep flight of stone stairs. I made an appointment for the ramp representative to come to our home and explain the ramp options and $4,000 cost to me. As we sat at the kitchen table going over brochures and local building codes, Alan came in from his nap and picked up a brochure. He went wild.

"I don't need this thing! This is for crippled people. There's nothing wrong with me. My wife and doctors make things up to keep me a prisoner ...," raving on and on, until he yelled, "Get out of my house now!"

Alan chased the salesman out to his car while I followed, snatching up his brochures and order forms.

As Alan yelled and the salesman locked his car door, I called out, "Come back Thursday and install the ramp, okay?"

They did come back, and the gleaming black steel ramp took up half of the back yard. Once Alan proved to himself that the ramp made him more independent, the whole enterprise became his idea.

He told friends, "I saw this ramp in a magazine and said we had to order it. It was my idea, right?" Right, Alan.

By the way, we had to pay for the ramp and almost all of the other equipment, since health insurance doesn't cover enough equipment to prevent accidents.

In July, as part of a thorough Parkinson's work-up, Alan finally had the first MRI scan of his head since the brain injury three years earlier. I was devastated when Dr. N. showed me the report. There were several areas where Alan's brain tissue had decreased in size due to disease or injury (atrophy), especially in the cerebral cortical sulci and temporal lobes. The basal ganglia appeared relatively small and were probably diffusely atrophic. Some structures appeared much smaller than normal. The formations of the hippocampus had wasted. There were no clots that would indicate strokes.

The radiologist's impression was that:

"There appears to be diffuse neuronal loss with greater central than peripheral atrophy, particularly prominent atrophy along the medial aspects of the temporal lobes. This may well all relate to the patient's previous anoxic event, but there is none of the typical findings of anoxic/ischemic injury. [He does not elaborate.] *The prominent atrophy in the temporal lobe areas can certainly be seen in Alzheimer's disease, but the hippocampal areas are also particularly susceptible to anoxic injury."*

Many of the areas the MRI documented were responsible for functions the 1998 neuropsychology evaluation results indicated might be severely impaired.

I felt like I'd been punched in the stomach. Even though I'd known for years that Alan had extensive brain damage, seeing the evidence that his brain was wasting away was hard to handle.

Everyone wanted to know if the brain injury caused the Parkinson's disease. Alan's doctors told me from the beginning that structural damage to any part of the brain increases the risk of other brain problems, such as strokes. Dr. N. explained that the area of the brain most affected by Parkinson's disease is the substantia nigra, where the neurotransmitter dopamine is produced. The substantia nigra is located near the watershed areas most prone to damage from low blood flow. There was no way of proving a definite cause and effect between the brain injury and PD. But the extent of damage made Alan more vulnerable than he probably would have been if the brain injury had not happened.

In July, Alan started physical therapy with Janine. We learned so much at every session. Janine showed Alan how to take a bigger step or to lift his knees to break the shuffling, accelerating gait (festination) that pitched his body forward. To my amazement, it worked temporarily and was an easy cue to give Alan. Janine even had Alan march down the hall while singing "Over there, over there ..." to decelerate the shuffling, and Alan practiced with gusto at home. She made him practice falling safely (be still my heart) and getting up again. She and the doctors credited Jeff's work with Alan for making him more flexible and stronger than most PD patients, which meant he could use his strong arms and quadriceps to pull himself up. That also relieved some of the strain on my back from lifting him.

Every area of daily functioning at home and in the community was addressed in PT, from raising the volume of his voice to stepping up and down from curbs. I became more hopeful that we could manage PD after all.

Exercise is an essential component of Parkinson's treatment, so Jeff and I integrated Janine's recommendations into a new exercise routine. We also increased Jeff's sessions to twice a week. In the evenings, Alan followed the numbered steps to play music on the stereo system and said, "Come on, wife, let's have a dance." As "Boogie Woogie Bugle Boy" boomed through the house, we side-stepped down the hall to swing band music. At the front door, I said, "Give me a twirl, handsome." We twirled each other a few times to practice turning smoothly and ended with a kiss.

I kept detailed records of his target symptoms, medication dose and time, moods, and functioning. The records showed that within two months, Alan had a very beneficial response from Sinemet. He walked and moved smoothly and naturally again. He even resumed walking Molly for the first time in months.

He said to her, "Molly, I'm better now, so let's get back to your education. Sit. Stay. Beg. Count. Speak."

It took weeks of coaxing and practicing together before Alan would write in his logbook again. For weeks, when he had micrographia, the entrees are in my writing. When he stopped writing, his skills regressed and had to be relearned with much effort. This was difficult because he'd never had the same fervor for writing that he did for reading.

Alan's functioning had also dropped off from the PD symptoms. The jobs he did daily were too hard now. He couldn't empty the dishwasher because bending and turning made him fall, and the dishes were too heavy to carry. When the Sinemet started working, Alan modified his jobs and went back to work. Now he emptied only the top dishwasher shelf so he wouldn't need to bend, and he decided to carry one plate at a time to the cupboard.

"I'll get more exercise this way," he said.

Our yoga tree poses may tilt, but we remain upright! (2000).

Unfortunately, the trade-off for Sinemet's benefits was the side effects. Alan became more confused and agitated, and had "information blackouts" where he couldn't access something he knew well. Dr. P. started a small dose of a different antipsychotic, and we got back on track. The Sinemet dose had to be increased to full strength gradually, so we alternated between a bit more Sinemet and a bit more antipsychotic. As the one who made these decisions, with the doctor's guidelines, I thought family caregivers should be granted a pharmacy degree from years of accumulated experience.

In early autumn, I hired a home health aide to help us six hours a day, three days a week. This was another big adjustment for Alan, even though I chose Raymond because he was close to Alan's age and they had some common interests. The idea of a stranger watching him shower or helping him dress was a problem for Alan. We had to phase in the more personal care while I emphasized that Raymond was a "trained medical professional," which was Alan's favorite designation.

Alan's sense of independence and control was already bruised by the PD, so we approached the issue of help by forming "Alan's Home Care Team," with Alan as the captain. We wrote everybody's names and job descriptions in his logbook. Alan dictated all the information he wanted them to know about him for the section I titled "The Life and Interests of Alan Cromer." We included his essential biography, explanations of the brain injury and Parkinson's, and updates on Alan's recent concerns. Jeff, Raymond, and the nephews who covered my time off all said they appreciated that information the most.

When Alan began to trust and remember Raymond, he was willing to go swimming at Curtis Hall together and out to lunch at the sub shop. However, one day he awoke from a nap and found me out and Raymond in the kitchen.

He lunged at Raymond, yelling, "Get out of my house. I don't need you here. I'm calling the police." He even tried to throw a punch.

I returned and calmed Alan down by bringing him to his office, away from the aide, and saying, "Stop. You can't punch anyone. That's dangerous and out of control."

He said, "I woke up and saw that guy here and thought you ran away and left me with him forever."

I reminded him that I would always come back from errands.

The next day, when Raymond returned, the three of us sat down to agree on a contract for respectful behavior, with Alan making most of the suggestions. It read:

1. *No one will yell or scream at the other person.*
2. *No one will hit or punch.*
3. *We will all treat each other with respect so we can all be safe.*

4. If Alan loses control and yells at Raymond, he will not be able to swim at Curtis Hall that week. (This clause was my addition.)

Alan, Raymond, and I signed the contract. Alan took it seriously and responded to the no-swimming consequence when reminded.

Sometimes, Alan drew Raymond into his conspiracies against me. Years earlier, I had enrolled Alan in the Alzheimer's Association Safe Return Program for people who wander. The program provides a national registry as well as detailed information for the local police in case Alan could not be found. He also carried Medic-Alert information in his wallet. Both programs distributed neck medallions and ID bracelets for participants, but Alan hated the "stigma."

One day while he and Raymond went swimming, Alan ripped off the medallion and bracelet, tore up the ID cards, and threw them all in the trash. "She'll never find that stuff in the locker room trash," he said to Raymond. I ordered name labels to sew in his clothes and different forms of identification by the carton.

Having Raymond as our home health aide worked well for a while, but I should have believed Alan's complaints earlier. Alan often complained about Raymond's driving when they went out to restaurants. But Alan hated not being able to drive, so I assumed he just felt bad when they were out together. One day, Raymond casually mentioned that he'd had a few tickets lately and was in an accident, but he didn't think it was his fault. As I listened carefully, I worried that Alan had been correct. I stopped asking Raymond to take Alan out.

Then there was a serious incident when they both relaxed on the porch chaise lounges and dozed off in the sun. Alan woke up first and took off quickly to escape being supervised. I came home at that point and began to frantically search for Alan on foot while Raymond drove along the usual walking routes. We eventually found Alan half a mile from home, seated on a park bench, talking to some young men outside a subway station where there had been recent gang activity.

Alan refused to get in the car and screamed at me, "I have no friends because you keep me a prisoner. I try to make friends and you stop me." He was furious and walked home at top speed, with me trailing him. By then, he was suffering from heat exhaustion and took hours of care to recuperate. The next day, I told Raymond his services were no longer needed. I also apologized to Alan for not taking his complaints about Raymond's driving seriously. He was a good judge of character, even with the brain injury.

Alan accepted my apology.

Throughout the year, we celebrated any step forward to counter Alan's depression about now having Parkinson's disease. In May, I cooked a special dinner when my first essay was published in *The Boston Globe*. The essay was about our trip to Bradlees to buy new dishes, and it was considered a breakthrough by our friends in the brain injury community because I had supplied the newspaper with statistics on the large number of people affected by brain injury who would be interested in this story. Alan was proud and said, "My new dishes will make you famous."

In June, we went to Legal Sea Foods when Alan received a royalty check for $545 for sales of his earlier textbook *Physics for the Life Sciences*, published in English and Korean. We bonded around our love of writing and supported each other's ongoing efforts.

When we woke up on August 7, I said, "Honey, today is my birthday. I'm fifty-two years old today. "

I'd been reminding Alan all week, but didn't expect him to remember.

He said, "Oh, my goodness, it is? I didn't get you anything. In my mind you'll always be thirty-five." That was my age when we met.

I said, "That's okay, you can pick out a card for me later at CVS," as I started to dress. I had to put down my jeans when I heard the most beautiful alto voice fill the room with a song I had never heard. I turned to see where this music was coming from. Alan sat on the edge of the bed in his blue cotton pajamas, singing:

"I look at you and suddenly
Something in your eyes I see ... It's that old devil moon in your eyes." Alan sang all the verses to the most romantic song I'd never heard him sing before.

I kissed him and said, "Alan, thank you so much! That's the best birthday gift you've ever given me!"

He replied, "Oh, you don't know that song? Glad you liked it."

Every year thereafter, I requested that Alan sing "Old Devil Moon" by E. Y. Harburg from *Finian's Rainbow* as my birthday present. I even learned all the words to sing with him from his book of lyrics.

In November, Sherry asked us to join her family at a hotel restaurant for Thanksgiving dinner. She was too sick to leave home, but wanted us to join her husband Jack in giving her children a festive holiday experience.

As we drove to the restaurant, I asked Alan, "Honey, what are you thankful for this year? Anything in particular that is in your life?"

He was quiet for a long time, so I thought he didn't want to play the game. But then he said haltingly, "I think I've come to accept my illness."

After a long pause, he then added, "I don't get so upset; maybe I don't hate myself so much when I make mistakes."

I exhaled and squeezed his leg as I said, "I am so thankful to have you here beside me as my husband."

20. The Loneliness of an Intimate Marriage

Throughout 2001, we spoke at a variety of programs. Our most popular speech was "The Impact of Disability on Relationships, Intimacy, and Sexuality." The program planners told us it was unusual and very valuable to have both members of a couple willing to talk about sexuality. Alan always opened his talk by saying, "It is a lot easier to talk about physics!" But to his credit, that never held him back:

"I think Janet and I have always kept love as the major point of our lives because we were older when we got married, thirty-seven and forty-nine. We had the same values and always had fun together. I think if couples had a lot of problems before one partner becomes disabled, it would be much harder to recover.... I got depressed about everything I had lost. I worried about getting back to a married sexual relationship. Even when I was very sick I felt sexual urges.... I remember that we had pretty normal sex. I don't remember all the pain from my heart, but I forget those things.

"We do many things to keep our marriage intimate. We say 'I love you' several times a day; we hug and kiss a lot.... We say, 'A kiss is our signal; a kiss means we're together.' I ask Janet why she loves me and she gives me a specific reason. Janet can be too serious. It is my job to make her laugh.... We say, 'I appreciate you for being this way, or for doing that.' When I was depressed about losing my abilities, Janet wrote me a love letter called 'Thirty Things You Can Do ...'

"I often say, 'We make love every day.' I mean you have to pay attention to your relationship and make your life good, and then you have a lot of love."

My speech focused on all the ways we used touch to connect, from the moment Alan came back to life. I told the story of our shared and different experiences with conjugal visits at Spaulding, and how we adapted sexual positions to reduce the strain on Alan's heart. I pointed out how medication side effects of fatigue, decreased desire, and difficulty maintaining an erection impacted us. I went on:

"I took an antidepressant for a time. My mood benefited, but it made me less responsive than I wanted to be. I also went through the changes of menopause in the last few years.... It has been important for us to label problems as related to side effects or a medical problem, not a personal failing or permanent condition ...

"When Alan goes through periods of intense anger and agitation, I am often the focus. Alan forgets the situation as soon as it is resolved. However, it takes me a few weeks to trust his predictability again and want to be intimate ...

"What approaches help us? We enjoy massage and practices that calm our minds and put us in synch like visualization and yoga. We use all our senses to enjoy a dinner of spicy Thai food or a bowl of raspberry ice cream. We don't say we're going out to dinner, we say we're going on a dinner date.

"I have a new understanding of 'living in the moment.' That is, that Alan's experience and our shared experience matters in this moment, for its own sake. Maybe it will become a memory or knowledge. Maybe not. But we savor the experience now.

"For me there is a very spiritual dimension to intimacy. This can be hard to describe, but I know when we have reached it. One day while we

were cuddling I said to Alan, 'This is such a luxury. When you were in the ICU, there was hardly a place on your body I could touch. All I wanted to do was hold you.' A beatific smile spread across my husband's face. With calm assurance he said, 'But you were always holding me.'"

Our intimacy talks always generated many questions from the audience, which Alan handled with aplomb. And for a few weeks after, I did see Alan and me more as others saw us: as a loving, courageous, open couple. I felt closer to him and more of the loving kindness between us and around us.

I often had my own versions of "all of the above is true." These feelings coexisted rather than contradicted each other. The same year we were publicizing our intimate marriage, I could no longer avoid feeling lonely in my marriage. The stirrings of loneliness must have been there for a long time, but now a cold chill wrapped around my shoulders and made me want a shawl.

What brought my loneliness to the surface was making the decision to sell our Narragansett home. The evidence had been mounting. It was crazy to be paying two mortgages out of our retirement and savings accounts. We were fortunate to own one home, never mind two. Alan could no longer be safe there, and Parkinson's even made it hard for him to swim.

But Narragansett was where I remembered my husband best. I could sit on the deck and visualize us as we used to be. We had so many blissful times there, being our outdoorsy and playful selves. Alan had a kayak a few years before I did. He loved paddling slowly upriver to a narrow crescent of shore, where he pulled over to enjoy a swim in the cool water along with his preferred snack of an apple and wine cooler. We canoed together often, so I didn't see the need for two kayaks. That changed when I rented a beginner's kayak and fell in love with gliding into narrow estuaries to watch egret chicks stretching their wings in the morning sun.

For my forty-fifth birthday, I gave myself a Sealution ocean-going kayak and christened it the "Midlife Sea-lution." Alan and I kayaked together from April to November, and I always appreciated his introduction to the sport.

Now the kayaks were long gone—passed on to nieces and nephews. Even though we'd found new ways to have fun in Narragansett, I felt an acute longing for the couple we had been even after three years.

Before contacting a Realtor, I had to convince myself that I was only losing a house, not the memory of my husband. But dementia kept altering the husband I tried to remember. I had a queasy sensation that I was practicing to be a widow. I took care of everything, handled all responsibilities, had the house repaired, managed our finances. And probably most telling, I took care of myself without expecting anything from Alan. That was the source of so much loneliness.

I wanted mutuality and understanding in forms that dementia would never allow Alan to be capable of, even when his physical symptoms improved. All of his improvements were relative, and I reported them to his doctors on my "Alan standard scale." I tried not to blame him when we gave up another part of our life that I treasured. Especially since Alan often said, "I'm sorry I screwed up our life. I'm sorry I ruined everything." I quickly reassured him that he wasn't responsible, or that a particular change didn't matter in the big picture. But I was only human, and sometimes I did blame him. On a better day, I blamed his illnesses and kept his person out of it.

At the last minute, Alan's nephew Tom decided to buy the house as a rental property. Alan was very sad about giving up his vacation home.

"Well, I suppose we didn't use it much anymore, but we loved the fireplace and our little beach, didn't we?" he said.

I told him, "We can always come back to Narragansett, stay in a bed and breakfast, and go to our favorite restaurant and theater."

But we both knew the changes were related to his health and we wouldn't be able to return often.

The times that elicited a tender swelling of love helped me feel alive with appreciation for Alan and less alone. At Christmas, we baked ginger cookies together. I placed one ingredient on the counter at a time. Alan measured the sugar, sifted the flour, and grated the orange rind with shaky hands.

"This is really technical," he said.

His face scrunched in deep concentration, he smiled when each step was completed successfully, like a kid allowed to do the job the older kids usually do. I felt very close and loving, a deep, warm couple feeling.

Alan thrived on praise from the youngest family members, the same kids he lamented not being able to help with their science homework. When our nieces visited during school vacation, we showed them the bookcase labeled "Alan's Archives" where we had arranged all the books Alan wrote during his career.

Cassie said, "Wow! Does that mean Uncle Alan is, like, a famous writer? That's awesome!"

I explained why that was true, and Sammie said, "Wait till I tell my teachers at school that my uncle is a famous scientist."

For weeks, Alan asked me to repeat the conversation. On a day when his Parkinson's symptoms were out in full force, he shuffled to the car laboriously but said, "Just remember, I'm awesome. My nieces said so."

Again, my heart pulsed with love and admiration for my husband.

Our nieces, Cassie and Sammie Caliri, always liven things up with their visits! (2000).

Throughout that year, we both talked more about the reality of Alan's complicated and progressive diseases and how they influenced end-of-life planning. I was in a spiritual struggle because the problems affecting Alan's brain seemed to be advancing faster than those affecting his heart. I couldn't understand what purpose it would serve if his heart disease could be treated with medications but his memory and thinking declined to the point where he lost even this person he'd worked so hard to become.

Over the three years of his illness, we had many conversations about what made Alan's life worth living with his current problems, and what treatments and situations would be unacceptable to him. I brought the subject up again each time a new diagnosis was added or after he'd had a bad spell. Media coverage of medical developments and famous people's medical issues also offered us a natural opportunity to explore our opinions.

Alan understood the issues and spent time on his own contemplating the big questions.

He told me a number of times, "I am of an age when I have to expect to die. I've had a good life and did everything I wanted to do. I probably couldn't do anything else I'd want to do now anyway because I'm sick."

He was disturbed by newspaper accounts of Vice President Dick Cheney's cardiac problems that were treated with an implantable defibrillator.

I asked, "Alan, would you want to live longer if it meant you had to have another operation or procedure?"

He replied, "No. They shouldn't put defibrillator things or other people's hearts in me."

Later that week, he added, "I wouldn't want to live in a nursing home where you could only visit but we couldn't sleep together. I wouldn't want to live if I lose my reading and writing again. I don't think I could get them back another time. I hope I don't live a long time and then get cancer or Alzheimer's. I don't want to get a stroke. I've already got enough old man diseases."

I wrote down and dated everything he said each time he said it.

We already had advance directives in place, but when we had appointments with Alan's primary care doctor and cardiologist, I said,

"We want to talk about signing a Comfort Care Order document." In Massachusetts, a Comfort Care Order covers specific treatments that a person does not want performed, particularly when the usual treatments for their medical problems have been exhausted. The order, signed by a doctor and the patient, absolves emergency medical providers from performing CPR if a person's heart stops.

Both doctors interviewed Alan at length about how he understood his diagnoses, his preferences, and treatment options. Since Alan had both dementia and the brain injury, they wanted to be sure he completely understood the document and signed it voluntarily.

When the doctors were satisfied that Alan was capable of making the decision, Alan signed the Comfort Care Order. When asked, I said that I understood the issues and agreed with Alan's decision. None of Alan's medications or treatments were changed that day. But we laid important groundwork for future discussions, and we received an order to hang on the refrigerator in case Alan had a medical emergency at home.

21. "Alan's Quality of Life Analysis"

One thing I knew for sure about Alan was that he had the power to rebound in appreciable ways from each series of medical setbacks. Once we found the magic combination of treatments, medications, and ways of helping him understand and participate, he was ready for his next adventure.

In February of 2002, we made our third annual trip to Sanibel Island, accompanied by nephew Tom, who offered both support and a guaranteed good time. Alan enjoyed showing Tom around the Sundial Resort complex and swimming in the warm turquoise water at the two pools. Parkinson's disease affected Alan's legs more than any other body part and made them "freeze" in the middle of an activity. One hot afternoon, the three of us were enjoying a swim when Alan called in alarm, "Help, help, I can't stay up; I'm sinking." Tom and I wrapped our arms under Alan's armpits and floated Alan to the edge of the small pool between us.

After a rest, Alan was able to walk stiffly, but he could never again trust his legs to swim safely. We focused on dry land pleasures like musical theater and sumptuous dinners in fancy restaurants instead, but this was another major loss for Alan.

When we returned home, Alan wasn't able to walk outdoors alone or do many familiar tasks without coaching. Some days he was fine, but other days he stumbled or fell and was more confused. On the challenging days, he needed help with personal care, dressing, and doing his favorite activities. I decided we needed to hire a home health aide forty hours a week to assist Alan and keep him safe. A friend who was a hospice social worker recommended Uche, a young Nigerian aide she knew. I met with Uche in a nearby café to explain Alan's problems and my expectations for safe and compassionate care.

When Uche came to our home for a full interview, Alan was livid.

"I don't need anyone on me; I'm fine, my wife just hires these guy to use up my money. I don't need any help."

During the interview, Uche told us about Nigeria, his family, and his plans to study nursing. I could tell Alan was getting intrigued with this warm and well-spoken young man. At the end of the formal interview, I suggested that Uche accompany us on Molly's walk since the job included walking with Alan and Molly.

As Alan bent down to harness Molly, he reared back up and looked at me with alarm.

"Wait! This isn't going to work," he said. "I don't want this guy to walk my dog. In Africa, they eat dogs, you know."

I was embarrassed and said, "Oh, Alan, I don't think that's true anymore."

But Uche chimed in sincerely, "Well, yes, they do eat dogs in some parts of Nigeria, but not in the part where I was born or where my parents live now."

I rolled my eyes, imagining a scene of Alan calling my cell phone yelling, "Come home right away. There's a guy here eying Molly's drumsticks."

"So you don't eat dogs?" Alan asked Uche.

"No, I've never eaten a dog."

I thought this must have been one of the strangest job interviews Uche would ever have, but characteristic of what working for us held in store. After the walk, I asked Alan, "What do you think? Can Uche come back tomorrow to help us out?"

Alan fixed Uche with a stern expression, "Yeah, I guess so, but don't eat my dog."

Alan tolerated having a home health aide when I framed Uche's presence as beneficial to us both. I explained that our doctor had told me I needed more help around the house so my strained back muscles could heal. I also said that since I was a nurse, I could supervise some of Uche's studies. Uche was already a U.S. citizen, but we proposed that Alan help him study U.S. history and government. Alan felt more comfortable when they each had clear jobs rather than feeling that Uche was supervising his every move.

He also tolerated Uche's company better when they went to interesting places in the community rather than just staying at home. Uche taught us so much about African history, geography, and culture. We spent afternoons at the kitchen table, tracking his lessons on Alan's globe and making notes for his logbook. In turn, Alan taught Uche about life in the United States, the local parks, evolution, history, and Shakespeare.

I spent hours explaining Alan's medical problems to Uche, what went on in Alan's mind when he said and did unpredictable things, his routines and preferences, how to read Alan's moods and nonverbal signals, and how to communicate with Alan effectively. We scheduled regular continuing education session on the topics Uche was most interested in and that I thought were important. I wrote out all the information in plain language in a communication book Uche and I shared. I emphasized the importance of treating Alan with respect and dignity, and how to minimize the episodes where Alan felt humiliated by needing assistance and reacted with anger.

We spent a lot of time on strategies to try to prevent the anger episodes and what to say when they happened in different settings.

"If Alan's jaw becomes tense, or he mutters obscenities under his breath, or looks like he suddenly doesn't recognize you, those are signs that the agitation is building," I said. "You need to say who you are and why you are with him, and ask what's bothering him."

I reviewed with Uche how to keep both Alan and himself safe when Alan was agitated, for example standing at least a leg's length away in case Alan tried to kick him, and suggesting that Alan go to his study and read a book for ten minutes. We talked about when to offer Alan extra medication for anxiety or agitation.

Even with our attention to preventing the agitated episodes, Alan periodically directed verbal and even physical aggression against Uche.

The precipitant was usually that Alan couldn't remember who Uche was or why he was in our home. He became paranoid about Uche being a robber, or a person hired to watch over him because I had abandoned him.

One intervention that helped was giving Alan an explanation he believed even when he was distrustful. Alan trusted an explanation already written on paper more than a verbal explanation. When Uche explained his presence, Alan said, "You're just making that up on the spot to trick me." But when Uche showed him the note in his logbook that said, "Uche is a good person and trained professional who is here to help Alan and Janet," Alan said, "Well, I guess I have to believe it if it says so in writing."

I reported these physical aggression incidents to Dr. P., Alan's psychiatrist, and we brainstormed how to help Alan understand and stay in control as well as medication issues.

One night after ruminating about his restrictions, Alan raged on about his need to run his own life without rules and interference. He roared so loudly that Molly fled from the living room to hide under the kitchen table.

I appealed to Alan's bond with Molly by saying, "Alan, stop! Do you see that you scared Molly? She's afraid of you because you are yelling and out of control. Molly and I don't feel safe when you yell like that."

As usual, Alan said, "It's your fault that I'm angry because you don't let me do what I want."

Since I often tried to give Alan an option for what he could do rather than just pronouncing what he could not do, I said, "Tell me one thing you want to do right now."

"I want to take a walk by myself and be left alone," he answered.

We compromised that Alan would walk around our block but I would follow several feet behind him in case his legs got weak. That worked, and he calmed down enough to watch a movie when we returned.

On our next visit to Dr. P., I recounted that Alan had been so agitated that Molly ran to hide for the first time. That got Alan's attention.

"I really did that? I scared my dog? That's a terrible thing to do. I don't want that to happen again," he said with genuine remorse. "How can I stop myself?"

We worked out that when I noticed Alan ruminating, I would suggest making something together or playing a computer game to shift his focus away from the growing internal turmoil. We made sure to have games and books around the living room, where he often sank into these whirlpools if he sat thinking for too long.

It never worked to say only that I was afraid of Alan, I had to include Molly to make the point. He felt more tender and responsible toward Molly, and he felt even less secure if I indicated that I couldn't help him control the anger that swept over him like a storm wave.

Appealing to Alan's love of Molly also snapped him out of his overtired rants about divorcing me. When he threatened divorce, I said, "Fine, Alan, if that's what you want. I'll move out and you can keep this house. Of course, I'll take Molly with me, since I inherited her from my mother and that matriarchal lineage makes her legally mine."

Alan's face took on an expression of grave recognition.

"Oh. Oh. Well, I guess Molly really is your dog legally since you put it that way. All right, you can stay. I won't divorce you today."

My matriarchal argument worked every time.

When Alan was feeling better, he continued to work out twice a week with his trainer Jeff and make craft projects. One of Alan's strengths was his desire to be creative. Alan, Uche, and I were regulars at Plaster Fun Time, a store where we could select a decorative item, paint it our chosen palette, and have it baked and glazed while we waited. The three of us shared a picnic table with young kids and their mothers. We took longer to complete our projects than they did, but we felt even prouder.

We even participated in a program that brought Spaulding Rehab doctors in training to our home to learn how disabled people function in the community. After some trepidation that the doctors would rehospitalize him for "not being smart enough and failing their tests," Alan thrived in his teaching role and appreciated their interest and the $100 honorarium check he received in the mail after each visit.

Alan and I both joined a Circle of Support for our dear friend Ginny's husband Bob, who had amyotrophic lateral sclerosis (ALS). Alan was distressed to witness Bob's progressive loss of motor strength and functioning, and asked me repeatedly, "Why can't Bob go to Spaulding where they can teach him to walk again?"

When he grasped the irreversibility of Bob's condition, Alan showed a level of empathy for Bob that I had not known he was capable of. He took an active role in reading to Bob, listening to classical music together, and cooking meals for Bob and Ginny with me.

There are certain elements that became so routine in our daily life after the brain injury that I forget to mention them. One was Alan's slow pace of doing anything and everything because he was easily distracted as well as slower at processing the steps. Parkinson's added its own set of brakes. We used checklists and verbal cues, but still he took forever to get dressed and ready to leave the house for an appointment.

One day when I chided him to hurry, Alan paused and explained, "I take my time getting ready to go somewhere because everything in front of me is much more interesting than anything ahead of me. That's because it's real."

I put more effort into describing what we would see and do at the upcoming destination.

Alan would say the highlight of 2002 was his opportunity to operate a crane on the "Big Dig" construction project submerging the major traffic arteries in Boston. My brother-in-law Jack was a master crane operator licensed to operate the tallest cranes manufactured. In February, Jack invited Alan and me to visit him on a Big Dig site for a lesson on how highway ramps are constructed. Sporting a yellow hard hat and orange safety vest, Alan managed to crawl up the treads to reach the control cab of the 1500 American crane with a small boom "only" five stories high. Jack's "pick" was steel beams coated with rubber called rebars, which he lifted up to the steelworkers perched on high beams that eventually became a bridge. Jack explained that later the rebars are covered with concrete wall forms. Jack performed the maneuver with the fine motor prowess of a surgeon. I noticed that the steelworkers didn't even flinch or duck as the rebar load swung toward them because they trusted Jack's skills.

Alan peppered Jack with questions about the hand signals the construction team communicated with, and how every part of the crane worked. Alan's finest moment came when Jack allowed him to raise and lower the empty boom using the controls.

Later Jack said, "I haven't seen that kind of sparkle in Alan's eyes since he got sick." He was right, and that sparkle and huge grin shone through in the copious photographs we took.

In July, Alan marked the fourth anniversary of his resuscitation. I had a tradition of sending an update letter about his progress to the doctors who had treated him along the way on each anniversary. This year, I substituted what I called "Alan's Quality of Life Analysis," because it summarized how Alan experienced life and what mattered most:

"Alan had been in the shower for a long time. I poked my head in and asked, 'Alan, are you okay? Do you have everything you need?' I was thinking about shampoo.

"There was a long pause. Then Alan's voice came from behind the curtain: 'I'm trying to answer your question. Do I have everything I need? Well, first ... I need a lot of love in my life. I have a lot of love in my life.

"'Second ... I need a good dog. I have a very good dog.

"'Third ... I need interesting books to read. I have plenty of interesting books. So, in response to your question, yes, I have everything I need.'

"I said, 'Honey, I'm so glad! But leave it up to you to come up with such a deep answer to the question.'

"'What?' he said. 'You're the one who's always asking me these deep questions!'"

The other high point of 2002 was the deepening romance between Tom and his girlfriend Claudia. They set their wedding date for November and planned a large wedding with family in attendance from around the country. Alan liked Claudia from the first time Tom introduced her to us. After that visit, Alan said, "Claudia is a very fine woman who will make a good partner for Tom. She's very warm and friendly and she joined right in with us."

Alan responded to Claudia's sunny Colombian nature and attentiveness to his comfort. But we were still surprised when Claudia made a special request of Alan as the wedding day drew near.

"Uncle Al," she said. "You know my father died several years ago, and I don't have anyone to walk me down the aisle when we get married. Would you do me the honor, please?"

My eyes misted up, but Alan knew exactly what Claudia meant. He drew himself up tall, bowed from the waist, and said gallantly, "The honor would be all mine."

On the day of Claudia and Tom's wedding, the church was filled with chattering family and eager children who bobbed up and down in their seats to get the first view of the bride. As the strains of Mendelssohn's wedding march rose to the rafters, Claudia processed slowly down the aisle on Alan's arm. The long aisle made for a difficult walk but he marched with dignity and aplomb to the front of the church. There wasn't a dry eye in the pews.

At the reception, Alan even offered the first toast. Raising his glass, he said, "May Tom and Claudia have a long and joyous life together."

Alan shone at festive ceremonial occasions.

Tom Cromer celebrates his marriage to Claudia with Alan and his father,
Richard Cromer in 2002.

22. A Place to Belong

We all crave a place to belong. A place where everyone knows our name, welcomes us in, accepts us as one of the gang. Where we share a common purpose or mission, can make a contribution, and feel good about ourselves. A place where we have certain rights and privileges because we've earned them. Belonging means being like everyone else and relaxing into being who we truly are.

After a brain injury, many people have trouble finding a place to belong. Alan's needs were shaped by cycles of recovery and illness, but he managed to find some of those essential places over time. Not long after he came home from Spaulding, Alan declared Sorella's to be "my very own place." Sorella's is a friendly neighborhood restaurant famous for heaping platters of ten-ingredient omelets and pancakes. Alan loved going there on Sunday mornings. No sooner was he seated than Ellie, one of the owners, wrapped him in a hug and asked, "Hi Alan, will it be the usual: blueberry pancakes and hot chocolate?"

Alan always grinned and said, "Is this a great place or what?" His mug of hot chocolate overflowing with whipped cream arrived promptly and was refilled mid-meal.

I only mentioned Alan's situation to Ellie once, intending to explain his discomfort with the loud noise and indecipherable menu. From then on, she gave us a table where Alan could sit with his back to the crowd and ignore the bustle of waitresses hoisting trays of food above our heads. Whenever his nephews visited, Alan said magnanimously, "Hey, let me to take you to my place. You've never had such great food. They know me there, so I get the special treatment."

Alan's home away from home was the Barnes and Noble bookstore, where he sat up straight in a leather library chair by the sunny front window and read aloud from Bill Clinton's autobiography or a children's book about the ocean. Before Alan became ill, we loved browsing in bookstores together. In contrast to other shopping expeditions, we never begrudged each other the time to linger, or the money spent on another armful of mixed category books. Now Alan's past and present identities mingled as he stroked the pages respectfully and said, "Look at the vivid colors of these fish. These illustrations are fantastic."

While I perused the latest fiction and psychology titles, he roamed from the test preparation section to history and over to self-help. One day, I looked up from a book about how women reinvent their lives after turning fifty to see Alan waving *How to Win Friends and Influence People* by Dale Carnegie. "Look what I found!" he called. "This will solve my problem with getting along with people." He bought the book and proceeded to discuss the advice with his friends. He was clear about what made sense and what instructions he thought would cause more problems.

One Saturday, Alan might pick a children's mythology book. On another, a complicated report on the Taliban or a dog training manual. As long as he could read the preface and tell me what he understood, I encouraged his choices. I knew the method that worked for him was to read only the preface of most books over and over. Alan cradled his choices in his arms as he shuffled to check out. Proudly stacking his purchases on the counter, he pulled his wallet from his suede bombardier's jacket and said to the clerk, "It makes a guy feel smart to be in a store with a million books. My plan is to read all these books eventually."

The clerk gave a short laugh and said, "Good luck, I'm trying to do the same thing."

Alan belonged on the water, be it a river, a pond, or the ocean. In his lifetime, he had owned a motor boat, canoe, and kayak, and he loved them equally. We thought those days were behind us until Spaulding Rehab started the Dr. Charles H. Weingarten Adaptive Sports and Recreation Program in 2002. Spaulding was situated right on the Charles River and became the first rehab hospital in the country with its own therapeutic recreation dock. I was apprehensive about Alan getting involved because the combination of Parkinson's disease and poor judgment made him so prone to injuries. He, of course, could not wait to get out on the water.

When we went for an orientation session, a young blind man set out on a windsurfer with dual controls steered by a staff member. On the other side of the dock, three staff members lowered a paralyzed woman's wheelchair into a specially equipped motor boat and took off into the wind. I'd never seen anything like this before, but the director explained the intensive training the staff received and the state-of-the-art equipment that made sports a powerful component of rehab treatment.

Alan's back and legs were so stiff that it took three people to secure him in a kayak, under the direction of a physical therapist. Launched from the ramp, he took a few tentative strokes while his companion coached him from an adjacent kayak. Suddenly, Alan the oarsman took over, and he glided with the sure, precise strokes I'd recognize anywhere. I stared through my tears, mesmerized.

"Oh, he's back. Alan came back," I said with wonder.

It had been four years since Alan held a paddle, but his procedural memory dipped the blades from one side to the other in a smooth arc as if it had been only four days. On the water, Alan was indeed his old self, the one he recognized and exalted in welcoming home.

"That was hard work, but I loved it!" he announced. "Did you see me? I was the best kayaker on the river."

I had given up hope of Alan and me kayaking together again. But one day the director said, "Do you want to go out with Alan? We have an extra boat today." Would I? Soon we paddled our kayaks under the bridge and along the Esplanade, sporting matching smiles. We were a couple again, an active couple sharing an activity we loved.

I said, "Alan, look at us! We're kayaking again."

He casually tossed back, "Yeah, I know; I do this all the time here."

For that hour, I was happier than I'd been for a few years. We were able to kayak together a few times that summer. Once we steered a double-seated kayak under the steel beams of the Big Dig construction far overhead, and we marveled at this nuts-and-bolts view visible only from the water.

As much as I craved the chance to participate, I had to admit that this was meant to be Alan's place to excel on his own terms, so I stopped asking to join in. I watched Alan's confidence and self-esteem billow like a spinnaker sail and listened as he telephoned reports of his latest adventure to his amazed family.

"I didn't think I could kayak again," he said. "But this program and my skills have exceeded my expectations."

As the program expanded, Alan tried most of the sports they offered. When the Parkinson's symptoms were better, he even strapped into a harness and ascended the climbing wall as the staff guided his ropes from below. He rode a reclining bike and a bike propelled by hand pedals for people with paralyzed legs. He paddled on a four-man team in a series of outrigger canoe races. As I gained trust in the staff's expertise, I let Alan and Uche, his home health aide, go to Spaulding without me. They both had a blast.

Alan announced to Molly, "I am officially an adaptive sports aficionado!"

Most of the dock staff were in their twenties and thirties, accomplished athletes, and dedicated to opening up outdoor opportunities to people with severe injuries or chronic diseases. I wasn't fully aware of the relationships Alan had cultivated or how the staff thought of him until we went to a fund-raising event for the program. On that Sunday, over a hundred people crowded the plaza overlooking the dock, jostling plates of barbecue, and boogying to the music of a Caribbean band.

Just as Alan was succumbing to stimulation overload, Matt, the program leader, clapped him on the back.

"Hey Al, great to see you. Are you gonna row on our team today?" he asked. "We need your muscle power in the boat!"

Then came Donald, who usually introduced Alan to new activities: "Professor! Could you tell this new gentleman about how you got back to kayaking? He had a stroke, and he's kind of nervous about the boats."

All afternoon, the jokes and easy familiarity went back and forth.

As he went to join the crew on the dock, Alan said, "See? These are my people now. They let me do what I want, and I even help the new guys."

I already appreciated how much happier Alan was, and how the exercise benefited his strength and coordination. But that day, I saw Alan the way the staff did: as the boating enthusiast who challenged himself beyond the limits of brain injury and Parkinson's. They respected him for his accomplishments and perseverance, while treating him like a regular guy. I stood aside and absorbed the genuine camaraderie and regard between Alan and the adaptive sports staff. There was not one hint of condescension or misplaced sympathy.

Alan was able to participate in the program for three summers. He was right: He did belong there.

23. Coping: The Good, the Bad, and the Ugly

First let me say that I could not have survived, let alone coped with, taking care of Alan without the boundless support of my women friends. Gail christened the group "The Stalwarts" for their abiding strength and loyalty. Just as each of Alan's family and friends offered him something unique, my friends brought me love, comfort, support, laughter, sustenance, reality testing, hands-on help, and a window to the broader world I could only sample vicariously. It took enormous mutual commitment to stay friends and refine what friendship meant at different junctures.

I could count on certain friends to listen if I called late at night worried or angry. Another friend brought me gourmet chocolate (nature's antidepressant) from wherever she traveled. One took on the unenviable job of confronting me about the need to pick a nursing home in case Alan's condition became unmanageable. Still another brought us dinners or homemade bread for years.

Alan raved about Marla's cooking and often told me, "You could learn to make this delicious food, you know."

I replied, "Yeah, but I'm not going to because it tastes so much better to me when Marla cooks it. You're missing the point!"

My friends found information and services we needed and saved me hours of investigation. They all told me stories about their personal and professional lives and asked my advice in ways that made me feel I still had something to contribute.

When I come up against a new situation or challenge, my first response is to call my friends, and my second response is to try to learn everything I can about this problem. To that end, I read many books on brain injury and many books about caregiving, written from different psychological and spiritual perspectives. I particularly welcomed memoirs by people who dealt with catastrophic illnesses. Their honesty and directness made them informed guides in this secret society.

I continued to attend the professional education conferences offering updates on brain research and dementia that I'd attended for years. I used to be interested in applying new ways of understanding brain problems to clients who struggled with mental illness, but now I scribbled notes applicable to my husband. I fulfilled my educational requirements, but left with a raging headache.

Hearing how other people approach major challenges and come to find meaning always expands my choices. Years before Alan became sick, I facilitated therapeutic support groups for people who had cancer and separate groups for their family caregivers. Now I remembered back to specific ways Bernice dealt with her husband's rage when he had a brain tumor, and how Eugene held on to his center when his wife's cancer recurred three times. I had tremendous respect for these strong and committed people when I worked with them and now applied some of their problem-solving strategies to our situation.

Finding support from those I could relate to was of paramount importance. To me, support meant honest, shared emotional exploration coupled with practical approaches to understand a problem and make the situation better. I was fortunate to have a few such venues. The first was BABIS, our brain injury support group. I met several people there who became good friends and confidants. I also facilitated a BABIS support group for family members. We learned so much from each other and, while opinions and choices often differed, most members found allies and even mentors. We shared resources for services, alternative perspectives, strategies for communication and behavioral problems, humor, and acceptance.

I found terrific information and camaraderie though family caregiver organizations, including the Well Spouse Association (www. wellspouse.org), a national organization for partners/spouses of a person with a chronic, progressive illness. At my first regional conference, two years into Alan's illness, I sat horrified when we went around the circle introducing ourselves. Many participants said they'd been caregivers for eight, twelve, or twenty-five years. I was shocked; could I do that? Would I have to? In fact, many caregivers measure their years of providing loving, complicated care in decades instead of single digits.

The discussion groups were frank and lively, and the workshops on caring for oneself and dealing with dreaded situations were thought-provoking and applicable. I started corresponding with online buddies late at night.

Through the *Caregiver* magazine Web site (www.caregiver.com), I found a Caregiver's Bill of Rights, written by Jo Horne. I'd been a caregiver for four years before anyone told me I had rights, which included:

"I have a right to maintain facets of my life that do not include the person I care for, just as I would if he or she were healthy.

"To reject any attempts by my loved one to manipulate me through guilt or depression.

"To receive consideration, affection, forgiveness, and acceptance for what I do for as long as I offer these qualities in return."

I spent a lot of time trying to make my attitude more constructive, my actions more organized, and my emotions less disruptive. Talk about a full-time job. I had extensive training in cognitive-behavioral therapy and integrated it into my clinical practice. Now I used it to check whether my thoughts were realistic and to keep my worries to a manageable size. I've always had a tendency to worry. That's why I started to meditate and use mind-body approaches when I was in my early twenties. But now I had plenty to worry about. After you've watched your husband die and come back to life, no worry feels like an exaggerated or distorted thought. I needed a technique that was as vivid and dramatic as my worries.

Back at Resurrection Medical Center, I designed an approach based on compartmentalization that served me well for years. My imagination became my therapist and turned my wild "what if" thoughts into sleek, black stallions. Then my imagination built "thought corrals" out in the meadow of my mind and rounded up the stallions. The thought corrals full of restless stallions could be in the periphery of awareness, but not raise havoc with my ability to think logically and take necessary steps. Over the years, the number of stallions went up or down, but I never dismantled the thought corrals.

I became good friends with disappointment. Disappointment doesn't get its due as emotions go, because it tastes like bitter green bile, and we swallow it fast. I didn't want to come across as ungrateful for all the care and support Alan received, but there were always losses and changes to get used to while forging ahead. But disappointment snagged me and held me in place a few times until I had to admit that Alan's latest diagnosis was a major setback for me too. Or that having a home health aide call in sick, when I had plans for a rare night out with friends, was disappointing as well as infuriating. Only when I had a dialogue with the disappointment could I decide whether to let situation go or do the necessary mourning that preceded adapting to a more serious change.

Over the years, I discovered more emotions than I knew existed. I called myself the "Queen of Coexisting Emotions," since I often said, "On one hand, I feel worried and apprehensive, and on the other hand, I'm happy and calm." Developing a high tolerance for a range of emotions proved useful and eased my confusion about having mixed feelings about many situations.

And when all the thinking and feeling got to be too much, I got out of my head and into my hands. In addition to painting small watercolors, I discovered the creative joy of making books with beautiful handmade papers from around the world. I became a familiar face at Paper Source, where I could touch the luxuriously textured or wildly patterned papers. When some women learn to knit, all their friends receive mittens for

Christmas. My friends received custom-designed journals and portfolios. Designing a book, making precise measurements, gluing in face papers, and stitching bindings was totally absorbing and meditative. And at the end, I held a finished piece I considered to be a work of art.

Hope and optimism often intertwined. I redefined both many times over the years. Early in Alan's illness, I could only be optimistic by focusing on one minute, one decision at a time. Small, predictable things kept me buoyed up: the predictable pleasure of making myself toast with cinnamon sugar and a cup of hot Irish breakfast tea in the morning. The comfort I counted on from wrapping the brown paisley shawl my sister gave me around my shoulders when I sat down to read.

As the years went on, Alan and I had some shared and some private hopes. I stopped hoping that he would return to being the person he was before the brain injury. Instead, I hoped that I could find attributes to love in this new person. By opening up to seeing those facets of Alan, and especially by letting him bring out new parts of me, I did fall in love with him again.

We both hoped that his illnesses would be manageable at home. But I knew that might not be possible, and so I made plans to handle multiple scenarios I thought could happen, such as hiring live-in help, or even considering moving to an assisted living facility together. The slogan "Hope for the best and plan for the worst" made sense to me.

Over time, our hopes transformed themselves into bright little stars that we could balance on the tips of our fingers because they were so close, not nebulous and distant. We hoped that the Parkinson's meds would help Alan walk well enough to go to Centre Street for ice cream tomorrow. I hoped that nothing would interfere with a nephew's promise to give me a few days of respite in two weeks. When Alan hoped that his sister would call on Sunday, that was easy to arrange. When something we hoped for happened, we stopped to notice and appreciate our good fortune.

A combination of hard work and finding the right resources often brought hopes to fruition. It wasn't just fate and fairy dust. My optimism rose when I found I could handle a new situation or call an expert for advice.

There was so much I had to learn to care for Alan every time his condition got worse or a new diagnosis was added. Each time we implemented a new behavior plan, I had to gather the background data on the problem, devise the plan, help Alan use the plan consistently, then review and revise it. Before you can give a new approach a fair trial, you need a transfusion of hope and optimism. When someone backed me up or helped me generate new ideas, I could keep going with the latest plan.

I believe caregivers would benefit tremendously from having skill coaches we can call at each critical juncture to teach and support us.

Daydreams kept me optimistic that I could have a small but separate life while caring for Alan, and that my life would go on after he died. I dreamt about staying out in the world later than the 4:00 PM curfew I had for years when we depended on home health aides. I dreamt about writing a best-selling book, about taking my nieces to New York now, to London later. About celebrating my sixtieth birthday in Paris.

Okay, I admit that many of my daydreams were about romance and tenderness. And not with Alan. In fact, I had more romantic and sexual fantasies than I'd had at sixteen. I had serial crushes where I admired and liked men from afar. Sometimes, they were men I knew. More often, they were men I didn't know and could therefore believe would be flawless suitors. My crushes let me pretend someone could find me desirable and interesting: the self-descriptors I used less as the years passed. I spent afternoons while Alan napped concocting romantic scenarios of restaurants where this week's crush and I would have dinner al fresco in a garden before adjourning to a hotel room with high-end linens. In my fantasies, nobody yelled, nobody was sarcastic, and nobody needed extra heart medication before making love.

In real life, the tedium of daily routines gets to be like a hospital smell that's in the air, but you don't notice it when you work there every day. My crushes and flirtations were like a window at the end of the hall being thrown open. I didn't complain about the hospital smell too often, but I perked right up when a gust of fresh air blew in.

Some nights after Alan was agitated all afternoon, I made up romantic fantasies of picnicking on the lawn at Tanglewood with an attentive man who fed me ripe strawberries as the Boston Symphony

Orchestra sent rhapsodies floating over the grass. These scenes were my buffer against being alone with an unpredictable man all night and gave me the illusion of being cared for.

One of the first and best memoirs I read was *Surviving Your Spouse's Chronic Illness* by Chris McGonigle. Chris devotes a whole chapter to "Sex: The Plaster Saint Syndrome" to explain the complicated changes the sexuality of both partners undergoes in chronic illness. Those outside the intimate relationship often assume the caregiver is a "saint" who agreed to selflessly devote him-/herself to the sick spouse and forsake their own needs for intimacy and sexuality.

Nothing could be further from the truth, in my experience and that of my caregiver friends. I resented Alan when his medical problems or moods made him withdraw from sex for weeks or even months. If a nice guy held the door open for me at the post office on my desperate days, I almost said to him, "Do you want to go away with me for the weekend?"

I wanted to be recognized and celebrated as a woman, to express myself freely, to have my needs met for a change. There came a point where I seriously considered looking for a lover, for lack of a better word. I talked it over with a few discreet confidants, who made suggestions and said they'd think about men who might be appropriate. Of course, being a caregiver with an early curfew had drawbacks.

There are many potential complications to affairs in this situation, but I really believed I could find a way to have what I needed without taking away from my love or commitment to Alan. Some family caregivers manage to do this, but I didn't find the right person or situation. In the end, I settled for enriching my relationships with male friends and enjoying their energy in nonsexual ways.

My yearnings made me aware of how much I had neglected the passion I always considered to be part of the life force and a wellspring for creativity. So I dove into workshops on coming home to one's body, the divine feminine across cultures and ages, celebrating sexuality at mid-life, and (my pleasure since the 1970s) belly dancing with veils and finger cymbals. It was affirming to stoke the fires of Eros again with a loving companion: myself.

While some forms of coping were very private and internal, others involved pilgrimages with large shopping bags. I went on shopping binges to do what I thought of as "providing for myself." This was different from retail therapy. While in providing for myself (PFM) mode, I felt an urgency to take in provisions as if the winter was coming and the cupboard was bare. Many of those purchases were comfort items such as eye pillows, spiritual books, relaxation CDs, and pale blue soy candles. Their presence in my home reminded me to take a breath and slow down, as if wrapping an encouraging arm around my own shoulder.

Sometimes, I was motivated by the rare opportunity to get out of the house without Alan tagging along. I'd stop to pick up a birthday card and say to myself, "I'd better get some cards for next month's birthdays because I might not get out again." When I reached the check-out counter, there would be eight cards for birthdays, sympathy, weddings, and baby congratulations in the basket. There would be gimmicky gifts, another mug with an inspirational quote, and a dog poster Alan might find funny.

I was dangerous in Staples, the office supply store. Ashamed of being so disorganized about filing papers and records, I fervently believed that a different organizing system or purple striped folders would motivate me to conquer the mess this time. My office looked like the annex of Staples, but the papers still slumped in piles on the floor.

I bought things I didn't really need, or too many of the ones I did. I was invited to a trunk show to meet the designer of elegant travel vests in exotic fabrics with many hidden pockets. The designer extolled the practicality of the expensive vests that freed women to walk city streets without carrying a purse. They were beautiful, and in my former life, I would have taken one on an international jaunt. But now I rarely even walked the streets of Boston.

I couldn't decide between an indigo blue batik vest or the garment made of gold silk and hand-dyed velvet. As I stroked them, I imagined a time years from now when I would be footloose and adventurous. So I bought them both, even though the price was outlandish in my circumstances. I wore the gold vest with jeans or over a black dress when I met with therapy clients. The blue batik stayed in the closet for years until I gave it away. It really was designed for traveling to distant shores.

Even when I made the connection that I was trying to give myself tangible objects to make up for what my husband couldn't give me emotionally anymore, I didn't particularly care. Any attempt was preferable to not making an effort to assuage the pain of loss and deprivation. And I liked using sustaining objects to assure myself I would have a life I could control filled with familiar pleasures again someday.

When I needed to rest quickly, I could rely on a glass of wine. Alan had so many problems sleeping that we woke up several times a night. By late afternoon, I was dragging and dreaded cooking dinner, then getting him ready for bed. I wanted a time-out from reality and responsibility, and on a good day, I might have a thirty-minute window.

I got into the habit of sipping a glass of wine as soon as Alan lay down for his pre-dinner nap. I got drowsy fast and stretched out on the couch for a quick snooze while he slept. Sometimes, I'd have a second glass late at night as I pecked e-mail notes to my buddies. I knew this wasn't the smartest approach, that it was wrong, that I should try meditation or a brisk walk instead, but the predictable relief cut into my motivation to change my habit for quite a while.

Caregiver organizations always warn their members about using short-term approaches like food or alcohol to deal with the long-term stresses of caregiving. They're right, and I wish I had followed that advice earlier.

There are healthier ways to retreat, and having a space to call my own was a better way. We had a cozy sunroom in the center of the house on the second floor. There was no door, but I was sheltered by the bookcases I stocked with only poetry and nature books. Although it was a sunroom, I kept the plants to a manageable number. During the worst of Alan's Parkinson's crisis, I came up one day to find four straggly plants withering away.

I took a hard look and declared my verdict: "I can take care of two plants, but not four plants. Sorry, but out you go."

Later, that appalled my gardener self, but I could only handle so much watering and fertilizing at that point.

I crept up to the sunroom while Alan was out with his aide and sat savoring the quiet as I gazed out the window over the neighborhood rooftops and trees. Sometimes I meditated, chanting from a book and bowing to Buddha and Kwan Yin on the small altar adorned with a shimmering brocade cloth from Tibet, playful crones, and spiritual symbols.

There were plenty of days when Alan said nasty, hurtful things to me, such as, "If I could get away from you I would. My life isn't worth living if I have to have you in it." I flinched, but shifted into figuring out the specific reason he was mad this time so we could deal with it.

But shortly after that, a burst of evil thoughts would fly through my head, including, "Go away, just leave before I kick you out. I wish you would die instead of threatening me all the time."

More than once I muttered, "Be careful what you wish for, Buster. I'll divorce you before you divorce me." When I was very frustrated and he wasn't wearing hearing aids, I just said it aloud.

Maybe the best thing I did was to stop pretending. I stopped pretending to myself and others that I had energy and compassion to give when I really didn't. By energy, I mean regularly replenished fuel for body and spirit. There were countless times over seven years when I was physically, emotionally, and spiritually exhausted, when Alan's twenty-four-hour care plus running our lives sucked up every drop of energy I had.

For years, one of my clinical specialties had been the effects of stress on physical and mental health. I developed many programs and classes to teach people to recognize and better manage the kinds of stress that could hurt their health. Imagine my surprise when I finally realized that my own stress measuring stick had grown to a distorted size and shape resembling Pinocchio's nose.

Like many caregivers, I became so accustomed to living with the shifting demands, medical roller coasters, and scrambled priorities of caregiving that my gauge of what was stressful had become warped. Now I didn't feel stressed until we'd had three nights in a row of disrupted sleep because Alan was confused or in a psychotic rage. Or until I felt my lower back go into spasm on the fourth day that week I picked him up off the floor after he insisted on standing up alone.

I told myself I was a "tough cookie," my family's badge of honor, and that I was already managing stress with walking, talking, yoga, meditation, and laughing at every opportunity. But those approaches weren't enough.

I finally stopped moving so fast and doing so much. I rested more and turned down several requests to help out in different organizations. I divided my reserves of compassion between the two of us, so I didn't chastise myself if I wasn't as patient or considerate with Alan on a particular day. I knew I'd like him better and have the mental energy to show my love the next day.

I began to strongly contradict the people who implied that our life was easy or took little effort because, as they said, "You're a professional who knows how to do all of this."

Nobody knows how to do all of this.

As caregivers, we all have to learn continuously. Alan and I dealt with the cumulative impact of heart disease, brain injury, Parkinson's, and dementia every day. I used everything I ever learned as a medical and psychiatric nurse to take care of Alan. And there were many times when I doubted myself or felt stranded by not understanding something or having the right resources. I always worried about family caregivers who had no medical background and were expected to do the same things that I was to keep their loved one safe, smart, and happy.

When I talked to family or friends, I started to lay out the truth about the darker parts of our life without worrying so much about protecting Alan's dignity by being discreet.

When I took more time to repair myself, nothing bad happened. Alan's condition didn't deteriorate, the bills waited to be paid, and the world kept spinning. I realized that overestimating my own importance in keeping our little universe in motion was its own stressor. It was a relief to give it up.

24. The Most Tragic Year

There are certain dates so momentous in their impact that they must be lifted right off the calendar and held aloft forever.

My sister Sherry had been very sick with several complicated diseases for many years. She agreed to try extremely invasive and involved treatments, some of which helped for a while. Sherry did everything she could to stay alive to be a mother to her four children for as long as humanly possible.

But in March 2003, Sherry was admitted to the intensive care unit of a hospital in Maine with worsening disease affecting every system of her body. I wanted desperately to be by her side night and day. To that end, one of Alan's nephews or Uche stayed with Alan around the clock so I could be with Sherry and her family.

I was with Sherry when she died on March 28, 2003.

My sister. My only sibling. My Sherry.

Janet and her sister, Sherry Caliri, celebrate Thanksgiving in 1999.

Marty and Larry came with Alan to Sherry's wake in Maine. Alan was very dignified and sad as he expressed his condolences to Sherry's husband and children. In the overheated funeral parlor packed with the kids' friends and teachers, my husband looked liked a stranger to me. We seldom were part of large gatherings anymore, so I'd stopped comparing him to men his age or people who weren't seriously ill. Even though he wore his suit jacket and tie, what I noticed now shocked me.

"Oh, Alan certainly has aged, hasn't he?" I asked Gail. "He looks like an old man bent by Parkinson's and confused to be here. His face sags and doesn't move. He looks so different from everybody else. He's aged so much."

Gail said gently, "Yes, Janet, he has."

It seemed we must have been living with his illness for a much longer time than I'd tracked.

The next day, I participated in Sherry's funeral while Alan stayed home. My friend Kathy said that seeing me twisted with grief and walking alone behind Sherry's coffin was one of the saddest sights she's ever seen. Even though she knew our situation well, she couldn't help but ask, "Where is that poor woman's husband? He should be with her."

Alan tried very hard to remember and support me. He could only allow himself to momentarily identify with the horror of losing one's sister.

He said, "I can't even imagine how horrible it would be if Barbara died. I don't even want to think about it because it makes me feel too sad."

But in a few weeks, the memory faded. When I moped around all day, saying I missed Sherry terribly, Alan said, "Oh, I'm so sorry; she's just not in my awareness. Tell me what happened to her again?"

A howling storm of grief overcame me. But the storm had to be set aside so that I could resume caring for Alan. I walked through our demanding but familiar routines like a robot, responding when Alan spoke, but frozen to express myself. In a numb state, I painted a large picture of my grief. A parched desert landscape with tough patches of dead grass fills the foreground. A narrow road snakes back toward an uninhabited horizon. Over the landscape, a blazing, relentless, unforgiving sun hangs menacingly. I was desiccated and cracked open. No tears left to cry.

Throughout 2003, we became more involved with Ginny and Bob as ALS ravaged more of Bob's ability to move the muscles of his arms and legs. Alan liked helping me prepare dinners to deliver on Wednesday nights and reading to Bob when they were both in the mood. Bob had a fierce courage and determination not to succumb to each diminution of the disease for as long as possible. Alan understood that drive in ways the rest of us could not. They shared some quiet conversations with a serious tone.

Even as Bob's respiratory muscles were affected, he planned a birthday party and directed us to inscribe his cake, "Forty-five and still alive!" That day we had a boisterous celebration of Bob and Ginny's shared joie de vivre. Bob stayed fully alive in mind and spirit right to the end of his life. He invited friends to come to scheduled meetings where he told each person why he loved them, and what he hoped would come to them in life. Bob showed us that it is possible to say good-bye and "I love you" with much courage and dignity.

Bob died on August 23, 2003.

After making every moment of his life count, recording his journals and leaving personalized gifts for those he loved, Bob even detailed his wishes for a series of memorial events. I was intent on participating in Bob's memorial service, but couldn't find anyone to stay with Alan that day. I convinced myself that Alan would want to attend since he'd been close to Bob. I could not have been more wrong.

Immersion into talk of death and remembrance was too much for Alan to bear. Alan's behavior throughout the service was atrocious. As the melodious voices of mourning friends filled the beautiful stone church with transcendent music, Alan yelled, "Do we have to sit here until my entire body goes numb on these awful benches? I don't have anything to do with these people. I'm getting out of here and going home now."

Just as Ginny began her full-hearted eulogy of her husband, Alan fled the church and ran two blocks attempting to get home. I was torn between staying to witness my dear friend's celebration of love and chasing after Alan.

As I ran, I said, "Just run, I don't care if you ever come back. Bob was my friend and you are ruining this service for me. I'm sick of your anger and acting out."

By the time I dragged Alan back to the church for the third time, my compassion and understanding were spent. I hated him and stayed angry at his behavior for days.

But eventually, I could reflect that Bob's memorial hit too close to home for Alan, who was aware that his own health was in decline. There was no way he could he watch a wife eulogize her beloved husband. I wondered if Alan was also remembering being the widower who buried his first wife Marge as he sat on those hard wooden benches.

When I asked him, he said, "I don't want to talk about any of that."

❧

Molly had not felt been well for a while, in vague ways that took some time to register. In January, the veterinarian diagnosed her problem as Lyme disease, a tick-borne infection, which had already damaged her kidneys. I had applied tick preventative medications monthly, but to my anguish and remorse, the disease was quite advanced by the time it was diagnosed. I felt guilty that I hadn't been able to protect her enough, and now she was suffering. For several months we tried medications, a special kidney disease diet, and holistic remedies.

On the days Molly was noticeably sick Alan worried and offered her extra attention. Her condition had a pattern of ups and downs, and sometimes involved discomfort and nausea. Karen, my acupuncturist, recommended a colleague, Janis, who specialized in acupuncture for animals. Janis made regular house calls to treat Molly's nausea and energy level. Molly didn't mind the thin needles at all. After offering Janis a warm greeting, Molly stretched across her favorite silk pillow to receive the treatment.

As the months went on, Molly's kidney disease worsened despite more treatments. I became frantic at the reality that she had a terminal illness. At night, my head swam with the implications: "Molly can't die ... Molly was supposed to go forward in life with me after Alan dies. Molly is my link to my mother. Molly's been Alan's closest companion every day for five years. Molly can't die."

But she did. Molly died on November 6, 2003.

Alan and I sat together on the couch, cradling Molly on our conjoined laps. Her breaths become slower as we stroked her soft apricot fur. Our tears fell on her peaceful body as we whispered our love and gratitude.

Alan and I sank into the deepest grief. I worried that without his dog, Alan would lose his will to live, so I brought him with me to see my therapist, Martha. As we talked about how to memorialize Molly, Alan framed the question that always stymied me.

"How do you know when to stop grieving?" he asked Martha. "How do you know when it's enough time?"

Martha told us about the Jewish tradition of sitting shiva, and we agreed to try that.

We nestled Molly's portrait and favorite toys into her bed and set a ring of candles and flowers around the well-worn plaid cushions. Many friends came to pay their respects by sitting with us on the kitchen floor as we all told Molly stories. Their love, tributes, and cards were a balm to our aching hearts. At the end of one week, I tucked Molly's bed into my mother's hope chest, where I kept my most precious mementos. After Molly was cremated, I kept her ashes in a raku pottery vessel on the mantle.

For two weeks, Alan blamed me daily for Molly's death.

"You were supposed to take care of her. You were supposed to make her better. You call yourself a nurse, but you let her die? It's all your fault," he lambasted me.

My explanations and pleas to support each other were no match for his grief. I could see his confidence in my ability to keep him alive ebbing away. To my horror, a few weeks later, Molly started to disappear from Alan's memory. When I mentioned her name, Alan knew who I meant, but he said, "Oh, that's awful, she's just not on my mind."

Once again, I withdrew into a cocoon of solitary grief.

At the end of that horrific year, two wonderful events brightened our lives when we needed it most. Tom's wife Claudia gave birth to their first child, Richard Alan Cromer. Alan was enchanted as he gingerly cradled the infant in his arms. "Good work, Tom. Good work, Claudia," he smiled.

And a new puppy decided to adopt Alan and me.

25. PARALLEL PATHS

When I read through the entries for 2003 in my journal and in Alan's logbook, the contrast between our experiences is striking. That year we traveled parallel paths for much of the time because our experiences were so different; we shared fewer activities and emotional connections. I was immersed in the devastating illnesses of my sister Sherry, our friend Bob, and our dog Molly. I provided either direct care or family support month after month as they each got sicker.

Alan, on the other hand, continued to be as active as possible depending on the waxing and waning of his Parkinson's symptoms. He enjoyed twice weekly workouts with his trainer Jeff and took interesting trips to local places with family and friends. He alternated between being Uche's teacher and student, and always had someone to talk to. We even enjoyed a touring Broadway production of *The Music Man*.

That summer, we hit the lowest point of our marriage. Late one Sunday afternoon in August, we had a terrible argument, after which Alan stormed into the bedroom. He climbed into bed still yelling and cursing at me.

When I came in to give him his antianxiety medication, I said, "I have your medicine here. I'll leave it on your table if you want to take it."

"I'm not taking any medicine from you," he snarled.

"That's your choice. I just didn't want you to have a stroke if your blood pressure gets too high." I turned to leave the room.

"I don't care if I die. My life isn't worth living if I have to have you in it!" he shouted.

His words stung like a slap on my cheek, and something inside me snapped. Looking right at him as he turned away from me in the bed, I ripped off my wedding and anniversary rings and flung them across the stifling bedroom. The rings narrowly missed the heating vent in the floor as they clattered to rest. After five years, I didn't feel married or loved anymore. I wasn't even sure I loved this version of Alan. I had run out of ways to define marriage.

I continued to take care of Alan with the same scrupulous detail, but I kept a shield around my heart to protect myself from his shifting moods and fluctuating ability to love me. I pondered how we could stay connected and loving as the dementia and other problems made him angrier and crazier.

Looking back, not wearing my rings gave me some protective detachment that kept my yearnings for Alan to be a supportive and reciprocating husband in check. Earlier in the year, I had introduced my friends to the phrase "married widow," which caregivers use to describe a marriage that is irreversibly changed but not over in ways that allow the widow to move on. Prolonged grieving that year left me more vulnerable to Alan's rejection. If Alan ever noticed the absence of my woven gold wedding band and diamond anniversary band, he didn't mention it.

As Christmas approached, my grief for Sherry was insufferable, and I wanted to feel part of a family again, part of a couple again. Alan and I both experienced the cumulative grief of the year as a heavy weight and sometimes comforted each other by snuggling on the couch to tell stories about Molly or just watch a movie. One morning, I opened my jewelry box and made the deliberate decision to slide the rings I'd always loved so much back on my left hand. I did still love Alan and feel a loyalty based on our formerly shared life, battles to reclaim him, and mutual determination to make each day the best it could be. And maybe I forgave Alan for not being in control of the hateful things he said when dementia had him in its heinous grip.

After Molly died in November, Alan and I had much less to talk and laugh about. We missed having a dog to smother with affection and conversation. So, one day in December while I was "just looking" at breeds in a pet store, a tiny shih-tzu male pup picked me out and convinced me to bring him home. I tiptoed into the living room and placed the three-pound ball of fur in the crook of Alan's elbow.

"Alan, this puppy followed me home," I said. "Can we keep him?"

"Well, he does look like a loveable sort," said Alan. We named the pup Nicky, and he and Alan quickly bonded.

After we adopted Nicky, Alan went to see his psychiatrist, Dr. P. We talked about how disturbed he was that his beloved Molly had died and was now slipping from his memory.

Alan said, "The human mind just can't take in mourning one person while loving another. It's too much for the mind to hold."

Dr. P. said, "Alan, you are serving Molly's memory well by giving your affection to a new dog." Alan liked the new dog, and over a few months, Nicky and Molly morphed into being the same continuous dog in Alan's mind.

26. "Less Grief, More Green"

As 2004 dawned, I was at one of the lowest points of my life. One January afternoon as I sat beneath a copper beach tree in the Arnold Arboretum, I realized that, after so much loss, I needed to give myself over to nature's turning of seasons and get involved with nature in new ways.

My New Year's resolution and mantra became "Less grief, more green." So I joined the Arboretum's volunteer school guide program, which educates Boston Public School students about nature. The bountiful training immersed me in biology and horticulture, and allowed me to be the student instead of the expert for a change. I relished guiding kids through the Arboretum grounds as we did experiments about pollination or made drawings of how Native Americans lived in this area.

Participating in the intensive training sessions and meeting my commitment to guide twice a week meant that I had to entrust more of Alan's care to Uche and be away longer. This was a big adjustment for us all, and a healthy one.

I brought home what I learned, and Alan and Uche were fascinated by dissecting a daffodil or looking at a magnolia ovule with a magnifying glass. Several friends commented on the transformation in my energy level and enthusiasm. Being an Arboretum school guide steeped in nature studies and the outdoors restored the balance I needed after years of belonging to only brain injury and caregivers groups.

Although I continued to grieve, my senses came alive and expanded, and I gained a connection to the world beyond myself and my family. I went on to be an Arboretum guide for four seasons and enhanced my identity as a nature lover who could now identify dozens of trees.

Although I did well as a guide, I flunked puppy training 101. I must have been out of my mind to buy a three-month-old dog while Alan's needs for care were steadily increasing. I had no idea how much consistent attention it takes to housebreak and socialize a puppy. Nicky teethed on every available hunk of wood, including the bentwood rocker and all the drawer knobs he could reach. I didn't even notice until weeks later.

I hired a dog trainer who made home visits to teach Alan, Uche, and me the same commands to use with Nicky. I figured that two out of three people being consistent isn't bad. We all enjoyed the sessions, but Alan had his own methods that resulted in plenty of mixed messages for Nicky.

Late one night, Alan accidentally dropped a handful of cardiac pills on the floor, and Nicky quickly gobbled them down. I couldn't make Nicky vomit the pills, so we spent an anxious night in the emergency room of Angell Memorial Hospital. Nicky spent twenty-four hours in intensive care connected to the same monitoring equipment used on people. The bill, with subsequent heart tests, came to $800, but we were both relieved that he was pronounced unharmed.

That year, I was piecing together a satisfying new career composed of paid and volunteer activities even as I continued my private therapy practice. I wrote regularly for publications that served healthcare professionals, facilitated a family support group, and spoke at conferences on medical ethics, brain injury, and family issues.

In June, I returned to the Fine Arts Work Center in Provincetown for a poetry writing workshop. As I browsed in Utilities, a gourmet kitchenware shop, I started to take tentative steps to prepare for a life after Alan passed on. I carried a cold stone of awareness that I would need to sell our twelve-room home and move to a condominium. Although the prospect of losing Alan was wrenching, the prospect of living on my own did not scare me. I was thirty-five when Alan and I met, and there were many parts of making a home for myself that I'd enjoyed and done well as a single person. My apartment in Harvard Square had been filled with fifty flowering plants, wild abstract paintings, and glass vessels whose colors refracted the light like jewels.

Now as I ran my finger over the etched designs on earthenware bowls, I got the idea to start a hope chest. A hope chest of beautiful objects I would bring with me to my new home and new life. I wasn't thinking of marrying again and didn't mean the kind of old-fashioned Lane cedar chest that my mother used to hold her trousseau as a newlywed.

No, I felt the words "hope chest" viscerally, as something solid that gave me hope that I could eventually recover and make a new life with purpose and joy after Alan died. I would collect objects to comfort me and feed my friends when I had to leave one home to start another. That day I chose a butter yellow serving bowl from Portugal with ripe fruits embossed on the rim.

Each time I returned to Provincetown, I chose another piece of pottery from that line. I designated a cardboard carton in a corner of the storeroom as my hope chest. I never used my treasures. I just trusted that they were there and would embolden me to make the necessary changes when the time came.

Alan benefited from close attention and interactions around the clock as his medical problems became more complicated. Uche worked with us forty hours a week, and my friend Gail proposed an innovative arrangement whereby she stayed with us a few nights every week when she worked at a local hospital. Gail had moved to a community an hour's drive away, and it was mutually beneficial for her to stay with us rather than face a long drive home after work. Gail, a psychiatric RN, contributed wise observations, suggestions, and her lively presence. I always slept soundly when Gail was in our house.

27. THE DEMENTIA CHRONICLES

In 2004, six years after the brain injury, Alan's ability to move through the world took some serious hits. His cardiovascular disease worsened and necessitated more frequent medication changes. On the eve of our annual trip to Sanibel Island, he had such bad chest pain that his cardiologist said it was no longer safe for Alan to fly. Alan was devastated when we had to cancel the trip and furious at one more assault on his freedom and mobility. The intensity of his reaction reminded me of his response to not being allowed to drive a car. He used a wheelchair outside the house more often because of angina and Parkinson's disease.

However, Alan focused on his perennial goal of being out and about, whether enjoying nature or ordering fried rice and kung pao chicken at his favorite Chinese restaurant.

He said, "All right, I'll use the chair if it makes me normal and not cooped up in the house."

One of Alan's strengths was his ability to protest another setback, then agree to adapt enough to maintain some control over what he valued most.

Parkinson's disease presented new challenges in more systems of Alan's body, including the ability to hold a steady blood pressure and heart rate. When Alan stood up from a chair, his blood pressure fell suddenly, making him feel dizzy and off-balance. He had enough problems staying upright without these sudden stumbling falls. The solution combined changing medications for both PD and heart disease, making sure he drank enough liquids, and cuing Alan to change positions slowly.

At his baseline, Alan had some amount of stiffness, freezing, trouble initiating movements, and extreme slowness. But hot humid weather made every symptom worse. We consulted with a physical therapist, who said part of Alan's gait problem was that he lost focus after five minutes. People with PD need to deliberately cue their movements by talking themselves through the activity. She showed Alan how to use a cane for balance and stability. Then Uche or I shadowed him, saying, "Alan, lift your feet when you walk, move your right foot and the cane at the same time."

Over time, I noticed small but mounting changes in Alan's ability to dress himself, do household chores, and figure out craft projects. I worried when each of his hard-won functional abilities started to regress.

One morning, he threw his dry cereal into the sink, saying, "This stuff tastes terrible. Something's wrong with it."

He couldn't remember the step of pouring milk on the cereal, even though he'd done it every day for years. He couldn't put two shoes that matched on the correct feet. Eventually, Alan was diagnosed as having Parkinson's dementia as well as vascular dementia.

That diagnosis saddened me, but let me adjust my expectations about how much I could teach Alan to regain those skills. Alan's priority was to choose his foods, so I set up his bowl, cereal, and glass of milk with a numbered card to help him follow the steps. We helped him with dressing by handing him items in sequence while having a pleasant conversation so the extra help didn't embarrass him.

Like many people who have dementia, Alan became less interested in bathing and afraid of the water. The pressure of a warm shower felt too out of control to him even when seated on a shower chair. He shrugged off the need to bathe until I figured out how to make the idea appealing while adjusting the routine to make him comfortable and secure.

One morning, I warmed the bathroom, drew a tub and said, "Alan, I read that in ancient Rome only the educated ruling class, the noble men, were allowed to bathe in the public baths. Bathing started out as an elite privilege."

"Is that right?" he said as he stepped into the tub. "Those were the same guys who invented government and roads." We talked about ancient Rome and Greece, his favorite subjects, as I lathered up his back.

During 2004 I became quite ill with three bouts of a mysterious type of kidney stones and injuries from a fall that happened walking Nicky at night.

Alan panicked when he saw me lying on the couch and shrieked, "You can't be sick. Get up from there! What will become of us if you get sick?" It was a legitimate question.

Alan felt temporarily reassured when I explained the plan that if anything happened to me, his nephews would oversee his care and find a good assisted living facility where he would be well cared for.

He said, "Oh, it's good that we've already thought of this, but don't get sick and don't die on me like my other wife did."

I assigned Alan to bring me lots of water every hour to flush out the kidney stones and read me a story to take my mind off the pain. He took the job seriously.

"I'm a professional husband so I'll just sit here and watch you sleep and make sure you wake up," he announced.

My doctors never figured out the cause of the kidney stones, but I'm sure a contributing factor was that my immune system was depleted by years of insufficient sleep and surges of high stress. When sick or injured, it was difficult to rest long enough to promote real repair.

My health problems forced the issue of how long I could continue to care for Alan at home as his problems worsened. I made a long list of scenarios that, to my mind, would justify placing Alan in a skilled nursing facility/nursing home. I brought the list to a therapy session with Martha but she halted my agonized obsessing with a simple statement.

"The only criteria that will matter is that Janet says, 'This is enough, I can't do this anymore.' And that will be perfectly legitimate," she said.

I did identify an Alzheimer's nursing home in our area in case we needed that option.

Our concerned friends rallied together to start a Circle of Support for Alan and me, using the "share the care" model we'd used for Bob and Ginny a few years earlier. I wished we'd known about these circles early in Alan's illness. I made a list of everything we needed help with from meals to visiting with Alan to cutting the hedges. One person volunteered to coordinate the schedule and requests so I didn't need to administer one more thing. There are many great tools available on the Internet to expedite scheduling. Alan benefited from new visitors who brought fresh ideas that intrigued him. For example, Paul shared his collection of audiotapes of famous political speeches, then he and Alan discussed the political era involved.

Over that year, Alan developed many more mental status problems both from his underlying conditions and adverse reactions to Parkinson's and psychiatric medications. He went through harrowing periods of psychotic rage, new delusions, paranoia, visual hallucinations, and tremendous fright. He tried to flee the house on several occasions and physically assaulted his home health aide. It was a full-time job to ascertain the causes and work out medication and behavioral approaches that would hold for any length of time.

I noticed that as Alan's dementia progressed, it became more difficult to balance his many medications so that the side effects of one did not counteract the benefits of another. We kept trying to find the best balance so that Alan still had dramatic improvements in cognitive processing and language when we hit the right combination.

In August, I wrote to his psychiatrist, *"After you increased the antidepressant, Alan started to 'think smarter' and 'talk smarter.' Within two weeks he was calmer and nicer to people with no agitation or hitting. Several family members visited and he handled the stimulation well. Although they noticed progression of dementia, his sister and nephew felt they had the best visit in several months because he was 'more reachable' and able to participate in a lively conversation with one person. He showed a range of normal emotions which matched his facial expression. Alan even said, 'I'm enjoying my thinking and being me again.'"*

But the side effects could be frighteningly dramatic. Mirapex, a Parkinson's drug, caused visual hallucinations that fed his delusions. Alan told me his second wife had visited.

"She said she'll teach me to drive again and give me lots of money. We're going to run away together, so I won't need you anymore."

At other times, the vivid dreams, hallucinations, and delusions tortured Alan.

"I can't tell what's real and not real," he said, clutching his head and shaking it from side to side to dislodge the visions. "Have I gone crazy or is this making me crazy?"

Alan believed what he read so I wrote in his logbook:

"This is what is real: Alan is not crazy. The dreams are a medicine side effect and will go away soon. Your second wife has never been in this house. She cannot hurt you. Alan and Janet have been married seventeen years, so you have not had contact with her in many years.

Alan can tell Janet when he has strange or frightening experiences. Janet will help Alan figure out what is real. Alan can stay focused on the present by reading the news and talking about current events."

Alan did find it helpful to have a concrete reality check while the medications were being straightened out.

We updated our communication strategies to reflect the Alzheimer's Association's 3 R's principles: reorient, reassure, redirect to comfort and connect with a confused person. I asked Uche and visitors to speak slowly in short sentences and to ask Alan easily answerable questions to start a conversation. When he was upset, we acknowledged the emotion, then suggested getting a snack or brushing the dog together.

Physical agitation continued to be the most dangerous problem. One day, Alan stood on the front porch screaming about not wanting anyone following him around. He swung his cane in wide arcs, daring Uche to approach him. His eyes were wild and he was momentarily strong. I coaxed him into the house and suggested doing exercises together after he took medication for agitation.

That was the first time he tried to use the cane as a weapon. I used to deal with these situations on locked psychiatric units, but being at home with a potentially violent man was even more dangerous. I asked my friend Kathy, a psychiatric nurse, to give Uche and me a refresher lesson on disarming an agitated person. Kathy showed us how to approach Alan and hold his arms while removing the cane from his grasp. This is an extreme situation to handle at home, but many caregivers need to devise strategies to de-escalate an out-of control person. We were able to prevent future agitated episodes from escalating to that point by observing and intervening earlier.

Fortunately, not all the dementia problems were that serious. The wackier incidents gave us a chance to just laugh. One morning, while I was doing errands, I had an urgent call from Uche.

"You have to come home right away; Alan insists on walking down Lamartine Street in your pajamas," Uche said.

Alan had gone upstairs and changed out of his pajamas and into my floral cotton summer pajamas. It was a snug fit, but he insisted on taking a walk while yelling at Uche to stop following him. Uche trailed him, carrying Alan's clothes.

Uche said, "Just come back and change into your own clothes and then you can go out again."

"What's the matter with the clothes I have on?" Alan asked in an annoyed tone.

"Those are girl's clothes. I have your men's clothes here."

Alan stood still, looked at Uche, and replied haughtily, "You obviously don't understand anything about this country!"

Eventually, we coaxed Alan into the house and his own clothes by chatting about a major news story as he dressed.

We had our own way of making perseverative issues bearable. Unfortunately, Alan had post-herpetic neuralgia, which affected his penis. The nerve pain was very bothersome, but pain medication specifically for neuralgia and a cold compress often helped.

Twenty times a day, he asked me, "What do you call this, jock itch?"

I would explain neuralgia, or just say yes. What really mattered was that I demonstrate that I knew he was uncomfortable and had a plan to deal with it. So I said, "Yes, you take pills for it, and I'll give you a cold pack to block the pain signals."

He also asked many other perseverative questions all day long.

One night, he asked, "What do you call this, jock itch?" But he quickly followed with, "I think I've asked you that before. That must drive you crazy!"

I said, "I'm glad to answer your questions, but let's make a deal. Every tenth time you ask me that question, you have to give me a rose."

Alan brightened right up. "Oh, that's fine," he laughed. "I'll just go out and buy a whole bunch of roses and keep asking you questions!"

We both laughed.

A few days later, we went through the question routine and I reminded Alan of our deal. He grinned and said, "How about a kiss every second time I ask?" I agreed.

Many times the perseverative questions served to make contact or let me know he was bored or worried. When he asked the jock itch question, I often asked if he felt pain. He thought for a moment and replied, "No, in fact I don't. I guess I was just wondering what you were doing." So we turned our attention to doing a word game or craft project together.

I started a "Frequently asked questions (FAQ)" section in his logbook for the answers to his big four questions:

1. What is this guy doing here? What is he supposed to do for me? (This referred to his home health aide.)
2. What is this pain in my penis?
3. How old is my dog?
4. Where did my wife go and when is she coming back?

Then we could direct Alan to consult his logbook for answers independently. He felt reassured when he read, "Janet went to guide the school kids in the Arboretum. She loves me and will come home at 2:00 PM."

Alan's perseverative behaviors were harder to manage than his questions. The worst one was letting the puppy chew on his hand constantly, to the point of injury. He lifted Nicky onto the bed with him and started teasing him by offering a finger. Of course, Nicky started biting with his needle-sharp teeth, and soon Alan screamed, "Come get this dog away from me. He won't stop biting me."

I removed Nicky from the room, but in five minutes I'd hear Alan coaxing the dog to jump up with him again.

"Don't take the dog up with you, he's going to bite you again," I said.

"No he won't, he loves me and wants to play with me," Alan insisted.

Inevitably I'd hear the yelps from Alan five minutes later, "Come get this dog off me, he's biting me!"

Alan's nipped hands looked like he pruned thorny rose bushes without gloves. Even when I pointed out the damage, he didn't make the connection or remember safer ways to play with Nicky. This predictable script exasperated me every night until I resorted to locking the dog in a separate room and listening to Alan whine that he couldn't get to sleep without Nicky.

Even as Alan's memory got worse, reading still provided his greatest joy. A friend asked why Alan bothered to read if he couldn't retain and remember material.

I said, "He reads for the sheer joy of being able to read, the pleasure of hearing his voice reading aloud, talking together about the subject, the normalcy and continuity of self that reading provides, and the stimulation of new information. With all those pleasures, not remembering what he reads hardly matters."

If there could be anything merciful about dementia, it might be that Alan reached a stage where he was no longer tormented by not remembering science. He thought that the few facts he could recall with satisfaction were all there was to know about the topic and that he was on equal footing with other educated men. He said, "I remember two of Newton's three laws, and the other one probably wasn't as important anyway."

Alan lost so many hearing aids that the insurance company first put us in the high-risk premium category, then cancelled our coverage. Replacements cost a few thousand dollars, only one of the many financial issues we dealt with related to long-term care for a person with cognitive impairments. We were very fortunate to have health insurance, but the co-pays for Alan's meds ran $700 to $1,000 a month. Our home health aides gave superb care that enabled me to keep Alan out of a nursing home, and believe me, they earned every cent of their salary. However, insurance did not contribute to the $30,000 per year cost of home care. Even though Alan's doctors credited his personal trainer Jeff with maintaining Alan's muscle strength, insurance did not cover that service.

I gave up my private practice that year because Alan could not be left alone for the hour I was with a client. Combined with the loss of two full-time incomes for seven years, that necessitated depleting our savings, living on retirement account funds, and paying for home care with our home equity loan. I knew we were better off than many families, but I became very active in educating policy makers and legislators about the exorbitant cost of chronic illness for families "in the middle" financially, and for the need to recognize and fund home care for people who have cognitive and memory deficits. This is a critical national healthcare issue.

That Thanksgiving, Tom and Claudia invited us to dinner at their home. It was getting harder for Alan to travel and be comfortable in other people's homes. But he loved Tom's family and wanted to see them. I encouraged him to rest all morning so he would have energy for the afternoon and be able to be a festive guest.

"What does 'festive' mean? Is that like joyous?" he asked.

I said, "Yes, a good holiday guest tries to be polite, kind, and even joyous if he's up for it."

Alan slumped tiredly in his recliner. "I used to be that, festive and joyous. But they put me in Spaulding for a long time and took that gene out of me," he said glumly.

When we modified everything we did to accommodate Alan's energy level and tolerance for stimulation, we could still enjoy carefully chosen activities. At Tom's home, Alan was quickly overcome by the sounds of lively children and several guests talking at once. He managed to avoid getting angry by cloistering himself in a bedroom and taking a nap until after dinner was served. Then he emerged, ready for a drumstick and a quiet meal with me at the kitchen table. I appreciated his efforts because I craved the camaraderie and celebration of family gatherings on holidays.

One day Uche, who was an astute observer and commentator on our marriage, watched as Alan and I laughed and enjoyed an affectionate moment. After Alan left to nap, Uche said to me, "When Alan dies it will be like the biggest, tallest tree in the forest falls. And you can never pick it up again."

28. "Am I Dying? I Forget."

One afternoon in 1999, when Alan was still recovering from cardiac bypass surgery, we sat in Finagle-a-Bagel eating lunch. Over the sound system came the melancholy strains of "September Song" by Maxwell Anderson.

Alan put down his turkey sandwich, tilted his head, and sang, "Oh, the days dwindle down to a precious few ... September, November ..."

"That song is about us, you know," he said matter of factly. "I might not live very long to be with you."

Back then, I didn't realize that he was so in touch with his mortality. Now six years had passed, time we often referred to as our bonus years. But Alan's heart disease had reached the point where medications were not controlling his symptoms well. The Parkinson's disease froze his legs and caused many other problems. Dementia was claiming more and more of his memory and intellect. Now Alan was in the November of his life. I felt that our parallel paths had converged again, and we shared the quest to make Alan's remaining time rich with love and connection. Somewhere along the line, I blended all the Alans from these years into a man I now called "My Alan," without distinguishing past and present.

Alan was tormented by increasingly frequent paranoid delusions and visual hallucinations of a gang of thugs who held him captive and beat him mercilessly. The psychosis led to anxiety and agitation beyond anything that had plagued him up until now. Sometimes, he had the same catastrophic emotional reactions he'd had shortly after the brain injury.

We chose to use psychiatric medications as a form of palliative care to help him have periods of peace and lucidity, free from torment. This came at the expense of being able to use optimal doses of Parkinson's meds, since they always cancelled out each other's benefits as Alan's brain became more affected by all the medical diseases.

At his worse, Alan often screamed at Uche and tried to hit him. In January, Alan locked himself in his office and called the police, yelling, "Come arrest this black guy. He broke into my house, beat me, and won't let me go."

I came home during the call and used the extension line to explain the situation and deflect the call.

Alan screamed, "We're having a domestic dispute, you better come settle it!" The police came, stayed twenty minutes, and skillfully talked to Alan until he was in control again.

Our local police were very helpful and responsive during subsequent episodes. Alan calmed down faster in their authoritative presence and seemed reassured that a force stronger than himself could control the rages that sent him out of control. Sometimes, the police even told him they had arrested the thugs in his hallucinations, so they couldn't hurt him anymore.

At other times, Alan could not differentiate between calling for help and planning to call. This led to some interactions a friend characterized as "straight out of vaudeville," and he was right.

At 2:00 AM one night, I opened my eyes to see Alan standing over me, wringing his hands.

"Oh, good, you're not dead," he said. "I thought you were sick so I called for help."

"Oh, you did? Who did you call?" I asked, bracing for another visit from an ambulance or fire engine.

"Don't worry. You need a nurse to take care of you. So I called a nurse. You know who she is. Our friend. She stays here. Don't worry, a nurse is coming."

"Did you call Gail, instead of 911?" I asked.

"Yeah, I called Gail. She's a nurse. She's coming here to take care of you."

"Oh, thank you, Alan," I said with relief. "Gail is a good person to call. That was a smart choice."

"Oh, she's good to call? You'll have to give me her number sometime."

In March, Alan had a long, frightening episode of chest pain. The medications we had did not relieve the pain for very long, and Alan's anxiety mounted.

"Shouldn't we go to the doctor?" he asked.

Later, he asked again, "Do you think we should go to the hospital? Why are we just sitting here? This hurts awful bad."

I reminded him that we had decided not to put him through more treatments, but I was angry and guilty that we didn't have a better plan for relieving his worsening symptoms at home.

Alan said, "Yeah, don't let them put needles in me. Don't let them put me in intensive care. If I'm going to die, I just want to stay home with you and Tom and my dog."

Eventually, I found a combination of meds that took the edge off enough for him to sleep. The next day, we went to see Alan's primary care doctor.

I said, "I know we said we don't want Alan to have more interventions, and he's probably not ready for hospice care. But there has to be something in between, and we want much better pain medication to treat these chest pains at home."

Dr. F. agreed and gave us prescriptions for morphine sulfate and antianxiety meds in liquid form. They worked much better.

I was reminded of how important it is to have a comprehensive plan in place whenever we shifted from one level of care to another. We'd decided not to pursue aggressive care, but hadn't thought through what to have on hand as his symptoms got worse. That was due in part to not being able to predict which symptoms would be most troublesome.

A few weeks later, we had the Big Talk on a night when Alan was very sad about his difficulty walking.

"I guess this just gets worse, this Parkinson's. Will I wind up in a wheelchair? I can't walk at all," he said.

I said, "Well, that might happen. Unfortunately, Parkinson's disease does get worse, and you have a bad case. You take medicine and there are more we can try. But sometimes the medicine doesn't help enough."

"Well, I guess this beats the alternative … being dead," he laughed ruefully.

"Let's sit down and talk about this," I said. "I know how hard it is for you to get through every day, and how much effort you put into everything you do. You do a terrific job, but it must be tiring. I want you to know that if it gets to be too much effort, you don't have to keep going for my sake."

Our eyes met and Alan listened attentively as I continued.

"When you die, I will miss you terribly," I said, stroking his cool hand between my warmer hands. "But I'll be okay. I'll be okay because you have taught me how to do everything, and you have provided for me. I love you very much, but I don't want you to stay alive just for me when it gets too hard."

"Oh, thank you for saying that," he said as he heaved himself up to try walking a few feet. "But it's not hard to make the right choice when you have a beautiful wife who loves you!"

"What's the right choice?" I ventured.

"Staying alive, of course! Don't worry; I'll be around for a while more!" He gave me a flirtatious grin and winked.

I kissed him, but wondered to myself, *Why would you want to stay alive when everything you do is so hard, and your abilities are slipping away from you by the day?* But so much of the decision-making took place within Alan, and he still found reasons to live.

He really did wake up looking forward to the day, starting with reading the newspaper and discussing the major stories. When a nephew or friends visited, he beamed. An unexpected phone call from his family made his afternoon worthwhile. Every night, I said, "Alan, the joy of my life is going to sleep with you every night. The joy of my life is waking up with you every morning." He grinned and went to sleep.

Alan relished all kinds of sensory pleasures that we shared that year. If a food was sweet and creamy, he was a happy man. Sitting in a velvet wingback chair in Starbucks, sipping a vanilla bean frappucino, made him sigh voluptuously. Stretching out in his lounge chair with the sun on his face any season of the year made him purr like a kitten. Best of all was cuddling Tom and Claudia's baby sons in his arms while singing them funny songs.

Alan still had long intervals of lucidity and eloquence interspersed with the psychotic outbursts. In May, we had another conversation about his health and decisions we might have to make.

Alan said, "I trust whatever you think is best. I trust your decisions. I think my family trusts your decisions."

Even after seven years, I was awed by the power and responsibility of making such important decisions for Alan and for us, and humbled by his trust and faith in me. Now I made decisions based on my full knowledge of who Alan was now, this year, this week. As his problems mounted, I considered both what I thought he would want and what I was capable of offering, especially with additional help. Even though I often thought clearly, there were times I said I had "mental whiplash" from being jerked between the reality of Alan's mortality and the reality of him continuing to live while the dementia progressed. I didn't want to lose him, but the only way his torments could end was in death. If he lived, he would only lose more and more of his fiercely reclaimed self to dementia. That price was too inhumane to contemplate.

I knew for awhile that Parkinson's disease and dementia would soon make it unsafe for Alan to sleep in our four-poster bed. But our bed had always been our life raft. There we could set aside the cognitive rehab, memory problems, and financial worries to make love or hold each other. One of life's greatest pleasures is to curl up at night close to the person you love best. In the world of catastrophic illness, not being able to sleep together is one more devastating loss and deprivation.

The only hospital bed insurers will pay to rent is a stingy single bed. Fortunately, we had the Cadillac of hospital beds waiting for us. When my friend Ginny's husband Bob was stricken with amyotrophic lateral sclerosis, they borrowed a queen-size hospital bed from an empathic and generous woman whose husband had died of ALS. Those first owners paid $10,000 for the bed. It was worth its weight in gold to each successive couple who slept in it.

When Bob died, Ginny held on to the bed until it was our turn. In May, I decided to make the switch.

Alan knew the hospital bed meant that he was getting much sicker. He liked things to be "normal, not like in a hospital." Alan respected good design, where form follows function. So I told him this was like the bed we slept in when we vacationed at Sundial Resort in Florida. Channeling Vanna White, I demonstrated how the head elevated so we could read and how the frame went up and down so he could climb in easily. The bed even had a side rail he could grip to get in and out.

Alan said, "Wow, this is really fancy!" as he jumped aboard.

Later, I bedecked the side rails with a string of large cowbells from India to alert me when Alan tried to get up. He fell sometimes because he couldn't remember that his legs didn't work. I placed the largest bell in Alan's shoe, figuring that if he circumvented the others, I would hear the cow bell as he kicked it out of his shoe. That night, I was working in the next room when Alan came stumbling in, gripping the bell in his hand.

"What the hell is this thing doing in my shoe?" he asked. None of the bells had made a sound when he got up.

Alan disliked my alarm systems, but adjusted easily to the bed because we maintained our family sleeping arrangement. We snuggled close together vertically, while Nicky sprawled horizontally across us.

Alan murmured, "Where's my dog? Where's my dog?" until his hand found Nicky's warm belly. "Ah, there's my dog!" he said as he drifted back to sleep.

I liked the hospital bed too. As the dark nights of Alan's life dwindled down, there was as much familiarity as there was strangeness in bed with us. The warmth, the touch, the curves and angles of body parts matching up like puzzle pieces. Along with my wakeful vigilance, there was Alan's smooth cheek, twinkling eyes, and whiff of Old Spice.

In late May, Alan qualified to start receiving hospice services at home because his heart had become so weak. We had a superb team made up of a registered nurse, social worker, chaplain, and two volunteers. Mary, the nurse, immediately asked Alan's doctor to triple the dose of medication for nerve pain, along with raising his chest pain and anxiety medications. Alan felt better and was more interactive and cheerful within days.

I requested volunteers to visit and read with Alan. The volunteers I'll call Judith and Rose were ideal matches for Alan's interests. Judith brought her background in biology and read about evolution and DNA from Alan's books. Rose knew so much about ancient Greece and Rome, and shared her photographs from her trips to see ancient civilizations.

They read on the living room couch until he tired and the volunteers picked up the story. Alan most enjoyed their rich conversations, and I loved listening to the sounds of their engaged voices going back and forth as I planted petunias and lizianthus in the porch window boxes. Reading remained what mattered most to Alan to the very end of his life. Three days before he died, he read aloud from *Huckleberry Finn*, slowly sounding out the tricky language with his volunteer:

"Tom poked about amongst the passages, and pretty soon ducked under a wall where you wouldn't 'a' noticed that there was a hole..."

That summer, Alan had the experience we both feared most. I was playing with the dog when he entered the living room and stared at me suspiciously. Towering over me, he planted his hands on his hips and demanded, "Who are you and what are you doing in my house?" I knew immediately that this was different from his usual post-nap confusion.

"Alan," I said, "I'm Janet. I'm your wife, Janet. I live here with you."

"I don't think so. I don't know you," he said, not backing down.

"Yes, I'm your wife, Janet. I love you and have lived here with you for many years," I said.

262 | *Janet M. Cromer*

"I guess I'll have to believe you," he huffed as he turned to leave the room. "I don't think so, but I suppose I have to let you stay."

I was distressed at this first episode of Alan's inability to recognize me. For years we had both hoped he would die before the dementia claimed this critical connection. I could imagine nothing more hellacious than knowing you were dying, suffering pain and delusions, and being deprived of the comfort of knowing the person you trusted and loved was with you.

29. May You Rest in the Sweetest Peace

Late on a Sunday afternoon in late July, Alan awoke from a nap calling, "Janet, Janet, where are you? Come here ..."

I ran to the bedroom and joined him on the edge of the bed, where he sat looking shrunken and terrified in his wrinkled undershirt and shorts. The room was almost dark behind the drawn curtains. Alan was afraid of the dark and often slept with a light on now.

"I didn't know where you were!" he cried. "I was scared those guys would come back and beat me up again. I didn't know where you were," his voice trailed off.

I wrapped my arms around his shivering body and pulled him close as I said, "Oh, Alan, I'm right here, darling. I will protect you in any way possible. Those guys won't hurt you."

Alan wrapped himself around my body so small and tight I thought he might crawl between my ribs and take refuge inside me. Then came his whispered voice: "I had a dream. I see myself naked and alone."

He had never said anything like that before. I swallowed the rock in my throat and said, "Oh, darling, that sounds so vulnerable and frightening."

"Yeah, I'm vulnerable; vulnerable and scared," he said.

We talked a bit more as I tried to reassure him that I would stay right beside him. In a few moments, he announced he was ready for dinner. Twenty minutes after that conversation, we were eating omelets at the kitchen table as he asked me questions from a newspaper article about the Israeli pullout from the Gaza Strip. He didn't remember his dream, but I was still shaken by our exchange.

Even though I was convinced that this was Alan's time to move on and be done with his suffering, it broke my heart when I couldn't take away his fear and aloneness. Even though I knew we all come into this world alone and go out alone, I hoped fervently that he could remember how it felt when we held each other, that he could retain that body memory for longer than ten minutes. Maybe that would be a small comfort to him, as it was to me.

A few nights later, he had a harder time standing up while I changed his clothes for bed. Alan said, "I guess I'm getting sicker and sicker. Am I dying? Am I going to die? I forget."

I said, "Yes, you are sicker in some ways. What bothers you most?"

"No, I don't feel sicker I guess. But much weaker," he said.

I said, "Well, honey, remember that you and I decided that you didn't want to go to the hospital anymore, have surgery, or be in intensive care? Your heart is getting weaker, but we don't know when you will die. It could be soon or down the line." Why do I always have to give him the hard news?

Alan thought for a moment before saying, "I know I'm getting weaker. I guess it will just keep getting harder and harder for you to take care of me, huh?"

"Alan, I want to take care of you, so I plan to get more people to help us out so I can be with you."

He straightened his head and grinned. "Well, that's good, because it feels so good when you take care of me." He buttoned his plaid flannel pajamas, crooked as usual, and kissed me as I tucked him in.

"I love you, Loverlump," he said.

"I love you, Loverman," I replied. Alan was asleep in five minutes and my heart ached with love for an hour.

On August 15, 2005, Alan celebrated his seventieth birthday. All summer, his family and friends visited from across the United States. Whenever we had company, we had a small birthday party to match Alan's lower energy level. He still liked unwrapping gifts and being the center of attention as he blew out the candles.

We all knew that those who loved him were paying their last visit. Maybe a hand lingered on his arm a few minutes longer, or there were tears shed on the trip back to the airport, but those visits were ripe with the same affection, laughter, and juicy conversations as previous visits.

Alan and I spent whole afternoons contentedly listening to Beethoven or Pachelbel, or acting out the words as Frank Sinatra belted out "I did it my way ..." We stayed in bed until mid-morning, holding each other quietly and circling fingertips over faces or hands. Every night, we sang our signature song, "I love you a bushel and a peck, a bushel and a peck and a hug around the neck ..."

Every night, I said, "Alan, the joy of my life is waking up with you each morning. The joy of my life is going to sleep with you each night." These times together were islands of refuge amidst the episodes of psychosis and anxiety.

Three weeks before Alan died, he declared, "Let's go out to lunch. Let's go somewhere nice. I feel like having a steak." So we drove to Charlie's Eating and Drinking Saloon in a nearby shopping center. The restaurant was one of our favorites because of the comfortable booths, juicy steaks, and apple pie.

I can see us now, in a dark corner surrounded by heavy oak paneling, only a few diners scattered across the large room in the hush following the noontime rush. We are a sweet older couple in casual summer clothes, holding hands across the table and smiling though the meal.

The gentleman dines from his wheelchair pushed under the table, yet waves his fork in the air to make a point as he speaks. The lady eases back against the banquette cushions after cutting his steak into small bites, then samples her salmon. Her eyes never leave her husband's face, and her expression is wistful and content.

We savored our afternoon together as much as Alan savored every last bite of his prime rib. I thought, *This is our last dinner date. Weren't we blessed to have so many? I didn't know we'd be given one more.*

Sliding my toes up Alan's leg, I said, "Alan, you're so romantic. You sure know how to show a lady a great time."

He laughed and said, "Well, I was always a suave guy who knew how to treat a gal."

We had a marvelously intimate date, undimmed by being our last.

Reviewing one's life can be so important yet so unavailable when dementia has ripped out half the pages. Alan wanted to take another look back and asked questions about his life daily. By this time, Alan could not generate any memories of his pleasures, accomplishments, loves, and greatest lessons on his own.

His life review took the form of inhabiting his most treasured memories by telling stories with family and friends, which we wrote in his logbook and read again. We poured over photo albums, and Alan chose a few photos to talk about each time so he wouldn't get overwhelmed. He enjoyed watching his video biography and videos of our nieces and nephews growing up. We pointed out Alan's attributes and influence that the younger generation now displayed.

The question that always thrust a knife in my gut was, "Did I ever amount to anything? Was I a good teacher?" I brought him to his office to see the "Alan's Archives" bookcases brimming with his titles or played the video from his retirement party where colleagues described his many contributions. When they visited, his nieces and nephews told him specific ways he enriched their lives and education, and I pointed out how many thousands of students he had taught.

Alan said, "Oh, good, I did amount to something. I was a good uncle and a good teacher."

Then he forgot until we repeated the ritual.

I talked to Mary, our hospice nurse, about how to make Alan's legacy more concrete. I thought knowing how his values and spirit would live on might make it easier for Alan to let go when his time came. I had a long-standing plan of establishing a fund in Alan's memory at Spaulding

Rehab that would provide resources to help adults with brain injuries learn to read, write, and think again. Alan and I had discussed such a fund over the years, and he liked the idea very much. My plan was to activate the fund after Alan died, but Mary had a better idea.

"How about involving Alan in setting up his legacy fund and asking if he wants to start it now?" she said.

That was excellent advice, and Alan readily approved the idea.

I said, "Our family and friends can contribute in honor of your birthday or other events right away, and later people can make donations in your memory."

"That's a great idea," Alan said. "Of course, I should go give them the first check!"

The Spaulding staff put together a reception befitting the occasion, attended by the speech-language pathologists who would oversee the new "Professor Alan Cromer Literacy Fund" and staff who knew us well through our BABIS involvement. Everyone was astonished at how well Alan looked in the charcoal jacket and silk tie he insisted on wearing. He didn't look like their image of a terminally ill man receiving hospice care. But Alan always looked strong and resilient when energized by purpose and determination.

Alan and I both offered remarks and then listened to warm reminiscences from the staff. Alan sat at the head of the conference table and delivered his remarks in his best professorial tone:

"In 1998 my heart stopped and I had a brain injury. I lost all my abilities. No one could really tell me what it would take, or how it would go. It took a long time. It was very depressing.

"I got over being depressed when Jennifer started teaching me to read again. I realized there was a plan going forward for me. I would consider my abilities now to be pretty much normal.

"We want to show our appreciation by starting the Cromer Literacy Fund to help other brain injury survivors learn to read, write, and think again.

"It is my pleasure to give you the first donation. Thank you."

Alan exchanged hugs and handshakes with the president of Spaulding Rehab. For the millionth time, I beamed at my husband with joy and pride.

Out in the lobby, Alan insisted on standing up for the group photograph. "I'll be damned if I'll be the only one in a wheelchair," he said. We propped him up by the elbows, and indeed he was the most distinguished person in the photograph Uche captured.

As soon as we arrived home, I rushed up to CVS to have the photographs developed into eight-by-ten-inch prints. When Alan got up from his nap, he asked, "I gave a speech today, right? I went to Spaulding and did something to help people like me, right?"

I pointed at the photo beside his recliner, and he smiled with satisfaction. Alan told everyone the story and truly seemed to find peace in establishing a memorial that would continue the work he championed.

A few days later, we received a card from Rick, a speech-language pathologist who took part in the presentation.

Rick wrote: *"Alan, the way you carried yourself, your stamina, and your presence at the head of the table all contributed to an unquestionable triumph over your illness. And Janet, your eloquence and love for Alan were shining."*

We both cherished Rick's words.

On Labor Day weekend of 2005, Alan got much sicker. At first I worried because Uche was on vacation and the agency couldn't supply home health aides to help us. But my friends stepped in to offer the most loving and tender care possible.

Alan's condition worsened all day Saturday. The hospice staff told me how to keep him comfortable with medications, but I was still distraught that my precious husband was now in his final hours. On Saturday evening, Gail, Ginny, and Jane joined us and kept a vigil in the living room.

I wanted to bathe Alan and change the sheets to make him more comfortable, so Ginny and Gail positioned themselves on one side of the bed and I stood on the other. As we turned Alan toward the friends he loved and felt so secure with, he opened his big blue eyes and smiled at them. They smiled back and spoke softly as I gently massaged his back. When we turned Alan back to me, his eyes looked deep into mine.

A smile spread across his face, and he said, "I love you," as he pursed his lips for a kiss.

I said, "I love you too, sweetheart. I love you forever."

Those were my husband's last words.

Throughout the night, I cradled Alan in my arms while I cooed my love and told him he could go whenever he was ready. I sobbed into the pillow as I gave what must be the most merciful yet painful permission to give. I could hear our friends talking quietly and occasionally laughing as they exchanged travel stories in the living room. I was glad that Alan might be hearing laughter and tales about travel. That would please him very much.

Alan held on through the night until Tom, "my nephew who is better than a son," came to lie alongside Alan and say his loving farewells. Bright sun streamed in the bedroom window and across our bed on a glorious Sunday morning.

Alan died on September 3 at 11 AM with Tom and me holding him close and his dog Nicky warming his feet.

I believe my husband had a good death.

After Alan died, Ginny told me that as Alan's last evening passed, she felt many things, some quite surprising.

She said, "I could feel Alan's life force returning as he was dying. As this started to happen, I held Alan's hand. I felt through his hand that Alan was summoning many of his parts of himself—little boy, student, writer, entrepreneur, professor—that he had not been able to experience in recent years due to his brain injury and illness. He gathered these parts to make his journey as one made whole again. Images of all these aspects of Alan flashed through my heart to the beat of his pulse in celebration of a tremendous life and of the tremendous love between Alan and Janet."

Ginny's experience and words captured everything I'd hoped for Alan and consoled me immeasurably.

Alan's nephew Marty told me that, during a conversation in July, Alan said that he wanted to live to attain his "three score and ten years," to reach the age of seventy. Alan, the atheist who was never oriented to time or his age after the brain injury, said the Bible designated seventy as the mark of an honorable life well lived. Hearing this, it made sense to me that Alan would hold strong his will to live against mounting challenges until three weeks past his seventieth birthday. True to character, Alan had accomplished his last goal.

We planned a memorial service for Alan that abounded in love, joy, and sorrow. Alan had been cremated and would be laid to rest in a plot at Forest Hills Cemetery under sweeping trees where birdsong graced the air.

Shortly before the start of Alan's memorial service, I withdrew a tiny packet of grey ashes from my pocket and approached the chapel altar, where Alan's ashes (cremains) now rested in a plain box. I opened Alan's box and slowly sifted the pure white essence of my beloved through my fingers. Then I opened the small bag and swirled Molly's ashes together with Alan's.

"There you go, sweetheart," I said. "You can hold your dog Molly on your lap for eternity. You can keep each other company wherever you go next."

Alan would have loved his memorial service. His family, closest friends, and I celebrated his life with stories from across the breadth of his seventy years on Earth. At the end of my remembrance, I read a poem I had written for us early in Alan's illness:

Ferocious Love

Ferocious love builds fortress walls
and dragon-filled moats around a kingdom
only the courageous may enter.
This love blazes in the dark, powers the body,
ignites the spirit, and fights for justice.

Ferocious love flinches and recoils when struck,
tires and wails, whines and screams,
sinks to the depths of despair,

and shakes its fist at the heavens above.
Yet in the end, proves indefatigable every time.

Ferocious love spreads a balm of honey
over the ravages of being, and
licks the soul until it is pink and pliable anew.
This love draws from the wellspring of passion, hope,
and love, and blesses the world with morning rain.

Ferocious love embraces the whole catastrophe
with compassion,
bows to the heavens above,
breathes in deeply,
grabs a partner, and dances all night.

At Alan's gravesite, we prayed, sang, and comforted each other as we sobbed our private and communal grief.

A few months later, I brought a drawing I'd done in 1995 of Alan paddling his kayak down Narrow River in Narragansett to an artist who customized gravestones. The artist used my sketch as the basis of an etched portrait on Alan's gravestone. Now Alan glides along the salt marsh shore of his favorite river, escorted by swans for all eternity. Alan is at peace. I smile when I visit his grave.

My Alan, I love you forever.

ACKNOWLEDGEMENTS

When Alan suffered a heart attack, cardiac arrest, and brain injury in 1998 we hoped and prayed for a *First Choice Recovery*. That meant complete physical recovery and restoration to the person he was before. Unfortunately, cardiovascular disease and extensive brain injury made a First Choice Recovery impossible. But we triumphed in a different and equally valuable way. Alan made a *Best Choice Recovery* when he and I invented a new way of being, contributing, making meaning, and having fun. We could not have shaped his Best Choice Recovery without the love, support, expertise, and involvement of many people.

We felt enormous gratitude and affection for everyone named here, and many other unnamed people who were kind and supportive in our encounters. I'll start with Alan's family: Thank you to Barbara and Sanford Kahn, Thomas Cromer, Martin Kahn, Larry Kahn, Richard and Pamela Cromer, and Burton Cromer.

Thank you to my family: Sherry and Jack Caliri and their children Brenton, Hank, Cassandra, and Samantha; my aunt and uncle, Marion and Elvin Lockwood, who supported me by telephone for years.

Thank you to our friends who stood with us in a hundred ways for seven years: Gail Cunningham, Ginny Mazur, Jane Mead, Marla

Lynch, Kathy Mc Donald, Don McCaffrey, Ann Marie Marr, Sue and George Sasdi, Jack Rutledge, Kathy Scully, Ronald and Marilyn Aaron, Eugene Salitan and Ellen Cole, Mike Glaubman, Kenneth Leavitt, and Karen Kirchoff. Our Jamaica Plain neighbors befriended and rescued us several times.

The friends who formed our Circle of Support gave us sustenance and peace.

Our dogs Molly and Nicky deserve a category of their own for their constant devotion and abiding love. The feeling is mutual. Nicky even sat at my feet every day as I wrote this book.

Legions of medical and rehabilitation professionals helped Alan survive and live fully. We are enormously grateful for your intelligence, compassion, and dedication. Starting in Chicago, Frank Pensa, MD performed CPR on the airplane. I thank the entire medical and nursing staff of the Resurrection Medical Center Intensive Care Unit, in particular these professionals I remember clearly ten years later: James Schneider, MD, Joseph Brawka, MD, Dr. Kovelinski, Robert Calabria, DO, and Kathleen Cantos RN, Nurse Manager.

In Boston, Alan's primary medical team was made up of Thomas Faldetta, MD and his office staff, David Pilgrim, MD and Steven Lampert, MD.

The mental health professionals who took time to know us and also learn from us were Pedro Politzer, MD, Steven Adelman, MD, Martha Bass, LICSW, and David Bullis, PhD.

At Spaulding Rehabilitation Hospital in Boston, Alan benefited from superb care from the Brain Injury Unit Team which included David Burke, MD, Jennifer Mello, CCC-SLP, Heather Palmer, OT/R, Beth Kenniston, PT, Kristen Simpson, BSN, RN, CRRN; Kevin Wallace, RN, Ron Calvanio, PhD, Alec Meleger, MD, Peg Frates, MD and Nasser Karamouz, MD. The entire staff of the Brain Injury Unit, including the certified nursing assistants, provides exceptionally expert care to patients and families whose lives have been shattered and need to be rebuilt.

We had our own home care team of skilled, creative, and devoted men who enabled Alan to be stronger, safer, and more independent.

Uche Ifedikwa, CNA cared for Alan daily for three years. Jeff Becker, Certified Personal Trainer was one of Alan's favorite conversationalists as well as his fitness coach for five years.

Many people in the brain injury world became expert guides and close friends. Marilyn Spivack, co-founder of the Brain Injury Association of America became a dear friend and mentor who convinced us to share our story to educate and give hope to others. Sally Johnson, LICSW, a founder of the Boston Acquired Brain Injury Support (BABIS) Group, became a close friend. Sally's dedicated guidance has been at the center of BABIS since 2001. We cherished our friendships with all of our BABIS friends, including Manya and Chuck Ozug, Andi and Tom Larsen, and Kitty and George Carroll.

A whole new world opened up to me when I started taking writing and book making classes at the Fine Arts Work Center in Provincetown. In Mopsy Strange-Kennedy's essay writing classes at Cambridge Center for Adult Education, I found my voice as a writer. My classmates were talented, energetic, and encouraging writers. Diane Butkus became a friend from that class, and served as Official First Reader for my manuscript. Thank you Diane for your thought-filled reflections and suggestions.

In Marcie Hershman's Monday Writer's Group I learned how to wrestle a voice and a mountain of notes into a book. I thank this group of scintillating and intelligent writers for all of their detailed suggestions and discussions that led to a more organized, focused, and crafted work.

I am very grateful to Marilyn Spivack and Therese O'Neil-Pirozzi, ScD, CCC-SLP, for writing the foreword, and for the work they do as clinicians, educators, and public advocates influencing policy and research for people with brain injuries and their families.

Thank you to Jim Anderson for his love and support while I completed this project.

Thank you, my readers, for spending your time with us. I appreciate your willingness to enter our world, take whatever may be of help to you, and leave your generous imprint.

To all those who live with a brain injury, may you be able to make your own Best Choice Recovery. To your family members, may you find the support, information, and strength within for your journey. Share your stories with everyone who will listen. Grab the attention of those who will not listen. Advocate for what you need. Alan would tell you, "Never stop loving, striving, and learning."

Thank you again to everyone who loved and helped us along the journey.

Janet M. Cromer

REFERENCES AND READINGS

Introduction
Rand Review, a publication of RAND Institute
"Stop Loss: A Nation Weighs the Tangible Consequences' of Invisible Combat Wounds"
Published in Summer, 2008
Information about the estimated numbers of veterans who may have TBIs.
www.rand.org/publications/randreview/issues/summer2008/wounds1.html

Chapter Three- Shattered Identity
Information about anoxic brain injury is from:
Sohlberg, M.M. and Mateer, C. A. (2001). *Cognitive Rehabilitation: An Integrative Neuropsychological Approach*. New York: Guilford Press.

Brain Injury Association of America publication on Anoxia by Nathan. D. Zasler, MD, FAAPM&R.
www.biausa.org.publications/anoxia.html

Chapter Four – Initiation into the Brain Injury World
Information on anoxic brain damage and brain function is from:
Sohlberg, M.M. and Mateer, C. A. (2001). Cognitive *Rehabilitation: An Integrative Neuropsychological Approach*. New York: Guilford Press.

Gutman, S.A. (2008). *Quick Reference Neuroscience for Rehabilitation Professionals: The Essential Neurological Principles Underlying Rehabilitation Practices (2nd Ed.)*.
Thorofare,NJ: SHANK Incorporated.

Information on executive functions is from:
Sohlberg, *op. cit.*

Zasler, N.D., Katz, D.I., and Zafonte, R.D. (2005). *Brain Injury Medicine: Principles and Practices*. New York: Demos.
In the chapter Cognitive Impairments after Brain Injury. By Eslinger, P.J., Zappola, G., Chakura, F., and Barrett, A.

Information on cognitive rehab is from:
Sohlberg, *op cit.*

Chapter Nine- Listen to the Sun on My Face
Information on errorless learning is from:
High,W.M., Sander, A.M., Struchen, M.A., Hart, K.A. (Eds.) , (2005.) Rehabilitation for Traumatic Brain Injury. New York: Oxford University Press.

For information on Restless Legs Syndrome (RLS) see:
National Institutes of Neurologic Disease and Stroke
www.ninds.nih.gov
Restless Legs Syndrome Foundations
www.rls.org

Chapter Twelve-Lurching toward Equilibrium
Information about neural plasticity is from:

"Can Brains Be Saved?" an article by Lee Woodruff in *Parade* magazine, July 12,2009.

Doidge, N. 2007. The Brain That Changes Itself: Stories of Personal Triumph from the Frontiers of Brain Science. New York: Penguin.

Sohlber, M.M., Mateer, C.A.- book above

A few excellent books on ambiguous loss are:

Boss, P. (1999). *Ambiguous Loss*. Cambridge, MA: Harvard University Press.

Bruce. E.J. and Schultz, C. (2001). *Nonfinite Loss and Grief: A Psychoeducational Approach*. Baltimore, MD: Paul H. Brookes Publishing Co.

Chapter Fourteen- Ceremony for a Second Marriage
While my ritual was my own creation, these are a few of my favorite books about personal rituals:

Imber-Black, E. and Roberts, J. *Rituals for Our Times*. (1992).New York: Harper Collins.

Wall, K. and Ferguson, G. (1994). *Lights of Passage: Rituals and Rites of Passage for the Problems and Pleasures of Modern Life*. New York: Harper Collins.

Chapter Sixteen- All of the Above is True
Information on vascular dementia is from:
The Alzheimers Association- Handout on Vascular Dementia
http://www.alz.org

Chapter Nineteen-Descent into Parkinson's
National Parkinson Foundation, INC.
http://www.parkinson.org
National Headquarters: Bob Hope Road
1501 N.W. 9th Avenue, Bob Hope Road
Miami, FL 33136-1494
Tel: 1-800-327-4545

Chapter Twenty Seven-The Dementia Chronicles
A few of the many good books available:
Capossela, C. and Warnock, S. (1995). *Share the Care: How to Organize a Group to Care for Someone Who Is Seriously Ill.* New York: Fireside.
Hoffman, S.B., and Platt, C.A. 2000). *Comforting the Confused: Strategies for Managing Dementia.* New York: Springer Publishing.
Strauss, C.J. (2001). *Talking to Alzheimer's: Simple Ways to Connect When You Visit with a Family Member or Friend.* Oakland, CA :New Harbinger Publications, Inc.

Note: There are now hundreds of books about brain injury, dementia, Parkinson's disease, and caregiving listed on Amazon.com.

Selected Resources
Brain Injury
Brain Injury Association of America- Information and links to 40 chartered state affiliates.
www.bia.usa
Tel: 703-761-0750

National Institute of Neurological Trauma and Stroke
www.ninds.nih.gov

Brain Trauma Foundation
www.braintrauma.org
Tel: 212-772-0608

National Rehabilitation Information Center
www.naric.com
Tel: 800-346-2742 or 301-459-5900

Brainline: A new, national, multimedia program offering information and resources about prevention, treatment, and living with TBI.
www.brainline.org

The Brain Injury Network
www.braininjurynetwork.org
Survivor operated non-profit advocacy organization for acquired brain injury survivors.

Dementia and Alzheimer's Disease

Alzheimer's Association
www.alz.org
Tel: 800-272-3900

Alzheimer's Foundation of America
www.alzfdn.org
Tel: 866-232-8484

National Institute of Mental Health
www.nimh.nih.gov
Dementia Advocacy and Support Network International
www.dasninternational.org

National Hospice and Palliative Care Organization
www.nhpco.org
Tel: 800-658-8893

Family Caregiver Issues

National Family Caregiver Association: Supports, empowers, and advocates for all caregivers.
www.nfcacares.org
Tel: 800-896-3650; 301-942-6430

The Well Spouse Association™: Advocates for and addresses the needs of individuals caring for a chronically ill or disabled spouse/partner.
www.wellspouse.org
Tel: 800-838-0874; 732-577-8899

Family Caregiver Alliance: A public voice for caregivers offers information, education, services, research, and advocacy programs.
www.caregiver.org

Veterans Issues
Defense and Veterans Brain Injury Center
Walter Reed Army Medical Center
6900 Georgia Avenue NW
Tel: 800-870-9244
www.dvbic.org

ReMind: A Bob Woodruff Foundation movement to provide resources and support to service men, veterans, and family members to successfully reintegrate into their communities.
www.ReMind.org

Parkinson's Disease
American Parkinson's Disease Association, Inc.: Research, education, and support.
Tel: 1-800-223-2732
www.apda@apdaparkinson.com

National Parkinson Foundation, Inc.
Tel: 1-800-327-4545
www.parkinson.org

Made in the USA
Middletown, DE
17 March 2018